THE OAKWOOD PRESS   SERIES X48

VERTICAL BOILER LOCOMOTIVES
AND RAILMOTORS BUILT IN GREAT BRITAIN

by

The Late

Rowland A.S. Abbott

NEWCOMEN SOCIETY

and

Edited by

James W. Lowe FIMechE

THE OAKWOOD PRESS

© Oakwood Press 1989

ISBN 0 85361 385 0

Typeset by Gem Publishing Company, Brightwell, Wallingford, Oxfordshire.
Printed by Nuffield Press, Oxford.

Dedicated to Nancy Abbott

All rights reserved. No part of this book may be reproduced or transmitted in any form or by any means, electronic or mechanical, including photocopying, recording or by any information storage and retrieval system, without permission from the Publisher in writing.

ABBREVIATIONS

AB – Andrew Barclay Sons & Co. Ltd
BAG – Bagnall W.G. Ltd
BE – Brush Electrical Engineering Co.
BE – Balanced Engine (Sentinel)
C – Compound
CE – Central Engine (Sentinel)
CT – Crane Tank
DE – Double Engine (Sentinel)
DG – Double Gearing (Sentinel)
DW – Driving Wheels
D – Dubs & Co.
F – Fireless
HP – Horse Power
HC – Hudswell Clarke & Co. Ltd
L – Locomotive (Sentinel)
LE – Lowca Engineering Co. Ltd
M – Metre Gauge
MW – Manning Wardle & Co.
N – Neilson & Co.
NG – Narrow Gauge
OC – Outside Cylinders
PSI – Pounds per sq. inch
RC – Railcar
RP – Ruston Proctor & Co.
RS – Robert Stephenson & Co.
S – Sentinel Waggon Works Ltd
ST – Saddle tank
TVB – Tank loco. vertical boiler
VBCT – Vertical boiler crane loco.
VBT – Vertical boiler tank loco.
VBTG – Vertical boiler tank geared loco.
VBTM – Vertical boiler tram loco.
VBTVC – Vertical boiler & cylinders tank loco.
YE – Yorkshire Engine Co.

Published by
The OAKWOOD PRESS
P.O. Box 122, Headington, Oxford.

Contents

Preface	iii
Acknowledgements	iv
Introduction	v
List of Builders	viii
The Locomotives and their Builders	1
Miscellanea	176
Index	177

Preface

The writer's interest in vertical boiler locomotives dates back to 1925, and this eventually culminated in a series of articles contributed to *The Engineer* during May and June, 1955, where examples built by 39 makers were discussed.

Over the last two decades much additional information has been assembled from many sources and the present work has been written in order to place on record in a more accessible manner both the original text and the results of later research. In addition all those railmotors and combined tramcars with this form of steam generator are now included.

At the same time it will be appreciated that in a number of instances the information available regarding some of the makes of locomotives mentioned in this narrative is fragmentary, and often contradictory, due mainly to the lapse of time and the destruction of records in recent years.

So far as the writer is aware, no previous attempt has ever been made to assemble in book form all that is known of the construction of the vertical boilered locomotive in Britain, and it is hoped that this contribution to locomotive history will prove a worthy reference book for all those engineers and historians whose interest lies in the study of unusual locomotives.

Old Botley, R.A.S. Abbott
Oxford

Note: The tracings from which *Figs. 33* and *34* have been made were acquired in the early 1920s but the present whereabouts of the original Stephenson drawings has not been located.

In the case of *Plates 55, 58* and *Fig. 32*, these came from an unknown source in the 1940s and in spite of diligent enquiries, it has not been possible to establish ownership of copyright, and for this omission the Author begs indulgence.

Acknowledgements

In gathering together the information contained in this book, over a period of 29 years, I have been greatly indebted to many persons with kindred interests and without whose help the work would probably never have been completed.

For this reason it is a great pleasure to express the most appreciative and grateful thanks to all those who, in varying degree, but with a common courtesy and willingness have assisted in the production of this book and it is sincerely hoped that none have been omitted from the following list:

C.J. Ashford, London
P.J. Ashforth, Silchester
R.J. Atkins, Sheffield
A.C. Baker, Maldon
J.H. Battersby, Bethesda
J. Benson, Marden
A.W. Brotchie, Aberdour
J.S. Brownlie, Kilsyth
T.S. Cardy, Gateshead
M. Carter, Barrow
R.N. Clements, Celbridge
A.B. Craven, Leeds
J.E. Davies, Penmaenmawr
M.I. Williams-Ellis, Blaenau-Festiniog
A.R. Etherington, Burton on Trent
A.V. Evans, Sandbach
Kenrich Evans, Caernarvon
E.D.Y. Faulkner, London
G.T.J. Fidler, Leeds
K.C. Fleming, Richmond
J. Fletcher, Godalming
P. Garnett, Leeds
R.D. Grant, Christchurch, N.Z.
P.H. Hawkins, Chesterfield
J. Hays, Newcastle
P. Holmes, Newcastle
K. Hoole, Scarborough
R.T. Horne, Croydon
G. Horsman, Leeds
J.M. Hutchings, King's Langley
A.R. Jones, Caernarvon
D. Jones, Penygroes
W. Kealey, Lincoln
Dr J. Kramer, Woolgoolga, N.S.W.
J.B. Latham, Woking

D. Llewelyn, Bethesda
R. Lord, Preston
J.W. Lowe, Cosby
M.J. Messenger, Truro
Mrs K. Moore, Arbroath
N. Nicholson, Glasgow
W.D. Ockendon, Sheffield
M.R. Pearce, Penmaenmawr
D.R. Pendleton, Sheffield
R.G. Pratt, Minehead
J. Proud, Lancaster
H. Pybus, Leeds
W. Rae, Arbroath
H. Richards, Dublin
M. Roberts, Nantlle
N.G. Robson, Newcastle
G. Russell, Motherwell
H.A. Samuel, Seaham
H.S. Smith, London
D. Stoyel, Tunbridge Wells
E.W. Taylerson, Reigate
D.H. Tew, Oakham
J.P. Thorpe, Ipswich
G. Toms, Loughborough
T. Wade, London
C.B. Walker, Wigan
J.F. Ward, Liverpool
R. Wear, Swindon
R. Weaver, Kenilworth
F. Whalley, Oldham
B. Wilcock, Bolton
Kyrle W. Williams, Allcannings
C.J.P. de Winton, Brecon
Y.N. Yeaman, Walkden

In addition, thanks are also due to all those firms, libraries and other institutions who have rendered assistance:

Alpha-Cement Ltd, West Thurrock
Edgar Allen Engineering Ltd, Sheffield
Baguley-Drewry Ltd, Burton-on-Trent
Andrew Barclay, Sons and Co., Kilmarnock
Institution of Civil Engineers, London

ACKNOWLEDGEMENTS

Derby County Record Office, Matlock
Richard Duckering Ltd, Lincoln
Editor of *Engineering*, London
Ewart Library, Dumfries
Fodens Ltd, Sandbach
Gateshead Central Library, Gateshead
Granada Publishing Co., St Alban's
Greenwood and Batley Ltd, Leeds
Hick, Hargreaves and Co. Ltd, Bolton
Hunslet Engine Company, Leeds
Hutchinson, Hollingsworth and Co. Ltd, Dobcross
Industrial Locomotive Society
Industrial Railway Society
Leeds Central Library
Leics. Record Service
National Coal Board, Walkden
National Library of Wales, Aberystwyth
North Western Museum of Science and Industry, Manchester
Markham & Co. Ltd, Chesterfield
Mitchell Library, Glasgow
Ransomes and Rapier Ltd, Ipswich
Thomas Robinson and Son Ltd, Rochdale
Science Museum, London
Seddon Atkinson Vehicles Ltd, Oldham
Sheffield City Libraries, Sheffield
Signal Tower Museum, Arbroath
W. Sisson and Co. Ltd, Gloucester
Stothert & Pitt Ltd, Bath
Walker Bros, Wigan
Yorkshire Engine Co., Sheffield

Introduction

Information relating to this type of locomotive is meagre and limited to widely scattered references in certain engineering journals, mostly confined to the later designs with certain exceptions.

The period of building extends from the Rainhill trial locomotive of Braithwaite and Ericsson (NOVELTY 1829) and Timothy Burstall's PERSEVERANCE built in the same year, to those built by the Sentinel Waggon Works from 1923 to 1957, when steam gave way to diesel power.

Builders and types can be divided as follows:

1 Railway company designs
2 Private locomotive firms
3 General engineering firms
4 Conversion from orthodox shunting locomotives
5 Crane locomotives
6 Tram locomotives

1 Railway Company designs

Apart from some early steam carriages, steam railmotors were initially introduced by the Great Western Railway in 1903 and by 1908 they had built 99 which were used on branch lines and short distance runs on main lines. Performance on their own met requirements, but when trailers were attached lack of power resulted. So some small tank locomotives of sufficient power to operate two to four coaches were "auto-fitted" and could then be controlled from the leading vehicle in direction of travel. Other railways built railmotors, some with vertical boilers and others with "loco" type boilers. Their main weakness was in the boiler design resulting in shortage of steam and rapid drop in boiler pressure— the usual working pressure was 160 lb. per square inch (psi).

2 Private locomotive firms

Quite a number of locomotive building firms built this type of locomotive as required, mostly for fitting on to coaches to form steam railmotors. There were a few builders who specialised, such as Alexander Chaplin, Clayton Wagons and de Winton, the latter principally supplying slate and granite quarries in the North Wales area. Chaplin's railway travelling cranes were easily modified in design to provide a useful shunter and a fair number were built, many going abroad.

The most prolific builder was the Sentinel Waggon Works Ltd, also well known as producers of steam road wagons with vertical boilers which had been highly developed. Their success was due to a high working pressure of 230 lb. psi using the well tried Super-Sentinel boiler with a superheater. Steam could be raised in three-quarters of an hour. So successful were the locomotives and railcars that approximately 545 locomotives and 285 railcars were built from 1923 to 1957, making the firm easily the largest producer.

3 General engineering firms

It will be observed that many engineering firms built one or more locomotives to shunt their own private sidings. The boilers were new or second-hand and built by firms who supplied industry with boilers for steam-raising for process plant, heating and other purposes, such as Cochran, Davy Paxman, Abbott and many others. It was realised that where facilities and machinery were available, a locomotive could be assembled at far less cost than by purchasing one from a locomotive manufacturer. In most cases the boiler, wheels and other details were bought out. Even wagon frames and wheels were used in some instances and adapted to support the boiler, water tank and cylinders.

4 Conversion from orthodox shunting locomotives

The conversion of an outside cylinder 0-4-0ST to a geared locomotive was carried out by removing the locomotive boiler and installing a Sentinel vertical boiler, and either connecting the steam supply to the existing cylinders or installing a pair of cylinders and gearing to one axle for transmission. One such conversion initiated the long line of Sentinel locomotives. From 1924 to 1936 at least 23 shunters were converted to vertical boiler types.

5 Crane locomotives

It is usually accepted that a crane locomotive, as distinct from a travelling crane, has conventional cylinders usually outside, with coupled wheels, steam being supplied by the same boiler supplying steam to separate cylinders operating the crane motions. The railway travelling crane, on the other hand, gets its travelling motion by means of gearing to one of the axles and a dog clutch or sliding gear.

6 Tram locomotives

Tram engines or "Dummies" as they were known were built in quantities by Wilkinson, Beyer Peacock, Kitson and Black Hawthorn most of which were built to Wilkinson's Patent. Tram engines presented some problems in design due to the strict regulations laid down by the authorities which included shrouding the wheels and motion. They had to be capable of being controlled from each end, with hand and steam brakes compulsory. No smoke or condensed steam was to be emitted, so that air or water condensers had to be fitted in most cases and coke was used as fuel. Building took place between the 1870s and 1890s.

The condensers were fixed to the roof and consisted of nests of tubes if air-cooled or exhaust passed into water tanks for water cooling. Governors were required to control the speed of the tram engine.

The Wilkinson design incorporated 6 in. or 7 in. diameter cylinders driving a crankshaft and motion was transmitted by means of gearing. There was no condenser, the exhaust steam being passed through a contrivance in the firebox which acted as a superheater from which the superheated steam was exhausted through the chimney.

Tram engines replaced the horse-trams and were in turn superseded by electric tramcars.

The practical advantage of vertical boiler locomotives was a lower financial outlay, quick steam raising, easy ash disposal and short wheelbase—the latter needed in traversing sharp curves encountered in industrial sidings and layouts.

Using the industrial type boiler was not ideal with a relatively low pressure and inefficient heat transfer and such boilers tended to prime. When more sophisticated designs became available with cross tubes, superheaters and higher boiler pressures, the saving in fuel was appreciable. There was, however, a limitation in size both in diameter and height, due to clearances and loading gauge restrictions.

It should be noted that in the works lists the first known customer is shown, but not transfers of location to keep the lists within reasonable bounds.

The identification of this type of locomotive has always presented problems and there is still much research to be done; what research has been carried out has been rewarding and it is hoped worthwhile.

It is deeply regretted that the late Mr Abbott cannot have the satisfaction of seeing the results of his labour in print, which it is hoped has filled a considerable gap in locomotive history.

J.W. Lowe
Cosby, Leics.

List of builders

Arranged alphabetically as they appear in the book.

	Page
William Bridges Adams, Bow	1
W.G. Armstrong & Co., Newcastle-upon-Tyne	4
Atkinson-Walker Wagons Ltd, Preston	5
Baguley (Engineers) Ltd, Burton-on-Trent	9
William Balmforth, Rodley	13
Andrew Barclay, Sons & Co. Ltd, Kilmarnock	16
Bedford Engineering Co., Bedford	18
Beyer Peacock & Co. Ltd, Manchester	19
J.L. Birley, Kirkham	21
Black, Hawthorn & Co., Gateshead	23
Blaenavon Co. Ltd, Gwent	27
Frederic Bradley, Kidderminster	27
Braithwaite & Ericsson, London	28
Bridgewater Collieries, Worsley	29
Timothy Burstall, Leith	30
Butler Brothers	32
The Butterley Co., Ripley	33
Caldow & McKinnel, Dumfries	33
Alexander Chaplin & Co., Glasgow	34
Clarke, Chapman & Co. Ltd., Gateshead	43
Clayton Wagons Ltd, Lincoln	44
Coalbrookdale Co., Coalbrookdale	49
Cochrane & Co., Middlesbrough	49
Cowans, Sheldon & Co. Ltd, Carlisle	51
A.F. Craig Ltd, Paisley	52
Darbishires Ltd, Penmaenmawr	52
R.E. Dickinson & Co., Birkenhead	54
George England & Co., New Cross	55
A.R. Etherington, Woodville	55
Falcon Engine & Car Works Ltd, Loughborough	57
Fletcher, Jennings & Co., Whitehaven	57
Fodens Ltd, Sandbach	59
Glengarnock Iron & Steel Co., Kilburnie	61
Great Central Railway, Gorton	61
Great Northern Railway, Doncaster	61
Great Southern & Western Railway, Inchicore	62
Great Western Railway, Swindon and Wolverhampton	64
T. Green & Son Ltd, Leeds	66
Greenwood & Batley Ltd, Leeds	68
Harrison & Son (Hanley) Ltd, Stoke-on-Trent	70
Head, Wrightson & Co., Thornaby-on-Tees	70
Hetton Coal Co. Ltd, Hetton Lyons	75
Benjamin Hick, Bolton	75
Owen Hughes, Valley	77

LIST OF BUILDERS

Hunslet Engine Co. Ltd, Leeds	78
Hutchinson, Hollingsworth & Co. Ltd, Dobcross	81
Kerr, Stuart & Co. Ltd, Stoke-on-Trent	82
Kitson & Co., Leeds	85
Liquid Fuel Engineering Co. Ltd, East Cowes	88
London & South Western Railway, Nine Elms	89
Manlove, Alliott & Fryer, Nottingham	91
Manning, Wardle & Co., Leeds	93
Marshall, Fleming & Co. Ltd, Motherwell	96
James Irving McConnell, Kirkconnel	96
Merryweather & Sons Ltd, Greenwich	96
Midland Railway, Derby	102
Neilson & Co., Glasgow	103
North British Locomotive Co. Ltd, Glasgow	103
Oliver & Co. Ltd, Chesterfield	106
Parsons & May, Jaywick	110
R.Y. Pickering & Co., Wishaw	110
Ransomes & Rapier Ltd, Ipswich	111
Thomas Robinson & Son, Rochdale	112
Rothwell, Hick & Rothwell, Bolton	113
George Russell & Co., Motherwell	114
Sara & Co., Plymouth	116
Sara & Burgess, Penryn	117
Savile Street Foundry Co. Ltd, Sheffield	118
J. Scarisbrick Walker & Brothers, Wigan	119
Sentinel Waggon Works Ltd, Shrewsbury	119
Alexander Shanks & Son Ltd, Arbroath	151
Silley, Cox & Co. Ltd, Falmouth	151
W. Sisson & Co. Ltd, Gloucester	151
J. Slee & Co., Warrington	155
T. Smith & Sons (Rodley) Ltd, Rodley	156
South Eastern Railway, Ashford	156
Robert Stephenson & Co., Newcastle-upon-Tyne	158
Stothert & Pitt Ltd, Bath	159
T.M. Tennant & Co., Leith	161
W. Wilkinson & Co. Ltd, Wigan	161
de Winton & Co., Caernarvon	164
Yorkshire Engine Co. Ltd, Sheffield	172

VERTICAL BOILER LOCOMOTIVES

Frontispiece: A Sara and Burgess locomotive built in 1860's possibly for use at Falmouth Docks.

R.W. Kidner collection

The Locomotives and their Builders

WILLIAM BRIDGES ADAMS
FAIRFIELD WORKS
BOW, LONDON

William Bridges Adams born in 1797 at Madeley, Staffs, was the son of a coachbuilder and became interested in railway engineering, setting up the Fairfield Works at Bow in 1843. The first vehicle produced was a hand-driven inspection car for James Samuel, the Resident Engineer for the Eastern Counties Railway who was a strong advocate of lightweight railcars. Samuel then designed, no doubt with the aid of Adams, a steam-propelled car resulting in the construction of a vertical boiler locomotive named EXPRESS.

It was delivered to the company in April 1847 and was not intended for traffic purposes, having been specially designed for the use of the Engineer and his staff to facilitate the carrying out of their inspection duties. This locomotive (*Fig. 1*) consisted of a four-wheeled carriage with the engine and boiler in the forward part, and seating accommodation for seven persons in the rear. The uncoupled wheels were 3 ft 4 in. in diameter, and the total length 12 ft 6 in. The two cylinders, 3½ in. in diameter with a stroke of 6 in., were placed on each side of the boiler inside the frames and drove the front axle. The vertical boiler was of 1 ft 7 in. diameter with a height of 4 ft 3 in.; the firebox of 1 ft 4 in. diameter was 1 ft 2 in. high. Thirty-five tubes (1½ in. dia. × 3 ft 3 in. long) provided a heating surface of 38 sq. ft, a further 5.5 sq. ft of firebox totalled 43.5 sq. ft. A water tank to hold 40 gallons was placed under the seats. The total weight including coke and water was said to be 1 ton 5 cwt. 2 qr.

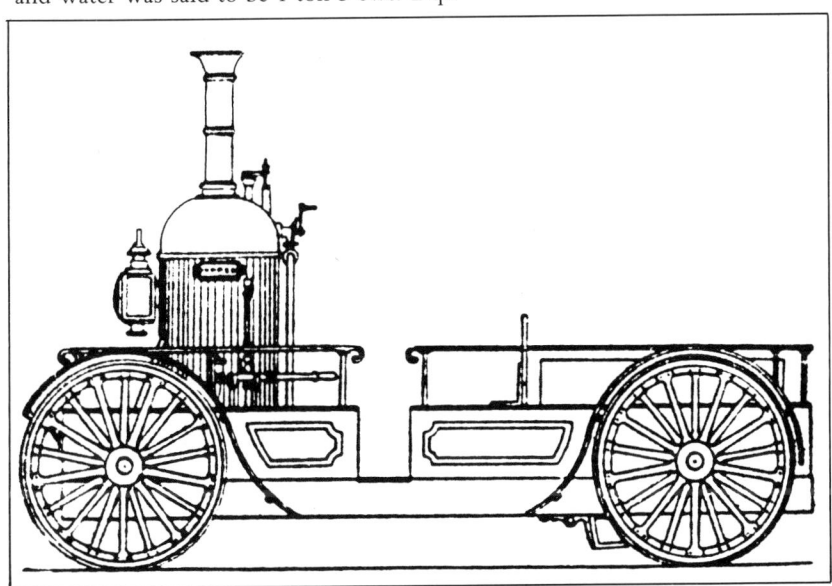

Fig. 1 Bridges Adams locomotive the *Express* built 1847 for the Eastern Counties Railway. *Ian Allan*

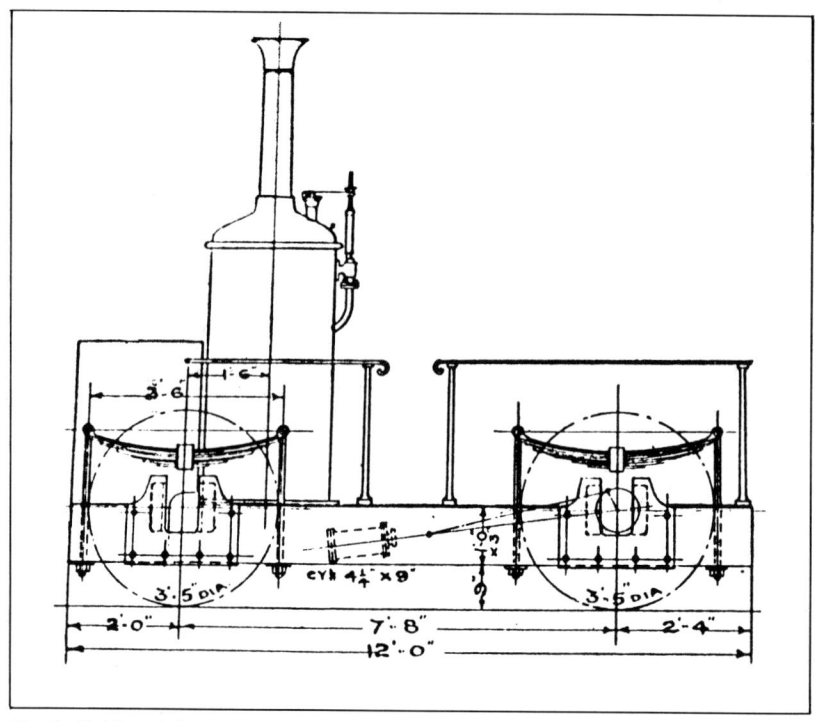

Fig. 2 Bridges Adams; an unidentified locomotive.   Ian Allan

Records of a second locomotive were brought to light by the late A.R. Bennett and an illustration of this is given in *Fig. 2*. It had a similar boiler and the external layout closely followed that of the EXPRESS, but internally it was very different having only one cylinder which was fixed under the footplate and drove on to the rear axle through a centrally placed crank. Steam distribution was by stationary link motion. The cylinder was 4¾ in. in diameter with a stroke of 9 in. The boiler was 2 ft dia. × 4 ft 6 in. high and worked at the unusual high pressure (for that date) of 130 lb. per square inch (psi). The four uncoupled wheels were of 3 ft 5 in. diameter on a wheelbase of 7 ft 6 in. and the frame of oak was 3 in. thick and 12 in. deep, hung below the axles on half-elliptic springs. The total wheelbase was 12 ft.

A small combined broad gauge engine and carriage was built in 1848 for the various branch lines of the Bristol and Exeter Railway. It commenced work in May 1849 and was named FAIRFIELD. The vertical boiler was 3 ft dia. × 6 ft high, the driving wheels were 4 ft 6 in. in diameter placed in front, driven by a pair of cylinders 7 in. or 8 in. dia. × 12 in. stroke, working a dummy crankshaft at the rear of the boiler, and coupled to the driving wheels by outside coupling rods. The exact position of the cylinders is not known. The carriage portion of

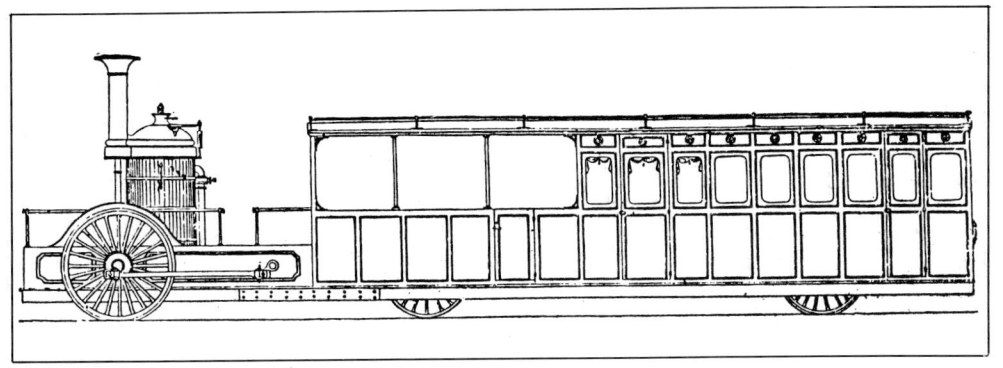

Fig. 3 Bridges Adams; combined engine and carriage *Fairfield* built in 1848 for Bristol & Exeter Railway.
Ian Allan

this vehicle ran on four 3 ft 6 in. dia. wheels and had accommodation for 16 first class and 32 second class passengers (*Fig. 3*).

At various times this steam carriage saw service on the Tiverton, Clevedon and Weston-Super-Mare branches but was evidently unsatisfactory, because some time in 1851 the locomotive part was separated from the carriage frame and a pair of 3 ft dia. trailing wheels fitted, the wheel arrangement becoming 0-2-2. A further rebuilding took place in 1856 when it was converted to a four-coupled locomotive and sold to Hutchinson and Ritson of Bridgwater. When sold by the Bristol and Exeter Railway the vertical boiler had been replaced by one of the conventional horizontal type.

A few other locomotives were built with ordinary locomotive type boilers including one for the Londonderry and Enniskillen Railway and two for the Cork and Bandon Railway. After 1850 building ceased and in the early 1850s the works were sold to Bryant and May.

Besides being the progenitor of the later steam railcars, the inventiveness of W.B. Adams was legion and his patent fish plate joint for the permanent way (1847), and radial axlebox (1863) formed the basis of all subsequent designs. W.B. Adams died in 1872.

References

The British Steam Railway Locomotive Vol. 1, E.L. Ahrons
Twenty Locomotive Men, C. Hamilton Ellis
English Pleasure Carriages, W.B. Adams
Engineering, Vol. 14, 1872.
The Engineer Vol. 34, 1872
The Locomotive 1943
Locomotive Engineering Vol. 1, Zerah Colburn

Fig. 4 Sir W. G. Armstrong & Co. condensing locomotive built in 1848. *Ian Allan*

W.G. ARMSTRONG and COMPANY
NEWCASTLE-UPON-TYNE

William·George Armstrong was born in Newcastle in 1810. He became a solicitor but with his partners, Armorer Donkin and a Mr Stable, formed a company in 1847 under the name of W.G. Armstrong & Co., on a site in the village of Elswick. Their chief products were hydraulic cranes and hoists. Later orders came in from the War Office which entailed the production of guns and mines. To add to the variety a vertical boiler locomotive was designed and built in 1848, being their first locomotive and the only one built with this type of boiler.

The novel construction is well shown by the drawing (*Fig. 4*) and the object of such a design was to increase the power of the locomotive by exhausting into a condenser, as the average boiler pressure, above the atmosphere, at this period was only about 90 lb. or so. By the use of a condenser it was hoped that an increase in effective pressure at the cylinders would be achieved if it could be arranged to exhaust into the condenser with a pressure of only about 4 lb. above zero. However, great difficulty was experienced with the supply of cold water for the condenser and the locomotive was not a success.

The only dimensions known are that the single pair of driving wheels had a diameter of 7 ft and that the vertical boiler was about 8 ft high. The driver's position was located between the condenser at the front and the boiler, while the fireman stood at the rear on the normal footplate. The cost of construction is said to have been about £2000.

Within a few years boiler pressures increased to a figure where there was no practical advantage in reducing the atmospheric pressure at the exhaust on normal locomotives. This locomotive ended this phase. The second phase was between 1860 to 1864 when twenty 2-4-0s were built for the East Indian Railway.

The company became Sir W.G. Armstrong Whitworth & Co. Ltd, in 1897 having amalgamated with Sir Joseph Whitworth & Co., of Manchester, the famous machine tool makers. The third phase of locomotive building took place during the period 1919-1938 when the Shell Factory at Scotswood was converted for this purpose. The Scotswood Factory was initially built in 1896 and closed in 1979. In 1927 the Firm joined with Vickers Ltd, to become Vickers Armstrong Ltd.

ATKINSON-WALKER WAGONS LTD
FRENCHWOOD WORKS, PRESTON

This company was established about 1908 as a general engineering concern, and entered the steam wagon building business in 1916, producing 540 undertype units up to 1929.

The Atkinson-Walker vertical boiler locomotives constructed at the Frenchwood Works are relatively little known, in that few details and specific information appeared in the contemporary technical press, and the firm's successors, Atkinson Vehicles Ltd, of Winery Lane, Walton-le-Dale, have preserved no records. The connection with the project by Walker Brothers (Wigan) Ltd, Pagefield Ironworks, Wigan, was mostly financial, together with the manufacture of certain mechanical parts and the supply of subsequent spares. They did not take part in the design.

These locomotives followed the usual practice in modern geared designs with the boiler at one end, water tanks at the other, and the engine in the centre, the whole being covered by an all-over cab. The total number of locomotives is thought to have been no more than about twenty-five and all were built between 1927 and 1931.

There were at least six different classes constructed, varying in weight from 5 to 40 tons, and these may be summarised as follows: class 'A', built for standard gauge had two cylinders 7 in. in diameter with a stroke of 10 in. and 3 ft diameter wheels; class 'B' built for the standard gauge had three cylinders 7 in. in diameter with a stroke of 10 in. on a wheelbase of 5 ft 6 in. The boiler had a heating surface of 125 sq.ft, a grate area of 7 sq.ft and a working pressure of 280 lb. psi. The water tank had the unusual capacity, for this type of locomotive, of 1000 gallons and the coal bunkers held 6 cwt. The overall length was 21 ft, height 11 ft 6 in. and a width overall of 8 ft. Weight in working order was 35 tons.

Class 'C' differed from all the others in having inside bearings for the axles and two horizontal cylinders, wheels 2 ft 3 in. in diameter, a boiler pressure of 230 lb. psi, and a weight of 10 tons. Class 'D' had a four-cylinder engine and ran on six wheels.

A locomotive was supplied to the 3 ft gauge Clogher Valley Railway in Ireland during 1928 (Works No. 114) and this had two cylinders 7 in. in diameter with a stroke of 10 in., wheels 2 ft 6 in. in diameter, a tube heating surface of 35 sq.ft, firebox heating surface of 25 sq.ft, and a grate area of 3.3 sq.ft; boiler pressure was 280 lb. psi. The length over buffers measured 17 ft, the overall width was 7 ft and the total height 9 ft 9 in.

The 3 ft gauge locomotive for the Ivybridge China Clay Co. Ltd was similar and from records that have survived it seems that the water capacity of this class was 300 gallons and that it was geared for a maximum speed of 16 mph.

Yet another design of narrow gauge locomotive was supplied to the Singapore Municipal Council, (Works Nos. 105–108), with the two axles coupled by external chain and fitted with an open-sided canopy cab. The engines fitted to all the locomotives were of the double-acting high-pressure, uniflow type, as developed by the makers in their steam wagons, and were totally enclosed with the big ends and main bearings lubricated under pressure, steam being admitted through ball valves controlled by cams and long pushrods.

The two-, three-, and four-cylinder engines were substantially similar, the bore being 7 in. in diameter, and the stroke 10 in., the various parts being standard throughout the range. With the exception of class 'C', the engines were set vertically on the longitudinal centre line of the locomotive, driving by enclosed bevel pinions a transverse shaft carrying a chain sprocket at each end, from which separate roller chains drove each axle, the axles being located by adjustable radius rods. In the case of class 'D', the axle under the water tank was driven by chain from the centre axle.

In the water-tube boiler riveted joints were entirely dispensed with, except for a double-riveted butt strap along the longitudinal joint of the top and bottom shell. The firebox, squared above the grate to receive the cross water tubes, was pressed in halves and electrically welded at the seams, the firebox then being welded to the outer shell by the same method, the whole construction being virtually one piece. The tubes, arranged crosswise, were inclined towards the front of the boiler to ensure active circulation of the water. Firing was effected through a chute, level with the footplate, fuel being distributed by a special firing tool, while a circular door in the front of the firebox was provided for cleaning the fire and "lighting-up".

A superheater consisting of a solid drawn steel tube in the form of a coil was housed in and supported by the cast iron uptake, and had sufficient heating surface to provide a temperature of 600 degrees Fahrenheit. Locomotives intended for passenger work could be fitted with feed water heaters.

Of the three designs illustrated here, *Plate 1*, represents class 'B' (Works No. 104 of 1928) when owned by Richard Briggs and Sons, of Clitheroe, while

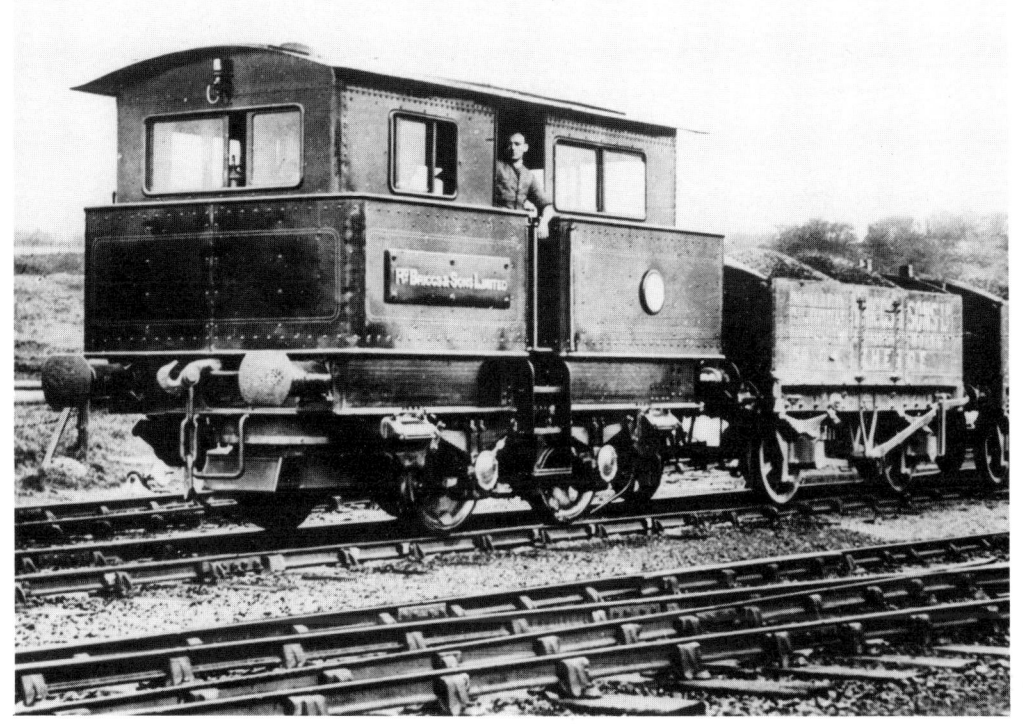

Plate 1 Atkinson-Walker Wagons Ltd class 'B' built in 1928.   *Seddon Atkinson Vehicles Ltd*

8 VERTICAL BOILER LOCOMOTIVES

Plate 2 Atkinson-Walker Wagons Ltd class 'C' built for Blaxter Quarries Ltd (113/1928).
D. Stoyel

Plate 3 Atkinson-Walker Wagons Ltd class 'D' for Oxford & Shipton Cement Ltd (110/1928).
D. Stoyel

Plate 2 shows class 'C' (Works No. 113 of 1928) as working at the Tottenham Works of the Eastern Gas Board. The solitary six-wheeled class 'D' (Works No. 110 of 1928), Plate 3, was photographed when working at Alpha Cement Limited, West Thurrock. A sectional side elevation of this large locomotive was published on page 243 of the Journal of the Institution of Junior Engineers for 1929.

Eighteen Atkinson-Walker locomotives are known to have been built and the following list gives details and original owners.

Works No.	Built	Class	Gauge	Customer	No./Name
102	1927	A	Std	Leatham Flour Mills, York	
103		B7	"	Walker Bros, Wigan	
104	1928	B	"	Richard Briggs & Sons, Clitheroe	LAZARUS
105	"		NG	Singapore Municipal Council	
106	"		"	"	
107	"		"	"	
108	"		"	"	
109	"	A	Std	Oxford & Shipton Cement Ltd	No. 2
110	"	D	"	"	No. 1
111	"	A3	3 ft	Ivybridge China Clay Co. Ltd	
112	"	B	Std	Shap Granite Co.	FELSPAR
113	"	C	"	Blaxter Quarries Ltd, Elsdon	
114	"		3 ft	Clogher Valley Rly	No. 8
115					
116					
117	1930	B	Std	H. Arnold & Sons, Doncaster	No. 1
118	"	"	"	"	No. 2
119	"	"	"	"	No. 3

References

The Locomotive Vol. 34 1928: description of class 'B' Locomotive, pp. 207–210
The Locomotive Vol. 34 1928: illustration of Singapore Locomotive, p. 210
The Narrow Gauge Railways of Ireland, H. Fayle: Clogher Valley Rly Locomotive
Institution of Junior Engineers 1929 p. 243: Sec. Elevation class 'D' Locomotive

BAGULEY (ENGINEERS) LTD
SHOBNALL ROAD
BURTON-ON-TRENT

Established in 1911 for the construction of lorries, railway rolling stock, internal combustion railcars and locomotives, the first steam locomotive was built in 1920 as Works No. 2001, and a total of 31 such locomotives were built up to 1928, together with 9 power-bogies for steam railmotors for Poland in 1931.

In the latter half of 1924, a light steam locomotive of unusually interesting design was built to the order of the Egyptian Delta Light Railways and delivered in September of that year. This locomotive, Plate 4, (Works No. 2028), was designed to haul one or two passenger coaches only on a suburban service at about 20 mph. Built to a rail gauge of 2 ft 5½ in. (75 cm), it had a vertical boiler

Plate 4 Baguley (Engineers) Ltd's geared locomotive built in 1924 for Egyptian Delta Light Railways.
Baguley-Drewry Ltd

at one end and a Vee-type compound engine arranged across the frame at the other end, the drive to all four wheels being through a clutch, two-speed gear, transverse shaft, and silent chains; the boiler and engine were designed by Mr Thomas Clarkson and constructed by Clarkson Steam Motors Ltd, Moulsham Street, Chelmsford.

Apart from the Clarkson thimble-tube boiler, this locomotive was unusual in that the engine was not intended to be stopped and started at each halt, but ran continuously as long as the locomotive was in use, movement being controlled by the clutch. The compound Vee-type engine had a high-pressure cylinder of 3¾ in. in diameter, and the low-pressure cylinder had a diameter of 6 in. and a 4 in. stroke. Steam was distributed by piston valves, and the cut-off was fixed; the engine ran in one direction only. There was no provision for running the low-pressure cylinder on high pressure steam as the gearbox provided ample torque at starting under all conditions, but the engine was thus not self-starting from all positions of rest, and also the fixed cut-off and the valve lead were designed for full speed running.

To overcome the starting difficulty, if this should arise, a specially designed foot-operated "barring-gear" was installed in the cab, and this was said to work with very little effort from the driver. Reversing was effected by sliding one or the other of a pair of bevels on the transverse shaft into engagement with the bevel on the drive shaft from the gearbox. Double sprockets were fitted to each end of the transverse shaft, and from these two silent chains on each side drove chain sprockets on each axle. Each axlebox was provided with slides for chain adjustment, and all chains were enclosed in sheet-steel casings. With an engine speed of 800 rpm the two gear ratios gave rail speeds of 12 mph and 24 mph, and the locomotive was capable of hauling a load of 8½ tons up a gradient of 1 in 12.

A full description of this Baguley-Clarkson design appeared in *Engineering* for 25th December, 1925, and was illustrated with 10 drawings and one photograph.

About 1929 Baguleys engaged a Mr S.R. Devlin, who had been chief draughtsman of Clayton Wagons Ltd, and when in 1930 the firm took over a Polish order for Clayton steam railmotors, a Baguley-Devlin design was developed. The order came from H. Cegielski of Warsaw, Poland, and the contract was for nine power-bogies; these were built in two separate batches, Works Nos. 2033 to 2037 were ordered on 1st March, 1930, and Works Nos. 2038 to 2041 on 8th May, 1930. The actual delivery dates are not known, but would have been early in 1931.

The first batch were of 100 hp and were single speed machines and, for a geared locomotive, had the unusual feature of a "step-up" ratio of 43 to 56 between the crankshaft and driving axle. The second batch, also of 100 hp had a two-speed drive between crankshaft and axle; the gear ratio required had to be selected while at rest and could not be changed when running.

These power-bogies, *Plate 5*, were modified considerably from the original Clayton design in that outside bearings were used, and the engine drove only the leading axle, which had spoked wheels, the other axle being provided with disc wheels. Single driving wheels were decided on as being much more efficient, for experience with large internal-combustion railcars had proved that coupled wheels were unnecessary for main line service over normal gradients. The frame length was 13 ft, with a wheelbase of 7 ft and the engine was a two cylinder, horizontal, high-pressure, totally enclosed unit with cylinders 7 in. in diameter by 10 in. stroke. The cylinders, crank-case and gearbox were bolted together so as to form one unit, supported at the gearing end by large bearings surrounding the driving axle; the other end was carried by a link attached to a pivot midway between the cylinders and crank-case.

Plate 5 Power bogie built by Baguley (Engineers) Ltd in 1931 for Poland. The axle-hung engine drove the front spoked wheels.   *Baguley-Drewry Ltd*

Plate 6 The engine and boiler of the Baguley-Devlin railmotor built in 1931 on test at Burton-on-Trent factory. *Baguley-Drewry Ltd*

The engine had piston valves operated by a modernised version of Dodds' wedge motion mounted on a countershaft below the crankshaft, and running in an oil-bath. The piston valves had separate heads, each of which was matched to its own half-liner so that the valve could be dismantled for cleaning and replaced exactly without the need for resetting; this engine appears to have been closely based on the Clayton design. The rare photograph, *Plate 6*, illustrates a single-speed engine and boiler set up on test at the Shobnall Works, and also shows how the oil pump, visible on the side of the crank-case, was driven off the valve gear countershaft. It will be appreciated that the extension carrying the axle supported bearings has been left off, and a fly-wheel fitted direct to the end of the crank-shaft.

The boiler was of the compact and efficient Spencer-Hopwood type, as used on steam cranes, and as it was bolted together it could be dismantled for cleaning and repairs. It was mounted at the rear of the bogie, behind the bolster which supported the coach. This was possible because the side frames of the latter extended forward from the body to attach to the bolster, which swung under the floor of the driving compartment. The frame extension and bolster thus formed a yoke surrounding the boiler below the floor of the driving compartment, an arrangement that gave a good weight distribution both with the coach attached and also without.

With the large external water tank located at the front of the bogie, and the engine laying horizontally to the rear of the driving axle, the boiler position just ahead of the rear axle, was in the right place to give the shortest pipe runs. The floor of the driving compartment was in line with the top of the frames at the front of the bogie, the latter being dropped to accommodate the bolster.

For details of these Baguley-Devlin power-bogies the writer is indebted to Mr R. Weaver of Kenilworth.

The firm became Baguley-Drewry in June 1967 until its closure in 1985.

WILLIAM BALMFORTH
PEELINGS FOUNDRY
RODLEY LANE
RODLEY, NR. LEEDS

The first mention of Balmforth appears in a Directory for 1820 and the following "titles" were mostly obtained from similar sources.

- 1820 Jeremiah Balmforth & David Smith; Calverley Bridge, Millwrights
- c1833 Became Balmforth, Booth & Smith
- c1840 Started building Cranes
- 1845 Balmforth, Smith & Booth
- 1847 Booth left and established the Union Foundry
- 1847–61 Balmforth & Smith
- 1864 William Balmforth (Engineers etc.) Peel Ings Foundry. (William was the Son of Jeremiah).
- 1881 Firm became Executors of William Balmforth
- 1897 Sons took charge becoming Balmforth Bros Ltd (James and Joseph)
- 1916 Firm failed, acquired by Samuel Butler & Co. Ltd
- c1922 Foundry closed and operations transferred to Butler's Albion Works at Stanningly.

Quarry and Contractors' plant, Scottish derricks, locomotive steam cranes, excavators and all kinds of lifting gear were manufactured and a small number of locomotives were built having vertical boilers, outside frames and cylinders which were inclined, the whole being carried on half-elliptical springs mounted above the frames as shown in *Plate 7*. The few dimensions were: diameter of wheels 1 ft 10 in., cylinders 8 in. × 14 in., the gauge of this particular locomotive being 3 ft. Connecting rods were round section with marine type big ends. When new the boiler had cross tubes and worked at 60 lb. psi, weighed 7 tons and the average load hauled with apparent ease was 60 tons. The curious arrangement of the valve gear was Stephenson link motion actuated through a rocking shaft, the long rod seen on the outside of the frames extending from the front of the locomotive right back to the valve chest.

The period of building this and other locomotives is difficult to ascertain. The locomotive illustrated working at Walney Island was purchased second-hand in

14 VERTICAL BOILER LOCOMOTIVES

Plate 7 Balmforth Bros' locomotive built c.1876 for Piel & Walney Gravel Co. *F. Jones*

Plate 8 Balmforth Bros' Ltd locomotive for Piel & Walney Gravel Co. showing conical smokebox/chimney. *F. Jones*

1896 and was said to be about 20 years old, which puts the building as c.1876. Another worked at Newbie Brickworks, Annan which came to this firm from Motherwell, Lanarkshire, in 1890 and was standard gauge. It bore the name IVANHOE and was scrapped in 1910. According to the firm's advertisement in *Engineering* in the 1880s the boilers then being made were fitted with Fox's patent corrugated steel fireboxes.

Two of these locomotives worked for many years at the Piel and Walney Gravel Co., Barrow-in-Furness. The proprietor of the site was Hunter who traded under his own name as a builder and contractor until 1926. He used the locos on various sites around Barrow in his capacity as an independent contractor and owner of the gravel company. The locomotive shown in *Plate 8* is distinguished by outside exhaust pipes, square topped horn guides and in later years by a conical smokebox/chimney. The boiler was replaced in 1956 by a conventional horizontal one taken off a Burrell agricultural engine and the loco rebuild was scrapped in 1960. The second Walney locomotive bore the name "Balmforth Bros Ltd", on the valve chest covers which indicates that the building date was 1897 or after, probably suggesting that Mr Hunter was pleased with his second-hand purchase, and bought the second one from Balmforth's as new. This had round-topped horn guides and other detail differences particularly in the arrangement of steam and exhaust pipework. The boiler was replaced in 1955 off a Marshall portable engine. It was scrapped in September 1960.

	Built	Cyls	D.W.	Gauge	
(1)	c.1876	8' × 14"	1' 1"	3 ft	Acquired second-hand by C.W. Hunter in 1896
(2)	by 1883	7" × ?		Std	Offered for sale at Parkeston, Harwich by Cochrane & Sons Contractors
(3)	by 1891	8" × ?		3 ft	Offered for sale 1.7.1891 by John H. Riddle, Glasgow
(4)	by 1892			3 ft	Offered for sale by auction 10.10.1892 at Contractor's Yard, Blackweir, Cardiff
(5)	1897★	8' × 14"		3 ft	Owned by Hunter (Piel & Walney Gravel Co.) possibly new
(6)	1897★			3 ft	Sheffield Corp. Longsett Reservoir. Here by 1900 nearly new? For sale 7/1906.
(7)	by 1911			3 ft	For sale 27.6.1911 by Wm. Kennedy, Glasgow

★or later

Of the above (1) and (3) could be the same locomotive and the same applies to (4), (6) & (7). On 18.3.1896 J. Bentley of Preston advertised a 3 ft gauge locomotive for sale and this could have been acquired by C.W. Hunter as his first locomotive. (5) was named THE DON. (2) could have gone to Edward Brooks, Newbie Brickworks, Annan.

References

Peter Holmes, Barrow-in-Furness (most of the above information)
M. Carter, Barrow-in-Furness
I.R.S. Handbook *Industrial Locomotives of Scotland* p. N 32
I.L.S. Journal Vol. 11 No. 3, May–June 1959, p. 7
Western Mail 4th October, 1892

ANDREW BARCLAY, SONS AND COMPANY LTD
CALEDONIA WORKS
KILMARNOCK

Established in 1840, the first locomotive to be built at the Caledonia Works was in 1859 and between this date and 1962 it is estimated that more than 2000 steam locomotives were built. The knowledge that Andrew Barclay was responsible for building one or more locomotives of the vertical boiler type comes from the text of a letter written by Barclay to the editor of *Engineering* dated 1st November, 1870. Apparently there had been recently published a description of a vertical boiler invented by J. Paxman, of Colchester, and the object of Barclay's letter was to point out that his own earlier patents were substantially the same.

The paragraph in which reference is made to a locomotive runs as follows:

> ... I enclose you a tracing of a boiler as made for contractors' locomotives by me, in which you will observe that instead of using the valves, as shown on the tops of the tubes in the boiler you illustrate to prevent priming, I make the roof of the firebox conical; this gives me room for a greater number of tubes, as you will see from the sectional plan of the tracing enclosed, and in the blue book for the year 1869, sheet 4, fig. 5; it also deflects laterally the current of water rising up, through the tubes being bent to the same angle as the roof...

The drawing of this boiler is reproduced in *Fig. 5*.

This information must have applied to the only two vertical boiler locomotives shown on the Works list.

Wks. No 105/1870 to H.C. Paterson, Agent, for Nova Scotia
Wks. No 156/1874 to Gray & Buchanan, Glasgow for Nova Scotia.

Both were 0–4–2 TVB with 5¼ in. dia. cylinders, no other details are known.

In 1905, Mr Pickersgill of the Great North of Scotland Railway, designed two railmotors, numbered 29 and 31, for service on the Lossiemouth and St Combs branches and these are illustrated here by *Plate 9*, but no photograph has yet been discovered showing the power-bogie only. The engine units were built by Andrew Barclay (Works numbers 1055/6 of 1905) and were equipped with the patent vertical boilers made by Cochran and Co. of Annan, the first and probably the only time that such boilers have been used in railway work. The firebox was almost hemispherical, pressed from a single flat plate, and there were neither stay nor rivet heads in contact with the fire. The gases passed through the side of the firebox over a brick arch and into the lower series of tubes, thence into a combustion chamber and back again through other tubes before passing to waste.

There were 295 horizontal return tubes 3 ft 11½ in. long and 1½ in. in diameter. The two openings in the furnace for firing and outlet were made without rivetted flanges, and the foundation ring was pressed from a flat plate. The boiler had a height of 9 ft 6 in. and the large diameter of 6 ft, and the dome shaped top gave these vehicles a very odd appearance. The heating surface was 500 sq.ft, and the grate area 9 sq.ft; the working pressure was 150 lb. psi. The Cochran design is a very fine example of intricate boilermaking and an official photograph of one of these rail-motor boilers taken at the time of construction is reproduced on page 199 of *The Locomotive* for 1905.

Plate 9 Andrew Barclay, Sons & Co. Ltd: railmotor with Cochran boiler built in 1905 for the Great North of Scotland Railway.
Andrew Barclay, Sons & Co. Ltd

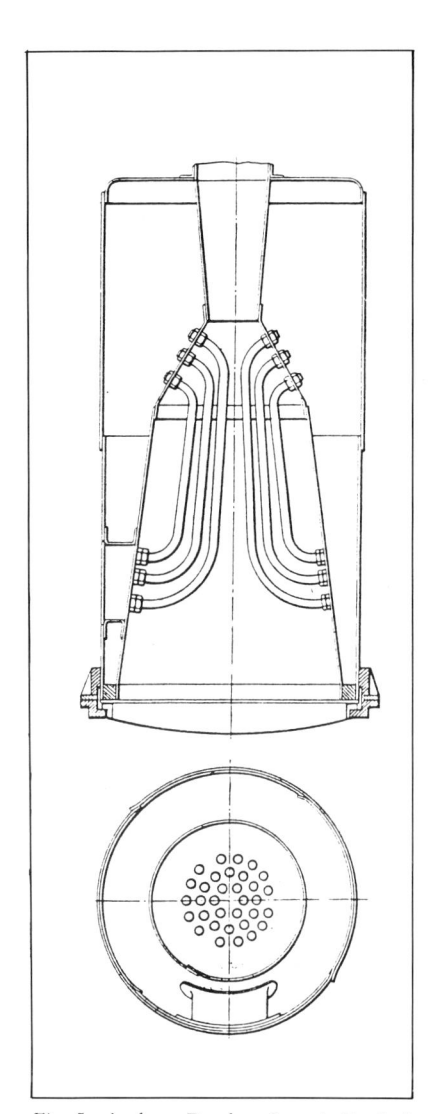

Fig. 5 Andrew Barclay, Sons & Co. Ltd: boiler for contractors' locomotives, 1869.
Engineering

The two horizontal cylinders, driving the leading wheels only, had a diameter of 10 in. with a stroke of 16 in., and the diameter of the driving wheels was 3 ft 7 in. on a wheelbase of 10 ft. The water tank had a larger capacity than was usual at this period and held 600 gallons.

The coachwork of these vehicles was constructed in the railway workshops at Inverurie, and had a seating capacity for 45 passengers on "garden" type chairs arranged on either side of an open saloon 34 ft 7 in. long. At the rear was a small compartment with side doors, by which the passengers entered; this space was the driver's position for reverse running. The overall length was 49 ft 11½ in., and the approximate weight in working order and with a full complement of passengers amounted to 47 tons. On trial between Inverurie and Aberdeen, one of these railmotors reached a speed of 60 mph and attained a speed of 30 mph in twenty seconds.

These railmotors are reported to have been complete failures in everyday service, for the boilers proved inadequate, and this is rather surprising in view of the high reputation that the Cochran type boiler has for being a copious generator of steam. After two years these vehicles were dismantled into their component parts; the bodies being converted into short bogie third class saloons, and the power-bogies into tank locomotives. As locomotives they did not survive long, and were withdrawn in 1909 and 1910.

The firm merged with the Hunslet Group in 1972 and the Works are fully utilised.

THE BEDFORD ENGINEERING COMPANY
AMPTHILL ROAD
BEDFORD

Established about 1890 at a site on the Ampthill Road near the Midland Railway main line, the Bedford Engineering Company primarily built steam cranes, but during the first decade or so of the present century it was also producing small vertical boiler locomotives, many details of which appear to have been constructed from standard crane components.

The locomotive illustrated in *Plate 10*, was built for an Indian railway of 1 ft 6 in. gauge about the year 1910, but these locomotives could be supplied for any gauge up to 4 ft 8½ in. The framing was of mild steel, mounted on steel-tyred wheels with volute springs, each axle having a steel spur wheel, both of which were in mesh with a large spur wheel on the countershaft; this latter was driven by a pinion on the crankshaft.

A two-cylinder horizontal engine with disc cranks had link reversing gear, while the boiler, which was of steel with water-tubes, had a working pressure of 130 lb. psi. A former employee, now deceased, stated that the firm built a number of these locomotives, but was unable to say whether any were for use in Great Britain; it has been suggested that several went to an Indian colliery company and presumably the locomotive illustrated was one of these. While it

BEDFORD ENGINEERING and BEYER, PEACOCK

Plate 10 The Bedford Engineering Co's design of locomotive as built c.1910. J.B. Latham

seems certain that only a few were built, the design was offered in three sizes as follows:

Cylinders:	4½ in. × 6½ in.	5 in. × 6½ in.	6 in. × 8 in.
Approximate speed on level:	8 mph	9 mph	10 mph
Tonnage hauled on level:	25	40	60
Tonnage hauled up 1 in 30:	5	7	11
Approximate weight in tons:	4	4½	5½
Price:	£275	£325	£375

The works of the Bedford Engineering Co. closed about 1932 due to declining orders and rising costs.

BEYER, PEACOCK AND COMPANY LTD
GORTON FOUNDRY
MANCHESTER

Founded in 1854 by Charles F. Beyer and Richard Peacock, the firm's first locomotive was built in July 1855. They quickly established a reputation for first class workmanship. Besides a healthy home market locomotives were exported

20   VERTICAL BOILER LOCOMOTIVES

Plate 11 Beyer Peacock & Co's Wilkinson type locomotive for Manchester, Bury, Rochdale & Oldham Steam Tramways Co.   *North Western Museum of Science & Industry*

to all parts of the World. They were later noted for their Beyer–Garratt types. As mentioned elsewhere a licence to manufacture steam tram locomotives under Wilkinson's Patent was taken up by Beyer, Peacock & Co. Ltd, and between 1883 and 1886 a total of 71 were built, of which 70 went to four tramway companies in England, and 1 was exported to Australia; *Plate 11* illustrates one for the 3 ft 6 in. gauge section of the Manchester, Bury, Rochdale and Oldham Steam Tramways Company.

The seventy-one locomotives were built as under:

Date	Works No.	Tramway	No.	Gauge
1883	2377–82	Manchester, Bury, Rochdale & Oldham	6	3 ft 6 in.
1883	2383–92	South Staffordshire Tramways	10	3 ft 6 in.
1883	2393	North Staffordshire Tramways	1	4 ft
1883	2411–29	North Staffordshire Tramways	19	4 ft
1885	2464	Sydney, New South Wales	1	4 ft 8½ in.
1884	2593–94	Coventry and District Tramways	2	3 ft 6 in.
1884	2595–2600	South Staffordshire Tramways	6	3 ft 6 in.
1884	2609–10	South Staffordshire Tramways	2	3 ft 6 in.
1886	2713–32	Manchester, Bury, Rochdale & Oldham	20	3 ft 6 in.
1886	2733–36	Manchester, Bury, Rochdale & Oldham	4	4 ft 8½ in.

The most successful tram locomotives built under Wilkinson's Patent were the final ones by Beyer, Peacock, who in 1886 fitted the more conventional air condensers similar to those developed by Kitson & Company rather than the type patented by Wilkinson. In the latter the exhaust steam was taken through a box fitted with horizontal tubes open at each end to the atmosphere, but positioned at right angles to the track. For details of the locomotives see the "William Wilkinson" section.

In 1961 the Works were re-organised to build diesel locomotives mainly with hydraulic transmission, but orders fell short of expectations, particularly when British Railways decided to standardise on diesel electric traction, a few of which were built. The Works closed in 1966.

MR J.L. BIRLEY
KIRKHAM
LANCS

Mr Birley who was the owner of a large factory in Kirkham owned an estate nearby. He was a man highly skilled in engineering practice and had built all manner of stationary steam engines, steam launches, and a home-made windmill. He also laid out a 20 in. gauge railway about 400 yds long and built a vertical boiler locomotive of unusual design consisting of a four-wheeled truck with a geared drive on to the rear pair of wheels. The boiler was a square multi-tubular boiler which provided steam to a vertical Willans compound engine. No dimensions are available but the "period" photograph (*Plate 12*) gives a good impression of the layout. The attached vehicle was also built by Mr Birley to accommodate passengers.

A second locomotive was built in 1893 with a more conventional horizontal boiler. The cabs of both locomotives were at least six feet in height. The second one built may well have used parts of the previous vertical boilered locomotive.

References

The Locomotive 5th September, 1903 p. 149
The Model Engineer 16th July, 1903 p. 62
Peter Holmes

Plate 12 J. Birley's 20 inch gauge locomotive built for his private railway.

P. Holmes Collection

Plate 13 Black, Hawthorn & Co's Wilkinson type locomotive built in 1883 for Alford & Sutton Tramway.

D.J. Sibley

BLACK, HAWTHORN & CO.
QUARRY FIELD WORKS
GATESHEAD

The Works were formerly occupied by Ralph Coulthard & Co. and were taken over by Black, Hawthorn & Co. in July 1865. The main products at first were stationary steam engines, boilers, pumps, winding engines and ships' engines. Locomotive building started in 1841 and gradually became the principal output of the works.

Works numbers were given to all types of production and a peculiarity of the system was that commencing at No. 190 no number was used ending in a nought with the exception of No. 730.

Four- and six-coupled tank locomotives were built for industry with a lesser number of larger types. The firm became a limited liability company in 1892 and ceased trading in 1896 and a partnership was then formed to take over the business with the title of Chapman & Furneaux. This only lasted until 1902 when the company went out of business following the death of the principal partner. The goodwill was taken over by R. & W. Hawthorn Leslie & Co. Ltd.

Black, Hawthorn & Co. were one of three firms who were granted a licence from William Wilkinson of Wigan to construct the latter's design of vertical boiler tram locomotives under his Patent No. 67 of 1881. A total of 33 were built. See the section on Wilkinson for description on his patented tram locomotive (*Plate 13*).

The firm had already built eight tram locomotives to other designs. All are listed together with the other vertical boiler locomotives built which include crane locomotives ordered by the Consett Iron Co. and the Dowlais Iron Co.

In *Machinery Market* for December 1890 a vertical boiler locomotive by Black, Hawthorn & Co. was advertised for sale, having 6 in. × 12 in. cylinders and a boiler of 3 ft diameter and 6 ft high suitable for 3 ft gauge, but this cannot be otherwise identified.

References

Manchester, Bury, Rochdale, & Oldham Steam Tramway, W.G.S. Hyde (Illustrations)
The Industrial Locomotive, Vol. 3, No. 26, pp. 55–6; No. 31, p. 160; No. 33, pp. 195–7
O.J. Sibley
A.C. Baker
Journal of the North of England Institute of Mining & Mechanical Engineers, Vol. XXIX, No. 506
Black, Hawthorn & Co – Works List, Allan C. Baker

BLACK, HAWTHORN & CO. VERTICAL BOILERED LOCOMOTIVES

Works No.	Date Ordered	Date Built	Type	Cyls	D.W.	Gauge	For	No. or Name
Wilkinson Type								
707	2.9.1882	1882	0–4–0VBTM	6¾"×10"	2'3½"	Std	City of London Contract Corporation for Gateshead & District Tramways	1
708	26.10.1882	"	"	"	"	"	"	2
709	"	"	"	"	"	"	"	3
711	"	1883	"	"	"	"	"	4
712	"	"	"	"	"	"	"	5
713	"	"	"	"	"	"	"	6
717	16.10.1882	"	"	6½"×9"	"	3'0"	North Shields & Tynemouth District Tramways Ltd	1
718	"	"	"	"	"	"	"	2
719	"	"	"	"	"	"	"	3
735	9.1.1883	"	"	7¼"×11"	"	2'6"	W.B. Dick & Co. London for Alford & Sutton Tramway	1
776	26.11.1883	20.2.1884	"	"	"	Std	City of London Contract Corporation for Gateshead & District Tramways	7
777	"	5.3.1884	"	"	"	"	"	8
783	28.12.1883	2.5.1884	"	"	"	"	"	9
784	"	16.5.1884	"	"	"	"	"	10
785	"	30.5.1884	"	"	"	"	"	11
786	"	13.6.1884	"	"	"	"	"	12
815	30.4.1884	1884	"	"	"	3'6"	City of London Contract Corporation for Manchester, Bury, Rochdale & Oldham Steam Tramways Co.	42
816	"	"	"	"	"	"	"	43
817	"	"	"	"	"	"	"	44
818	"	"	"	"	"	"	"	45
819	"	"	"	"	"	"	"	46
821	"	"	"	"	"	"	"	47
822	"	1885	"	"	"	"	"	48
823	"	"	"	"	"	"	"	49
824	"	"	"	"	"	"	"	50
825	"	"	"	"	"	"	"	51

Works No.	Date Ordered	Date Built	Type	Cyls	D.W.	Gauge	For	No. or Name
827	12.8.1884	"	"	"	"	Std	Gateshead & District Tramways	13
835	15.1.1885	"	"	7½"×11"	"	4'7¾"	Corporation of Huddersfield Tramways	7
836	17.1.1885	1.5.1885	"	7¼"×?	"	"	South Kensington Exhibition to Corporation of Huddersfield Tramways	WILMENSEN 9
842	31.3.1885	5.1885	"	6½"×9"	"	4'8⅛"	Antwerp Exhibition	
849	12.5.1885	1885	"	7½"×11"	"	4'7¾"	Corporation of Huddersfield Tramways	8
964	11.1.1889	1889	"	"	"	Std	Gateshead & District Tramways	14
965	"	"	"	"	"	"	"	15

B.H. Vertical Boiler Locos

Works No.	Date Ordered	Date Built	Type	Cyls	D.W.	Gauge	For	No. or Name
506	14.6.1879	1879	0-4-0VBTM	C 7"×11"×12"	2'0"	Std	Experimental, C.Lund, Newcastle (for overseas?)	
522	31.10.1879	"	"	C 6"×11"×11"	2'2"	"	?	
579	6.1880	1880	"	10"×15"	3'6"	"	F.C. Winby, Notts. for Tynemouth Tramways (possibly not delivered)	
581	"	1881	"	"	"	"	"	
582	"	1880	"	"	"	"	"	
589	14.10.1880	1881	"	7"×12"	2'4"	M	Hugh Wilson for shipment. Liverpool probably to Brazil	
624	2.1881	"	"	10"×15"	3'0"	4'	W. Lyster Holt, London for North Staffordshire Steam Tramways (possibly not delivered)	CONDE
625	"	"	"	"	"	"	"	
1084	3.4.1893	1893	0-4-0VBT	4"×5"	1'4½"	1'6"	J. Kensington for Minas Huelle Santander, Spain	CARBARCENO

Vertical Boiler Crane Locomotives

Works No.	Date Ordered	Date Built	Type	Cyls	D.W.	Gauge	For	Tons Lift	No.
831	15.10.1884	1885	CT 0-4-0VB	OC 8"×12"	2'9"	Std	Consett Iron Co.	2	D No3
897	6.1.1887	1887	CT 2.4.0VB	OC 13½"×21"	3'	"	"	12	E No1
898	"	"	"	"	"	"	"	"	E No2
931	27.1.1888	1888	CT 0-4-0VB	OC 12"×21½"	"	"	Dowlais Iron Co. Ltd, East Moors, Cardiff	7	E No3
986	8.10.1889	1890	"	"	"	"	"	"	1
987	"	"	"	"	"	"	"	"	"
1048	18.8.1891	1892	"	"	"	"	Consett Iron Co.	"	E No5
1049	"	"	"	"	"	"	"	"	E No6
1051	"	"	"	"	"	"	"	"	E No7
*1206	11.12.1900	1901	"	"	"	"	"	"	E No10

Note: 7 ton cranes had 8"×8" lifting cyls, 6"×7" slewing cyls.

*Chapman & Furneaux

BLAENAVON CO. LTD.
GWENT

The Blaenavon Iron & Coal Co. was formed in 1836 and eventually consisted of two blast furnace and coke oven sites, one going over to steel production in 1878; numerous collieries and a limestone quarry were served by a network of internal railways ranging from standard gauge to 3 ft 4 in., and 3 ft. In the early days plateways and tramways were used. Connections were made with the Monmouthshire Railway and Canal Co., and the London and North Western Railway at the Forgeside site. The Forgeside furnaces were dismantled 1934–5 but the locomotives remained principally for colliery duties, some six conventional locomotives eventually becoming N.C.B. property.

Changes in title were:

Blaenavon Iron & Coal Co. 1836–1864
Blaenavon Co. Ltd 1865–1870
Blaenavon Iron & Steel Co. Ltd 1871–1879
Blaenavon Co. Ltd 1880–1957

The company went into voluntary liquidation on 21st June, 1957 but the original furnaces remain in the guardianship of the Secretary of State for Wales.

Three geared Vertical Boiler Locomotives were at some time used for coke oven work, two of which appear to have been built by A. Chaplin & Co. with the third possibly made by the Company.

References

The Engineer, Vol. 51, 25th February, 1881
J. Fletcher
P. Ashforth

FREDERIC BRADLEY
CLENSMORE IRONWORKS
CLENSMORE, KIDDERMINSTER

This firm of general engineers is recorded in the 1864 P.O. Directory as John Bradley and Company, Ironfounders, Clensmore, and in the same Directory for 1868 as Frederic Bradley, Ironfounder.

The brief connection with locomotive engineering by this concern came about under the following circumstances. In 1814 the town of Ryde in the Isle of Wight had invested in a pier with the unusual length of 580 yds, and in 1861 the pier company widened the structure to carry a 4 ft 8½ in. gauge tramway, and this was opened with horse traction in 1864. Later, in 1871, an extension was completed to the St John's Road terminus of the Isle of Wight Railway, but this section was closed in 1880 and the tramway curtailed to serve the pier only.

During 1880 Mr F. Bradley of the Kidderminster Works had a contract for repairing Ryde Pier, and as by June of that year the pier company had decided to try steam traction on its tramway, an order was placed with Mr Bradley, who rebuilt two of the horse tramcars with vertical boilers and engines driving the four wheels through a jack-shaft and coupling rods. Both boilers were fitted with gas furnaces, but when tested at the Kidderminster Works these burnt 3000 cubic feet of gas per hour, instead of the estimated 1000 cubic feet.

The Directors of the Pier Co. therefore decided to have the boilers converted to coke burners at a cost of £40 each before delivery, which took place on 6th January, 1881: both vehicles then proved very successful and economical, consuming five cwt. of coke daily. By 1884 both boilers needed new fireboxes and tubes and from October of that year the Directors decided to again work their tramway with horse cars. In 1886 the Ryde Gas Company bought both steam cars for £42 and after repairs and the fitting of wagon-type bodies employed them hauling coal and coke about the works until May 1896 when they were sold to a Mr W. Ferguson of Leytonstone. No drawing or photograph of these steam cars has been discovered up to the time of writing in spite of enquiries over many years.

By 1921 an amalgamation had been effected between the businesses of F. Bradley and the ironfounding firm, established in 1831 by George Turton and his brother Richard, the new undertaking becoming Bradley and Turton Limited, engineers, Stourport Road and Clensmore Foundry.

In 1979 the address of the firm was Bradley and Turton Limited, Caldwell Works, Kidderminster.

BRAITHWAITE & ERICSSON
NEW ROAD
LONDON

John Braithwaite had a workshop in New Road, London, and when he died in 1818 it was carried on by his two sons, John and Francis. Francis died in 1823 and in 1827 John took John Ericsson, a Swede, into partnership. Ericsson was an Engineer and in 1829 they designed and built a locomotive for the forthcoming Rainhill Trials and named it NOVELTY.

It resembled basically a fire engine, designed and built currently with the locomotive. The boiler was mainly vertical but had a horizontal section 15 ft long × 15 in. dia. equipped with a return tube through which heated air was passed. It had two vertical cylinders 6 in. × 12 in., wheels 4 ft 2⅕ in. diameter and a water tank holding 120 gallons; boiler pressure was 50 lb. psi. Forced draught was applied by bellows and the pair of wheels adjacent to the boiler were driven by means of bell cranks, see *Plate 14*.

Unfortunately NOVELTY was constructed in a hurry and no trial runs were made before arriving at Rainhill. After some adjustments it was steamed and startled the audience by reaching a speed of 28 mph following which it broke down; after numerous attempts to get it going again the trials were abandoned.

In 1830 two more vertical boiler locomotives were built for the Liverpool and Manchester Railway. They were named WILLIAM IV and QUEEN ADELAIDE respectively, both carried on four wheels with boilers similar in design to NOVELTY, but without bellows, relying on the exhaust draught and a small fan. Neither succeeded in meeting the conditions laid down—to haul 40 tons in two hours between Liverpool and Manchester using not more than 1½ lb. of coke per ton mile.

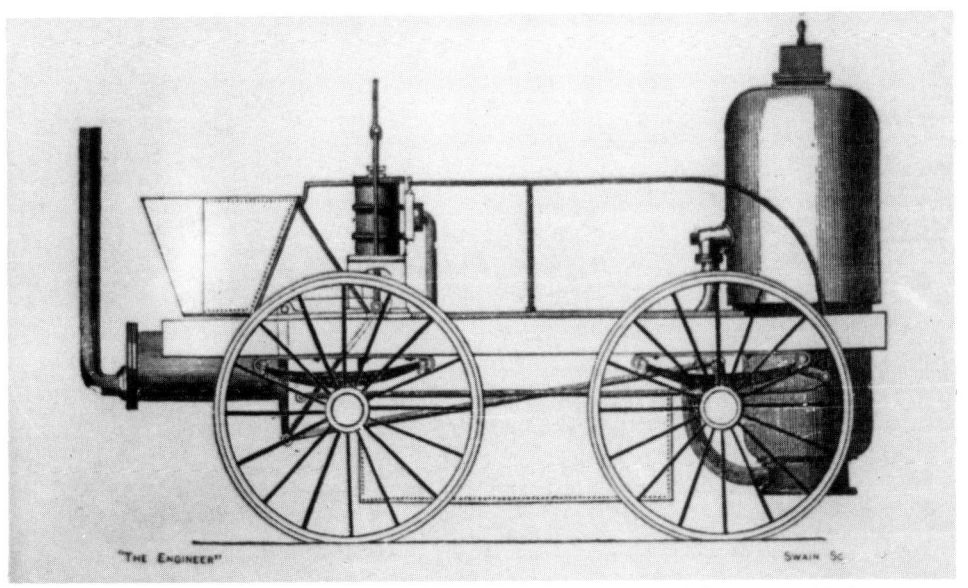

Plate 14 Braithwaite & Ericsson's *Novelty* built in 1829 for the Rainhill Contest. *Engineer*

NOVELTY was rebuilt with a new tubular boiler in 1833 and all three may have been sold to the St Helens & Runcorn Gap Railway.

More conventional locomotives were subsequently built, the majority being the 0–4–0 Bury type and at least sixteen went to America, with six 0–4–0s and six 2–2–0s to the Eastern Counties Railway.

The firm failed in 1836/7 but carried on building until 1841, probably under Receivership.

BRIDGEWATER COLLIERIES
WORSLEY

The provenance of the locomotive illustrated by *Fig. 6*, is unknown, but according to the inscription on the original drawing was the "first locomotive on Bridgewater Collieries, 1880. The locomotive worked at Worsley Yard and Worsley Tip only. Makers unknown, but not made at Worsley or Walkden Yard. Coupled wheels about 2 ft in diameter. Reversing probably by gears. 1 cylinder about 8 in. bore. Gear ratio 4 to 1. Working pressure 80 lb. per square inch". The drawing is date-stamped "Engineering Department, Walkden, 25 Jan. 1951".

It is said that this locomotive was in use at Worsley Shops when they were transferred to Walkden in 1900; later it is understood to have done some work at Walkden.

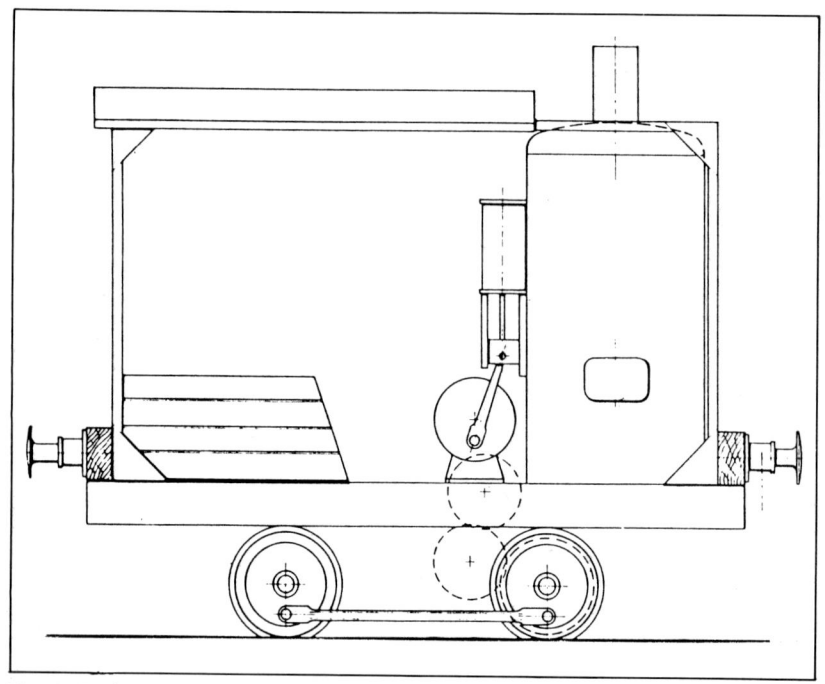

Fig. 6 Bridgewater Collieries' locomotive of unknown origin and date.

National Coal Board

Referring to the Author's article and drawing in the *Industrial Railway Record* No. 36 and subsequent correspondence in *I.R.R.* Nos. 42 and 50 there seems conflicting evidence as to whether the locomotive in question was a basic steam crane with the crane removed as indicated on the drawing or whether it was a Chaplin conventional vertical boiler locomotive, (Works No. 1643 of 1873), with centrally placed boiler. Apparently there was only one locomotive of this type working on the Bridgewater Collieries system so further investigation is required.

TIMOTHY BURSTALL
LEITH

Timothy Burstall, an engineer who had built a steam road coach in 1824 and a second one in 1827, entered a locomotive for the Rainhill contest held under the auspices of the Liverpool and Manchester Railway in 1829.

Until the mid-1920s few details of its construction were known except that the boiler was not tubular, but the late C.F. Dendy Marshall finally discovered a

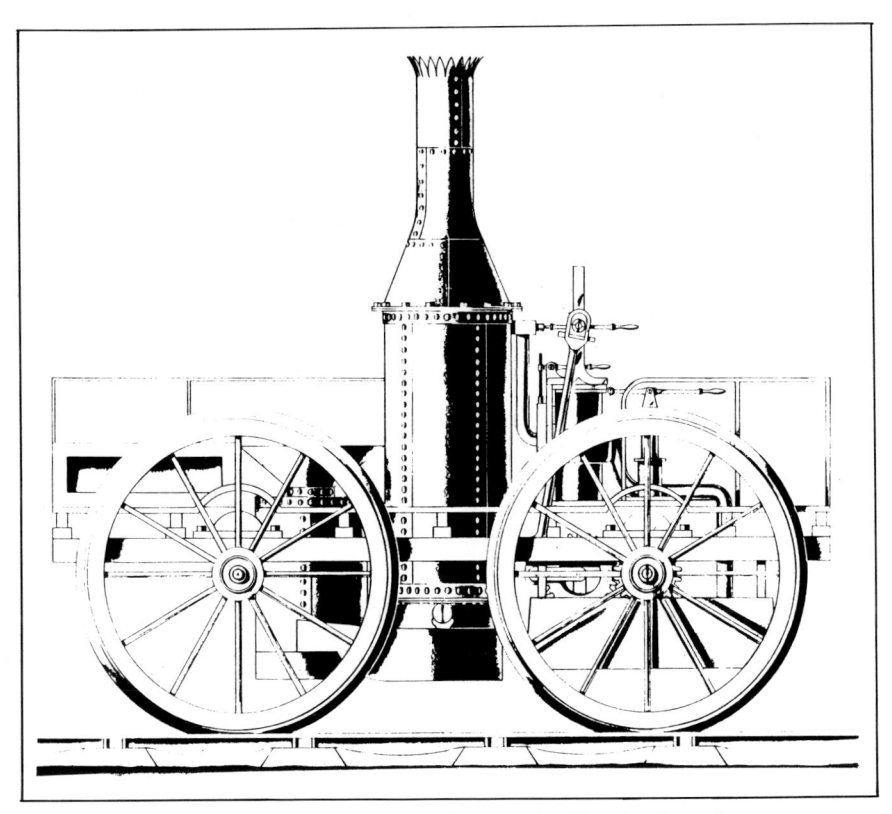

Fig. 7 The locomotive built for the Rainhill contest by Timothy Burstall.
Science Museum, London

lithograph in the possession of Mons. Charles Dollfus, of Paris, which is now generally considered to represent this locomotive, which was named PERSEVERANCE. This lithograph is reproduced on page 53 of *A History of Railway Locomotives down to the year 1831* by Dendy Marshall, 1953, and from this early print the excellent drawing, *Fig. 7*, had been built up by the Science Museum, London. No dimensions are known except that the weight was 2 tons, 17 cwt. and the drive was described as similar to that applied to the second steam road coach which had been built by Burstall and Hill.

From the drawing it will be observed that the piston rods of the two vertical cylinders worked through the top covers and were attached to crossheads, from which return connecting rods passed on either side of each cylinder to drive the crankshaft, which would therefore have had four cranks. From the crankshaft the drive was by gearing to one axle. The PERSEVERANCE was almost completely ignored in all the accounts of the trials, and its poor performance must be attributed to the inefficient form of boiler. The fuel appears to have been fed into the grate from below and in the words of Nicholas Wood when referring to the boiler of this locomotive "the heated air and flame escaped up the chimney without any flues to abstract the redundant heat".

With such a boiler it is understandable why the highest speed that was attained was only about 5 mph but this may not have been the only reason, for there is a Minute of the Liverpool and Manchester Directors, dated 5th October, 1829, the day before the commencement of the trials, which records that the locomotive met with an accident when being unloaded at Rainhill. In consequence of a chain coming loose, the machine fell to the ground and fractured one of the cranks, together with a pipe, so that although repairs were carried out in time, the whole locomotive must have been severely strained. The Board of the railway afterwards presented Burstall with £25 in aid of his expenses.

BUTLER BROS (?)

Notice of an auction sale by S. Hinder to be held on the 20th and 21st November, 1877 at the yard at Dauntsey station, GWR, re Budd & Holt, contractor for the Malmesbury Railway appeared in the *Engineer* for 9th and 16th November, 1877. The plant for sale included a 6 wheel tender locomotive and a 9 hp vertical locomotive on "Chaplins principle" by Butler Bros. A photograph (*Plate 15*) of an unidentified vertical boiler locomotive on this contract dates from 1876 and presumably is the same locomotive offered in the sale.

No company styled Butler Bros can be traced. There was a company John Butler & Co. of Albion Works, Stanningley with rail connection to the GNR and latterly the headquarters of Geo. Cohen's 600 Group. They were established in 1840 and early products included railway bridges as well as cranes. An offshoot was Samuel Butler & Co. Ltd (whose works were opposite those of John Butler Co.), who built steam cranes about the period of World War I and later (see also William Balmforth); seemingly too late to be considered the builder of this particular locomotive.

References

The Industrial Locomotive No. 23, Autumn 1981, Vol. 2, p. 185
The Industrial Locomotive No. 28, Winter 1983, Vol. 3, pp. 97–98
J.S. Brownlie

Plate 15 Unidentified 9 hp vertical boiler locomotive reputed to have been built by Butler Bros on the Malmesbury Railway contract.

THE BUTTERLEY COMPANY
RIPLEY
DERBYSHIRE

This company was formed in December 1792 by two civil engineers, Benjamin Outram and William Jessop, a coal owner Francis Beresford, and a banker John Wright.
Until 1823 the business was carried out under the title "Benjamin Outram & Co.". The main spheres of production were ironworks, collieries, quarries, stationary and marine engines. The Butterley Company was incorporated in 1888 and became a public limited company in 1901 and finally divided and reorganised in 1968.
To work its extensive railway systems not only at Ripley but at the Codnor Park puddling furnaces and rolling mills, quarries, etc. the company constructed locomotives in its own workshops at Ripley. Between 1860 and 1907 it built at least 26 locomotives most of which were four- and six-coupled saddle tanks. In addition six vertical boiler four-wheeled locomotives were built. They had a geared drive with a ratio of 3:1 with small 4 in. dia. cylinders. No further information has been forthcoming due to the destruction of their early records. Fortunately the drawing (*Fig. 8*) was discovered in private ownership and is now preserved in the Derbyshire Record Office.
About 1860 steam traction was introduced on the 3 ft 9 in. gauge system at Hilts Quarry. A 0-4-0 tender locomotive was used at first, later replaced by a 0-4-0 VBT apparently one of six bought (?) in 1871, Butterley Nos 14-19. Only one Chaplin loco is known to have been supplied (Works No. 1109/1869) so that it is probable that one or more of the remaining five could have been built by Butterley.
No. 23, a standard gauge VB locomotive built in 1870 was at Hartshay Colliery.

References

I. R.S. Pocket Book E, *Industrial Locomotives of the East Midlands*, pp. E.12 & 13
The Butterley Gangroad by "Dowie"

CALDOW AND McKINNEL
PALMERSTON FOUNDRY
DUMFRIES

The above firm built two vertical boiler locomotives of which no details have survived. One was for the standard gauge, and had a geared drive, and was supplied to Thompson and Company, of Catelawbridge Quarry, near Thornhill in Dumfriesshire. It was scrapped *c.*1910, and the quarry closed *c.*1914.
The other locomotive was built for the 2 ft 6 in. gauge line of the Kelhead Lime Co. near Annan in Dumfriesshire. This locomotive was scrapped in 1919, and the quarry closed in 1925. According to McDowell's "Visitors Guide" for the year 1860, the above engineering business was engaged in the manufacture of steam engines (both fixed and portable), railway wagon wheels, railway water tanks, signals and girders, and had been established by James A.B. McKinnel in 1818.

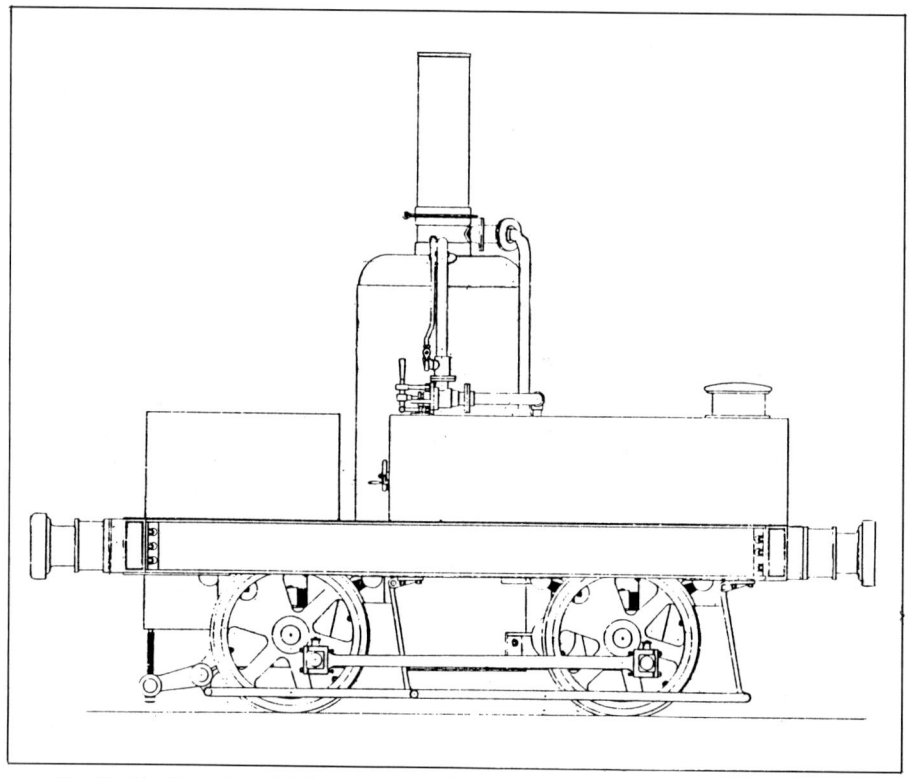

Fig. 8 The Butterley Co's locomotive built for own use c.1870.
Derby County Record Office, Matlock

ALEXANDER CHAPLIN AND COMPANY
CRANSTONHILL ENGINE WORKS
PORT STREET
ANDERSON, GLASGOW

Established in 1849 by Mr Chaplin as a general engineering works engaged in the repair of steam boilers, portable engines and pumps, new production commenced in 1857 with the building of contractors' plant for railway and dock undertakings. The once fairly numerous vertical boiler locomotives patented by Mr Chaplin were made in several sizes and for a variety of gauges from 2 ft 6 in. to 4 ft 8½ in., and although essentially alike in general layout, differed in details, and *Figs 9* and *10*, illustrate these variations. Some had spoked wheels, others disc; some dished-top boilers, others conical smokeboxes. A few may have had

ALEXANDER CHAPLIN & CO.

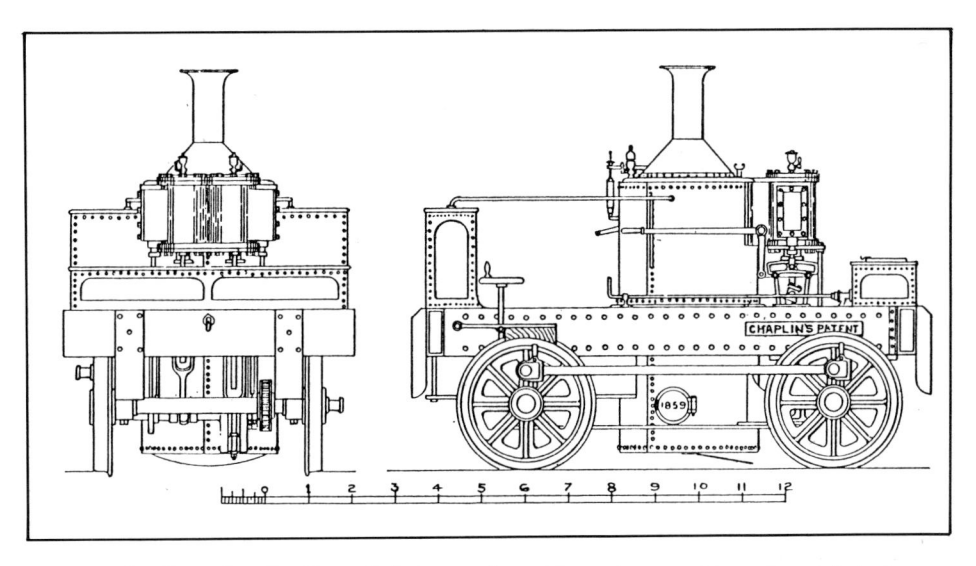

Fig. 9 Alexander Chaplin & Co's locomotive with marine type big ends and forked coupling rods. *Ian Allan*

Fig. 10 Alexander Chaplin & Co's locomotive showing variations in design from *Fig. 9* and *Plate 16*. *Ian Allan*

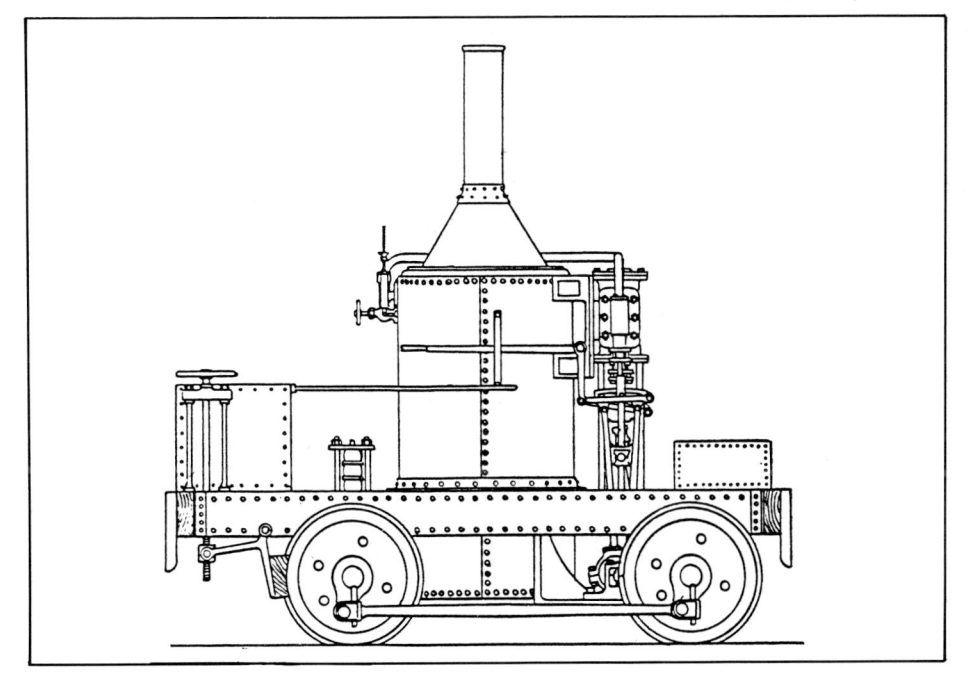

Plate 16 Locomotive 2368/1885 built by Alexander Chaplin & Co. for Northampton Gas Co.
Author

piston valves, others had balanced valves of semi-circular section; while cylinder dimensions of 4½ in. × 9 in., 6 in. × 12 in., 9 in. × 12 in., 7 in. × 14 in., and 9 in. × 16 in. have been recorded and the horsepower ranged from 6 to 27.

Other details that varied were bushed side rods in conjunction with cottered big ends to the connecting rods, or cottered side rods and connecting rods with marine type big ends. Furthermore, the connecting rods were sometimes forked, the piston rods being prolonged and working through guides, while at a later date the engines were of the design shown in *Plate 16*, which illustrates a Chaplin built in 1885. The coupled wheels varied from 2 ft 1½ in. in diameter to 3 ft in diameter and three different wheelbases are known, i.e. 5 ft 7 in., 6 ft 6 in., and 7 ft. The gear ratio was generally 2 to 1. The narrow gauge design had outside bearings to the axles, and the coupling rods worked on disc cranks.

Perhaps the most unusual feature of these locomotives was the boiler, which incorporated hanging tubes, patented by Mr Chaplin. The upright boiler had an internal firebox, in the slightly arched roof plate of which were screwed a number of wrought-iron tubes welded up at their lower ends, and it was the disposition of these tubes that formed the chief peculiarity of the boiler. They were all inserted in the arched top plate of the firebox at right angles to it, and their lower ends thus inclined inwards. The interval between the inner circle of tubes was filled up by a plug of fireclay, and the flames from the fire were thus caused by the action of the draught to strike against the sides of the firebox; after being deflected from it they passed in between the tubes to the central flue leading to the chimney. When working, the steam generated in these tubes discharged in a series of sudden bursts or minor explosions and this was found effectual in driving out any sediment that might have collected in the bottom of the tubes.

Another advantage claimed for this boiler was that it had ample space above the grate for complete combustion and was therefore well adapted for use with small coal, wood or even peat, and was found to generate steam very freely. The working pressure was 100 lb. psi.

The date when locomotive construction commenced was 1860 and a Patent, covering vertical boiler locomotives had been taken out by Mr Chaplin in 1857, and Works No. 140 of 1860 was the first built while the specification of a second Patent of 1866 described the use of double flanged wheels as an aid to greater adhesion, and a locomotive fitted with such wheels is said to have been built in that year.

The business was transferred to Helen Street, Govan, in 1890 and finally closed down in 1930. Some vertical boiler locomotives were attributed to McKendrick, Ball & Co. John McKendrick was a Partner in the Firm of A. Chaplin & Co. Ltd, $c.1860$ and Henry Ball was the London Agent, the address being 63 Queen Victoria Street, London E.C. These two gentlemen formed the company and eventually took over the engineering side of A. Chaplin under the original company name. During this time some locomotives bore the Works Plate: McKendrick, Ball & Co.

References

Leicestershire Records Service
J.S. Brownlie

ALEXANDER CHAPLIN & CO.
LIST OF VERTICAL BOILERED LOCOMOTIVES BUILT

Works No.	Ex Works	H.P.	Cyls	Gauge	Customer	Note
140	9.3.1860	12	6"×13"	Std	Meeson & Co., Stratford	
146	28.4.1860	6	4¼"×9"		Wm. Bird & Co., London	
152	16.4.1861	9	5¼"×11"	Std	York & Co., London per J.B. Brown & Co.	(a)
153	c.1860/1				Contractor	
156	27.12.1860	12	6"×13"		Henry Wrigg Nr. Kirkby Stephen	
177	21.3.1861	15	7"×14"	Std	R. Brotherhood, Chippenham per J.B. Brown & Co.	
178	19.12.1860	6		4'8"	John Frederic Bourne for Demerara	
188	2.3.1861	21	8"×14"	4'6"	Meeson & Co., Grays, Essex per J.B. Brown & Co.	
191	29.3.1861	21		4'6"	Stewart & Co., Isle of Portland	

Works No.	Ex Works	H.P.	Cyls	Gauge	Customer	Note
232	19.6.1861	15	7"×14"		John Martin Nr. Loughborough	(b)
239	16.3.1863	9			2nd hand to Smith & Knight, 1, Gt. George St., London	★
240	14.10.1862	12			Wm. Howie, Union St., Glasgow for John Coghill & Co., Renfrew	(c)
244	12.12.1861	6		4'8"	Spence & Buddon, London for Demerara	
275	29.11.1861	15	7"×14"	4'0"	Law & Blount, London	
277	31.3.1862	4			Hor. Engine Loco. for Wm. Bird & Co., London	(d)
305	1.1862	12			Thos. Vaughan, Southbanks Ironworks, Middlesbrough	
317	2.9.1863	9			Cochrane & Co., Middlesbrough	
358	7.4.1863	9			Cochrane & Co., Middlesbrough	
369	17.4.1863	12			York & Co., London	★
370	2.9.1863	12			Edward Bros, Belfast	(e)
371	8.3.1864	12			A. & K. McDonald, Wick	(f)
379	15.5.1863	15			Landré & Glinderman, Amsterdam	
381	7.10.1863	9			Cochrane & Co., Middlesbrough	
382	7.10.1863	9			Cochrane & Co., Middlesbrough	(g)
431	19.11.1864	12			James Watt & Co., London	★
432	8.2.1864	15			R. Sharpe & Sons, Westminster	★
458	14.3.1865	9			Forrest & Barr, Glasgow	(h)
466	28.6.1864	15			A. & K. McDonald, Park House, Paisley Road	
557	15.3.1865	12			Ireland & Co., Contractor, Montrose & Bervie Rly	(i)
574	18.2.1867	12			D. Graham Holt, Northfleet, Kent	★
581	14.3.1865	9			W. & T. York, Albert Harbour Works, Greenock	(j)
595	6.7.1866	9			Landré & Glinderman, Amsterdam	
708	6.8.1866	9		Std	Liebig's Extract of Meat Co., London per S. & W. Lellan	(k)
812	31.7.1867	15			Wimshurst & Co.	
828	23.11.1866	9			Baglan Hall Colls Co., Briton Ferry, Glam	★
852	8.1.1867	21			Smith, Fleming & Co., London. To U.S.A. (Michigan?)	★
909	6.1.1868	12			Bahia & San Francisco Rly. Co. Ltd, 11 Broad St., London	
985	30.12.1867	9		3'7½"	Wimshurst & Co.	
988	8.1.1868	9		2'2"	Wimshurst & Co. for Bourne & Robinson, Peasley Cross Colls.	
989	1.5.1868	12			J. & H. Keyworth & Co., Liverpool	
1034	30.6.1868	15			A. & K. McDonald	
1043	30.5.1868	15			Davy & Co., Königsberg, Prussia: BOB	
1056	28.7.1869	12			Wimshurst & Co. for D. Murray, Blisworth	(l)

ALEXANDER CHAPLIN & CO.

Works No.	Ex Works	H.P. Cyls	Gauge	Customer	Note
1095	6.3.1869	6		Wimshurst & Co.	
1102	4.5.1869	15		Pierre Devu, Polvolocźiska, Austria, Galicia	
1106	21.4.1869	9		Smith Fleming & Co., 18 Leadenhall St., London. To U.S.A. (Michigan?)	
1109	24.6.1869	6		Butterley Co., Alfreton	
1159	27.6.1870	12		H. Davy & R. Donath, Berlin: OTTO	
1162	11.10.1869	9	Std	Danish State Rly. per H.W. Casperson, Newcastle-upon-Tyne	
1163	11.10.1869	12	Std	Danish State Rly. per H.W. Casperson, Newcastle-upon-Tyne	
1181	19.9.1871	6	3'3"	Wimshurst & Co. for Johore Steam Saw Mills Co.	
1182	26.4.1870	12		G.E. Stevenson, Liverpool	
1184	15.3.1870	9	2'8"	Wimshurst & Co. for R.Campbell, Buscot Park, Berks.	
1185	27.6.1870	9		Humphrey Davy, Berlin: BRUNO	
1206	2.5.1870	6	3'6"	Redfern, Alexander & Co., London	
1207	6.4.1870	6	5'6"	Robinson & Majoribanks, Bothwell St., Glasgow for Russia	
1208	26.4.1870	6	5'6"	Robinson & Marjoribanks, Bothwell St., Glasgow for Russia	
1220	17.9.1871	6	2'8"	W.M. Gregory, Glyn Neath, Glam	
1227	12.7.1870	12	7' or Std	W.M. Gregory, Penallt Coll., Glyn Neath, Glam	
1233	12.5.1871	12		J. Perry & Co., Pensford, Nr. Bristol	
1241	15.12.1870	9	Std	Wimshurst & Co.	
1254	11.8.1870	9		Wimshurst & Co. for Budden, Jennings & Co. for Demerara	(m)
1290	9.1.1871	12	Std	Geo. Wilson & Co., Glaisdale Iron Works	(o)
1307	24.11.1870	12		G.E. Stevenson, Liverpool	
1394	15.11.1871	12	Std	Wimshurst & Co.	(p)
1406	16.12.1871	12	Std	Danish State Rly, Aarhus, Denmark	
1425	30.1.1872	12	Std	Danish State Rly, Aarhus, Denmark	
1443	6.6.1872	12	3'2"	Losh, Wilson & Bell, Newcastle-upon-Tyne	
1455	11.9.1872	9	3'6"	Wm. Briscoe & Son, Wolverhampton. To Otago, N.Z.	(DD)
1458	4.4.1872	12	Std	Archibald Hood, Lasswade for Glam. Coal Co. Ltd, Llwyn-y-Pia	
1476	26.8.1872	12		Wimshurst, Hollick & Co. for H. Simon, Manchester	
1477	11.1872		Std	Wimshurst, Hollick & Co. for The Colonial Co. Ltd.: EDITH	(q)

Works No.	Ex Works	H.P. Cyls	Gauge	Customer	Note
1481	28.2.1872	9		Wimshurst, Hollick & Co.	
1482	23.12.1872	12	Std	Wimshurst, Hollick & Co. for The Colonial Co. Ltd: MABEL	(q)
1483	9.4.1873			Wimshurst, Hollick & Co.	
1504	11.10.1872	9		S.W. Perrot Junr., Herne, Wesphalia	
1505	23.10.1872	12	Std	Belfast Harbour Commissioners	
1517	20.12.1872	12		Wimshurst, Hollick & Co.	
1518	24.3.1873	12		Wimshurst, Hollick & Co.	
1520	7.6.1873	12		Wimshurst, Hollick & Co.	
1523	1.7.1873	12		Wm.F. Burnley & Co., Glasgow	
1533	13.12.1872	15		Compagnie Miniere Belge. De Vignaes Svignies Antwerp	
1554	31.3.1873	9		A. Malcolm & Co., Princes Dock Chambers, Hull	
1584	12.4.1873	15		Sir John Goode, the Col. Gov. of Cape of Good Hope	(r)
1585	22.4.1873	9		Thomas Allan & Sons, South Stockton-on-Tees	
1596	7.10.1873	12		Davy, Donath & Co., Berlin	
1597	10.4.1873	12		Edward Woods, London	
1598	10.1.1874	12		Davy, Donath & Co., Berlin	(s)
1640	10.1.1874	12		Davy, Donath & Co., Berlin	
1643	20.11.1873	15		Bridgewater Trustees, Bolton-le-Moor	(t)
1651	6.1.1874	6	2'4"	Wolsingham Park, Dinas & Co., Newcastle-upon-Tyne	
1657	17.4.1876	9		A. Malcolm & Co., Hull	
1668	30.5.1874	12	Std	Seend Iron Works, Seend, Wilts per Osborne Aldes	
1670	17.4.1874	15	3'6½"	A. Malcolm & Co., Hull	
1675	27.4.1874	9		Wimshurst, Hollick & Co., London	(u)
1681	22.5.1874	9		Wimshurst, Hollick & Co., London	
1685	2.4.1874	9	3'0"	Rochdale Corp. Waterworks, Rochdale	
1694	30.6.1874	15		Sir John Goode, the Col. Gov. of Cape of Good Hope	
1756	29.9.1874	9		Wimshurst, Hollick & Co., London	(u)
1757	15.10.1874	9		Wimshurst, Hollick & Co., London	(u)
1768	13.11.1874	15		The Bedworth Coal & Iron Co., Bedworth	(v)
1775	12.12.1874	9		Wimshurst, Hollick & Co., London	
1776	23.3.1875	12	Std	Wimshurst, Hollick & Co., London	
1797	16.3.1875	9	3'6"	J.J. van Bruam, Holland	(w)
1810	25.5.1875	9	Std	Wimshurst, Hollick & Co., London	
1831	9.6.1877	12		Wimshurst, Hollick & Co., London	
1847	31.8.1875	9	2'6"	Nicholls, Matthews & Co., Tavistock	
1848	17.5.1877	12	Std	Fraserburgh Harbour Comm. J.H. Bostock Engineer	(x)

Works No.	Ex Works	H.P.	Cyls	Gauge	Customer	Note
1858	8.9.1875	9			Wimshurst, Hollick & Co., London	
1877	20.1.1876	9			Wimshurst, Hollick & Co., London	
1886	26.5.1876	9			Wimshurst, Hollick & Co., London	(y)
1890	10.5.1876	9		Std	A.&J. Hellibors, Kronsas, Sweden	(z)
1896	31.3.1876	15		Std	Edinburgh Gas Light Co. 1	
1939	15.6.1878	9			Michael Brodie & Co., Hawick	(AA)
1940	22.6.1876	15	Special	4'3"	Wm. Lee Son & Co., Halling, Rochester, Kent	
2057	22.2.1878	15		Std	Edinburgh Gas Light Co. 2	
2090	2.6.1879	12			McKendrick, Ball & Co., Dublin	(BB)
2097	19.8.1882	9		3'6"	Wm. Briscoe & Son, Wolverhampton. To Otago, N.Z.	(DD)
2117	21.6.1879	15		7'0"	McKendrick, Ball & Co. for E. London Harbour, S. Africa	
2129	26.12.1879	15		7'0"	Sir John Goode for E. London Harbour, S. Africa	
2134	18.5.1880				Belfast Harbour Commissioners, 26 ton loco steam crane	
2159	26.3.1881	15		Std	James Brown & Co. Ltd, Penicuik	
2184	1.1882	12			Société Anonyme des Acieries de Longwy	
2288	1.8.1883				A.L. Elder & Co., London to Wallaroo Copper Co., Adelaide	
2300	5.10.1883	12			J. Kenyon Rogers, Liverpool, Alogoas Rly Maceió, Brazil	
2304	24.10.1883	9			Hogg Curtis Campbell & Co.	★
2368	22.12.1885	15	7"×12"	Std	Northampton Gas Light Co.	(CC)
2416	14.7.1887	12	6"×?		Board of Public Works, Dublin	
2426	19.10.1887	12	6"×?	Std	Swanston & Co., London	
2447	1.9.1888	9		3'4½"	Wimshurst, Hollick & Co., London	
2461	11.5.1889	6		2'6"	W.A. Harley, Montevideo	
2489	16.12.1889	6		2'6"	W.A. Harley, Montevideo	
2586	23.2.1892	6	4½"×9"		James & Shakspeare, London	
2695	10.6.1896	18?			Swanston & Co., London for Canary Islands (Canarias)	
2788	7.6.1899	15		Std	W. Sommerville & Son Ltd, Milton Bridge nr Penicuik	

HP/cylinders
 6 hp – 4¼ in. or 4½ in. × 9 in.
 9 hp – 5¼ in. × 11 in.
 12 hp – 6 in. × 13 in.
 15 hp – 7 in. × 14 in.
 21 hp – 8 in. × 14 in.

ALEXANDER CHAPLIN LIST NOTES

(Dates are dates of letters to A. Chaplin)

*	Per London depot
(a)	19.9.1872 in possession of Mountsorrel Granite Co.
(b)	19.9.1872 in possession of Mountsorrel Granite Co. "Sold some 5–6 years ago"
(c)	25.10.1871 adapted to work pump
(d)	For H.M. Commissioners-international exhibition
(e)	5.6.1870 spur & wheel ordered by Connor & Alley, 17.7.1870 owned by Mr Carlye Contractor, Belfast
(f)	12.12.1873 in possession of the Stevenson Iron & Coal Co., Wishaw
	In Oct. 1876 in possession of Easton Gibb & Co. at Skipton
	15.2.1877 J. & W. Granger nr Kirkintilloch. 7.1881 John Logan & Co., Candie Colly, nr Linlithgow
(g)	1.6.1871 in possession of A. Gabrielli, Chatham
(h)	27.7.1869 in possession of Charles Brand & Son, Cumnock
(i)	7.1877 in possession of Mr Scott, Leith
(j)	21.9.1872 in possession of Hanna Donald & Wilson, Paisley
(k)	9.7.1870 in possession of Oswald & Co., Pallion High Road, Sunderland. 3.1874 Kilsyth Coal Co. (Successors to J. Wallace & Co.) working at Solesgarth Mine
(l)	14.9.1870 at Castle Dyke Iron Ore Co., Stowe nr Weedon
	26.9.1878 at Henry Mobbs, Vulcan Ironworks, Guildhall Rd, Northampton.
(m)	1890–3 probably used on Bristol & Radstock line for GWR
(n)	Fitted with hanging tube boiler
(o)	Std gauge altered to 2ft 8in. gauge
(p)	For Joseph Yeoman, Bransford Station, Worcester & Hereford Rly.
(q)	With Spark Arrester, Ashpan etc. for Cane Fields
(r)	For East London Harbour
(s)	24.5.1877 sold to August Egeling Maurermewter, Buchau, Magdeburg
(t)	19.10.1883 & 10.12.1886 at Saunderson's Siding Wortley.
(u)	Built specially low to go through archway
(v)	Returned after trial; 18.2.1876. Sold to Bosanquet Curtis & Co., London for Demerara; 27.4.1883 new boiler to Hogg Curtis & Campbell
(w)	Bought for his son J.A. van Bruam, British Honduras
(x)	12.1885 "For some time past owned by Gartverrie Fireclay Co., Glenboig"
(y)	Advertised for sale 8/1883. Some time at Tintern Abbey Tinplate Co.
(z)	At A.B. Saw Mills Bomhus nr Gävle, Castrikland
(AA)	9.1882 on hire to John Jackson, Contractor, Wicklow
	3.1885 at Llwydarth Tinplate Co., Glam.
(BB)	Later to E.J. Jackson, Contractor, Rathmines, Dublin
(CC)	With gear for driving coke crusher. Preserved.
(DD)	Nos. 1455 and 2097 went to David Proudfoot, Dunedin; a Railway Contractor. Briscoe, the agent set up a branch office in Dunedin. No. 2097 did not start work until 1898 and was employed by the Christchurch Meat Co. at their Islington Works and transferred to Timaru Works in 1927.

Main agents: Wimshurst & Co. later Wimshurst, Hollick & Co., London
             McKendrick, Ball & Co., London

Possible additions to the list are the two coke drawing locomotives supplied to Blaenavon Company Limited. (See also entry under their heading.) According to *The Engineer*, Vol. 51 25.2.1881 p. 139 the second locomotive was of 6 hp with two horizontal cylinders driving gearing to the hauling barrel by a worm and worm wheel, a clutch on the worm wheel disengaging the barrel when it was desired to move the engine along the line of the railway. The four-wheeled locomotive was not coupled. It was reported that a small engine of the same general construction also made by Chaplin had been made for the Blaenavon Company some years earlier.

CLARKE, CHAPMAN & CO. LTD
VICTORIA WORKS
GATESHEAD

Two vertical boiler crane locomotives were built in 1907, Works Nos. 7519 and 7520 for the Consett Iron Co., their running numbers being E. No. 11 and E. No. 12.

The gearing, pillar, and all principal castings were of cast steel and the jib was the swan-neck type, built up of mild steel plates and angles and also the carriage. There were three sets of engines—one for lifting the load and varying the radius, one for revolving, and the other for travelling; the latter comprising two outside cylinders driving four coupled wheels (*Plate 17*). They were withdrawn from service in 1953 and 1962 respectively. In 1968 Clarke, Chapman & Co. Ltd acquired the Clyde Crane & Booth firm, and in 1969 Sir William Arrol & Co. Ltd and Wellman Cranes Ltd formed a crane division titled Clarke, Chapman Crane & Bridge Division. This became the largest crane building manufacturers in the British Isles.

References

Clarke, Chapman & Co. Ltd
J.S. Brownlie

Plate 17 Clarke Chapman & Co. Ltd's 7 ton crane locomotive for Consett Iron Co. No. E No.11. *Clarke Chapman & Co. Ltd*

CLAYTON WAGONS LTD
ABBEY WORKS
LINCOLN

The Company was registered on 4th April, 1920 to acquire from 1st April, 1920 the Titanic Works, Abbey Works, and Clayton Forge under an Agreement between Clayton & Shuttleworth Ltd, and Clayton Wagons Ltd dated 15th April, 1920. Abbey Works occupied over 20 acres for the production of railway carriages and wagons with the Forge using 10 acres and supplying the necessary forgings and drop forgings. On the south side of the GCR Lincoln–Barnetby line to which it was connected was a common siding serving the other Clayton & Shuttleworth Works. Financial difficulties of the parent company were felt by the subsidiaries and by 1928 only the Forge was in use.

Clayton Wagons Ltd went into liquidation on 28th October, 1929 and the Forge was sold in 1929 to Thomas Smith's Stamping Works Ltd of Coventry who formed a new subsidiary, Smith-Clayton Forge Ltd. The plant and machinery was moved from the Abbey Works by George Cohen, Sons & Co. Ltd, in 1930 and the buildings were finally sold to Smith-Clayton Forge Ltd in 1935.

The original founders of the parent company were Nathaniel Clayton—born in 1811, died December 1890—who at the age of 31 commenced business with Mr Joseph Shuttleworth in a small smithy on the outskirts of Lincoln. In 1843 the company of Clayton & Shuttleworth Co. turned out the first portable threshing machine.

Clayton Wagons Ltd designed a series of vertical boiler locomotives, but due to the small number built and apparent lack of interest taken by the technical press at the time exact details of these locomotives are now very difficult to obtain. However *The Engineer* for 8th April, 1927 did publish a description and a report of the trials of the first of their Type 'A' design (pp. 381 & 382). The general arrangement comprised boiler at one end of the frame, a horizontal two-cylinder engine beneath the floor of the cab, with the water tank and coal bunker at the other end. The boiler was very similar to the early Sentinel design, except that it had twelve rows of cross water tubes instead of eight, while the superheater consisted of eight coils in place of five, as in the Sentinel. The boiler was 4 ft 10⅜ in. high, and had a heating surface of 85 sq.ft. It was constructed with the inner shell attached to the outer shell by means of two machined flanges with asbestos joints and bolts, so that it could be dropped down through the bottom for the scaling of the tubes. Two safety valves were fitted and the boiler worked at a pressure of 275 lb. psi, while the superheating coil in the top of the firebox supplied steam at a temperature of about 600 degrees Fahrenheit. The feed water could be supplied either by a direct-acting pump or by an injector, and means were provided for warming the water from the exhaust steam (*Plate 18*).

The engine was a two-cylinder, horizontal, high-pressure, totally enclosed unit, with cylinders of 6¾ in. bore by 10 in. stroke. The cylinders, crank-case and the gearbox of the reduction gearing were bolted together so as to form one unit, and the combined set was supported at the gear end by bearings surrounding the main driving axle, while the other end was carried by a swinging link attached to a point midway between the cylinders and crankcase, and fixed by

CLAYTON WAGONS LTD

Plate 18 Clayton Wagons Ltd's type 'A' 100hp locomotive built c.1927.
Richard Duckering & Co.

spherical washers and rubber buffers to one of the crossbearers of the main frames. This link was arranged in such a position that it carried a large part of the weight of the engine, which was thus spring borne. The engine had piston valves arranged below the cylinders to ensure drainage, and the valve gear was rather unusual. There were only two eccentrics, one for each cylinder, and they were mounted on a lay-shaft driven off the crankshaft by gear wheels. In order to reverse the engine, the eccentrics were moved across the shaft from one side to the other. This lay-shaft was hollow and contained a sliding shaft in which notches were cut to form two inclined planes at right angles to each other—one for each eccentric. By moving the sliding shaft endways the eccentricity could be varied from full ahead to full reverse.

It will be understood from this brief description of the valve gear that it was yet another variation of the old Dodds wedge motion. Other particulars of Type 'A' locomotives were: total length over buffers, 18 ft 4 in., width between frames 4 ft 0¼ in., wheelbase 7 ft, coupled wheels 3 ft 6 in. in diameter, gear ratio 3 to 1; speed at 500 rpm, 20.5 mph; weight with half capacity of coal and water 20 tons. It is thought that only two or three of these Type 'A' locomotives were built, one of which was purchased by G. & T. Earle Limited, for their Hessle Quarry, Hull. The locomotive was returned by Clayton Wagons Limited and later it went to Pilsley Colliery in Derbyshire, and was finally bought by Downings of Barnsley for re-sale, it was in this firm's yard in August 1950. A second locomotive built circa 1926 was taken over by Smith-Clayton Forge Limited, Lincoln, who took over the Clayton Forge from the Receiver. The locomotive was there in a derelict state in July 1950 and sold for scrap c.1954.

In addition to the locomotive described above there was also another design known as Type 'C'. As will be seen from *Fig. 11* these were different in appearance and were for narrow gauges. This Type 'C' was available in two sizes, both of which had short wheelbases of 3 ft 6 in. and 5 ft respectively, and had 2 ft diameter wheels hidden behind a "skirt" of sheet metal. The two-cylinder, horizontal, totally enclosed engine developed 100 brake horse power (bhp). These locomotives were intended for gauges of 2 ft up to one metre, and had a water tank to hold 200 gallons, a bunker capacity of 5 cwt. and could be supplied weighing 6, 8, or 10 tons in working order. It will be noticed that the drive to the coupled wheels was by rods from a jackshaft—rather on the lines of a modern diesel locomotive; the exact position of the engine in this design is not known.

Concurrently with the locomotives a series of railmotors was also manufactured at the Abbey Works, and the design of the power-bogie the whole unit was basically the same as the Type 'A' industrial locomotive except that the wheels were 3 ft in diameter, and the water tank and coal bunker held 550 gallons and 15 cwt. respectively. It should be understood that the railmotors and the locomotives were direct "off-shoots" of the Clayton "undertype" steam wagon, of which 44 units were built between 1921 and 1928, the boilers and engines being the same.

In 1927 the London & North Eastern Railway undertook extensive tests with a railmotor in the Spring of that year, trials being made between York and Whitby over the Scarborough coast line, and on the Newcastle and Ponteland branch. The trials of this first car, which weighed 25 tons and seated 60 passengers, together with a luggage compartment, having proved favourable, the LNER ordered ten more, the dates, names, together with the withdrawal dates being as under:

Date	Name	Seating Capacity	Withdrawn
1927	PILOT	60	1936
1928	RAPID	64	1932
1928	ROYAL SAILOR	64	1936
1928	WELLINGTON	64	1936
1928	WONDER	64	1936
1928	UNION	64	1936
1928	COMET	64	1937
1928	CHEVY CHASE	64	1937
1928	RAILWAY	64	1937
1928	BANG UP	44	1937
1928	TRANSIT	64	1937

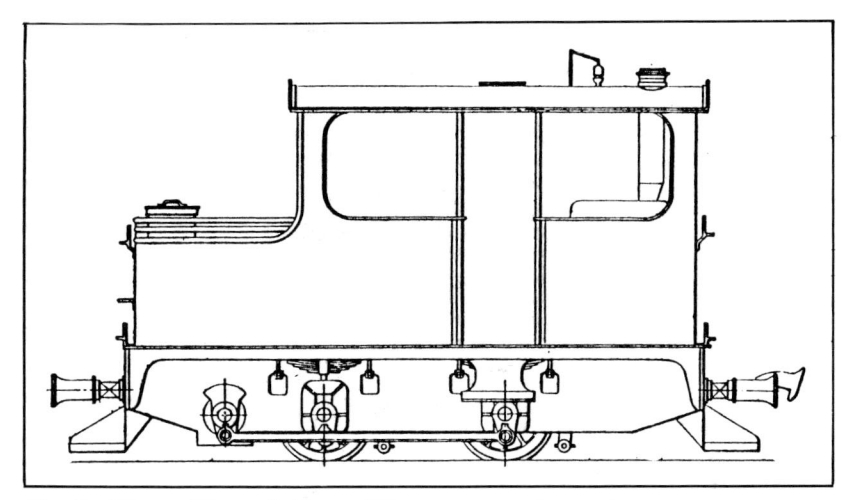

Fig. 11 Clayton Wagons Ltd's type 'C' narrow gauge locomotive.

Richard Duckering & Co.

The railmotor BANG UP is illustrated by *Plate 19* and it should be explained that the names bestowed on these vehicles were intended to perpetuate those carried by some of the early stage coaches. The coal consumption averaged only 10 lb. per mile, and they were reported to be capable of a speed of 45 mph but their average life of only 8 years would appear to indicate that the design was not entirely satisfactory.

One of these railmotors was ordered by the Egyptian Government Railways and delivered about August 1927. As a result of its performance five additional ones were sent out during the Autumn of 1928, but these were double-ended articulated vehicles, i.e. each consisting of two bodies on three bogies, the centre one being the four-coupled power-unit with two separate swing bolsters. The overall length was 101 ft 7 in. with the bogies set at 41 ft 10 in. centres, and a weight in working order of 54 tons, 15 cwt. A photograph appeared in *The Locomotive* for 1928 on page 309. Six of the standard type were built for the Great Southern Railways of Ireland in 1928, and other orders included some for Poland. Altogether a figure of 80 railmotors built has been quoted, but the writer is unable to confirm this. After the demise of Clayton Wagons Ltd, in 1930, the drawings, patterns, and templates passed into the hands of Richard Duckering Ltd, Waterside Works, Lincoln, who then undertook to supply spare parts for both the railmotors and the industrial locomotives.

References

P.J. Ashforth
The Engineer, Vol. 143 pp. 381–2, 8/4/1927 (Type 'A')
The Engineer, Vol. 129 layout of Abbey Works p. 422, 23/4/1928

Plate 19 The railmotor *Bang Up* built in 1928 by Clayton Wagons Ltd for the LNER.
British Rail

THE COALBROOKDALE COMPANY
SHROPSHIRE

It is well known that the famous Coalbrookdale Co. (established in 1709) built a number of locomotives for use at the Dale and associated works, and of these three were for use on the 2 ft 4 in. tramplates from the Dale Works to Lightmoor, the Castle Works at Dawley, and thence to Horsehay.

The first of these narrow gauge locomotives was a vertical boiler design, but in spite of much diligent local enquiry no details of its construction have come to light.

COCHRANE & COMPANY
ORMESBY IRONWORKS
MIDDLESBROUGH

After 27th December, 1889, the firm became a Limited Company, then Cochrane's Limited. After 1st June, 1962, the firm was known as Cochrane's (Middlesbrough) Foundry Limited. At some time the firm may have been Cochrane, Grove & Co., date unknown.

Until the middle 1930s there were nine vertical boiler locomotives among the firm's stud, dating from the 1860s to the 1880s. Four of these were built by Alexander Chaplin all in 1863 (Works Nos: 317, 358, 381 and 382). The remaining five were built by Cochrane & Co., and this was confirmed in a communication from the firm which stated that they were unable to say when they were built or to supply dimensions, as all drawings relating to them had been destroyed some years ago. The Chaplin locomotives were probably the first to be used and Cochrane & Co. added to these as and when required for traffic requirements.

The photograph (*Plate 20*) was taken when this particular locomotive was working at the Linthorpe–Dinsdale Smelting Co. Ltd, Dinsdale, Co. Durham where it started work c.1945 and was scrapped c.1950. Another of these 0–4–0VB locomotives built in 1871 went to the Loftus Iron Co., Carlin How in 1876 and was scrapped c.1934. The other photograph (*Plate 21*) is of quite a different design with outside inclined cylinders, boiler with horizontal smokebox. At least one was totally enclosed apart from the water tank and access for the driver/fireman. The wheels appear to be the same as in *Plate 22* so the cylinder would be vertical and attached to the boiler. This particular locomotive is shown built in 1871. This locomotive had 7 in. × 14 in. cylinders, 2 ft 6¼ in. diameter wheels, 5 ft 6 in. wheelbase and operated at a boiler pressure of 100 lb. psi. Gear ratio was 2.5 to 1. It has also been reported that Cochranes built vertical boiler locomotives for overseas, two being noted in a private siding in France.

References

B.L.C. Pocket Book K. *Industrial Locomotives of North Riding of Yorkshire* p. K.47. (Photographs of loco at Skinningrove Works)
I.R.S. Handbook L. *Industrial Locomotives of Durham* p. 125
R.G. Pratt

Plate 20 Cochrane & Co. locomotive built for their own use photographed in 1933 whilst working at the Linthorpe–Dinsdale Smelting Co. Ltd.　　　　　　　　　　*B.D. Stoyel*

Plate 21 Cochrane & Co: a locomotive built for their own use. Note boiler design and normal coupled wheels and outside cylinders (photo c.1902).　　　　　　*R.G. Pratt*

Plate 22 Cochrane & Co: an earlier locomotive built for own use c.1860–1880. Design features are similar to the A. Chaplin & Co. locomotive. *F. Jones*

COWANS, SHELDON & CO. LTD
ST NICHOLAS WORKS
CARLISLE

Founded at Woodbank, near Upperby, Carlisle in 1846 by John Cowans and Edward Sheldon, the factory was intended for general engineering and forgings. The rapid growth of output necessitated the purchase of a larger factory which was effected in 1857. Construction of cranes of all types commenced in 1859 and they soon became the principal product of the firm gaining a world wide reputation.

Among the special cranes designed for steelworks was a locomotive crane of Black Hawthorn design. Two were supplied to the Consett Iron Co.:

Works No. 1749/1892 Consett No. E.No.4 withdrawn 1932
Works No. 4101/1920 Consett No. E.No.14 withdrawn 1961

No record of others has been traced.

A.F. CRAIG AND COMPANY, LIMITED
CALEDONIA ENGINEERING WORKS
PAISLEY

This firm built a unique vertical boiler locomotive for their own use sometime in the 1870s, (the years 1871 and 1875 have been quoted). It worked on a 3 ft 1½ in. gauge track in and around the foundry, which was engaged in making heavy castings for marine and other work. As built the locomotive was fitted with a standard Cochran vertical cross-tube boiler placed on a girder frame and supplying steam to a vertical engine having cylinders of 6 in. diameter with a stroke of 8 in. A fly-wheel was fitted and two speeds were provided; the crankshaft had a sliding pinion at each end and engaged with spur wheels of different diameters on a countershaft, which in turn carried a centre pinion. This pinion engaged with the crown-wheel of a differential gear on the axle; the wheels were not coupled. The other axle, under the boiler could be slewed by means of a handwheel, and as no footplate was provided the driver walked alongside with his hand on the boiler stop valve. The four wheels were 2 ft 8 in. in diameter, and the wheelbase 3 ft 6 in. The water tank was originally mounted on the boiler top over the engine, and the exhaust steam passed through piping in this tank before reaching the chimney. The coal box was below the frames at the extreme front at the engine end.

Apparently this locomotive was rebuilt at least three times; in 1895, 1918 and 1947, and on comparing the photograph with an official works drawing, the arrangement of the cylinder framing seems to have been altered during one of these rebuilds. The original Cochran boiler was replaced in 1895 by the second-hand cross-tube one shown in *Plate 23*, when the water tank was placed on the frames above the coal box. The engine worked very much better after this, as the exhaust was allowed to go free and was not passed through the smokebox. With a wheelbase of 3 ft 6 in. on a gauge of 3 ft 1½ in. and a height of about 11 ft 6 in. it is remarkable that this locomotive proved so stable, and was able to pull heavy loads round almost 90° bends. It ran so successfully that it was not withdrawn until 1966.

DARBISHIRES LIMITED
GRAIGLWYD QUARRIES
PENMAENMAWR

Although built as long ago as 1905, the scaled-down version of a 3 ft gauge de Winton locomotive shown in *Plate 24*, has hitherto been almost unknown until recent years. It was built by the firm's foreman fitter, a Mr Redstone, in the maintenance workshops at Penmaenmawr. Named REDSTONE, it had cylinders 4 in. in diameter with a stroke of 6 in.; wheels were 1 ft 11 in. in diameter and the locomotive was built for a gauge of 1 ft 10¾ in.

It was used on a length of track in Mr Darbishire's grounds at Plas Mawr house, and was later transferred to Trevor Quarries, but proved to be too small for serious work. It is now preserved by Mr A.J. Hills originally at Llanberis, and latterly at the Brecon Mountain Railway at Pontsticill.

Plate 23 A.F. Craig & Co. Ltd's unique locomotive built c.1875 for own use.
A.F. Craig & Co. Ltd

Plate 24 Darbishires Ltd: de Winton type locomotive built for own use in Penmaenmawr workshops in 1905. *F. Jones*

R.E. DICKINSON AND COMPANY
CLEVELAND WORKS
BIRKENHEAD

In the late 1870s considerable interest was shown by a number of Scottish tramway undertakings in the possibility of operating their systems by steam power, and among the early experimenters with steam traction on street tramways were R.E. Dickinson of Birkenhead, who are known to have built two combined steam tramcars, with vertical boilers for trials in Scotland.

In 1877 one of these cars was built to the designs of two young Glasgow engineers, Robertson and Henderson, and this vehicle had a vertical boiler and a 3-cylinder semi-compound engine at one end, and a condenser under the floor at the other. In May 1877 it conveyed a party of ladies and gentlemen, including the Lord Provost Jamieson of Aberdeen, between Partick and Whiteinch on the Vale of Clyde Tramways in a very satisfactory manner, while in December of the same year another trial was made between Greenock and Gourock. It was then transferred to Leith where it was again successfully tried.

It appears that this car was originally ordered by the Edinburgh Tramways Company for use on their lines between Portobello and Edinburgh, but at that period the company had no powers to operate cars by mechanical means, although it was tried in that city during January 1878. In July 1878 this combined steam tramcar was sold by the makers, to the Stirling and Bridge of Allen Tramways Company, but its career after this is unknown.

The Dundee and District Tramways Co. Ltd applied for permission to use steam power on the East End lines of their system and authorization for this was granted by the Police Commissioners for one year from April 1880. A second combined car was built by R.E. Dickinson and Co. and this arrived at Dundee in July 1880, and a trial trip was run in August, but it was returned to the makers in December of the same year and, like the car at Stirling, its later history is not known.

This second combined steam tramcar, *Fig. 12*, was described as of the "Grantham" type and was very similar to the one built in 1877, but whether Robertson and Henderson had any hand in its design cannot now be ascertained. It was four-wheeled, single-ended, and double-decked, with the vertical boiler at one end and the stairway at the other, where there was a 190 gallon water tank under the floor to balance the weight of the boiler. This boiler, which had a working pressure of 130 lb. psi was enclosed in a semi-circular wooden case. The length of the vehicle was 22 ft, and the carrying capacity was 40 passengers.

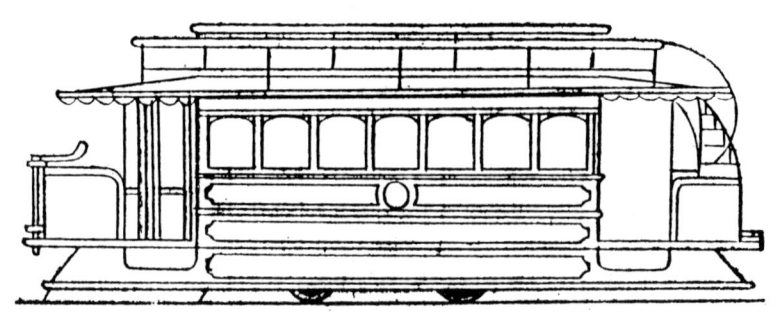

Fig. 12 R.E. Dickinson & Co's steam tramcar built 1880 for trials in Dundee.
N.B. Traction Group

GEORGE ENGLAND & CO.
HATCHAM IRON WORKS
POMEROY STREET
NEW CROSS, LONDON

The Works were established about 1839 but it was not until 1849 that locomotive building commenced. After building over 100 locomotives most of which were four-coupled well, side and saddle tanks, a new company was formed in association with Robert Fairlie in September 1869. The partnership comprised—Robert Fairlie, George England Junior, and J.S. Fraser, the title of the firm becoming Fairlie Engine & Steam Carriage Co., with the object of building Fairlie's patent double boiler locomotives, but after building five such locomotives and a Steam Car the new firm ran into financial difficulties. The business was closed down and the machinery sold by auction on 14th May, 1872. Further Fairlie locomotives were built by other firms including Sharp Stewart & Co. Ltd, Yorkshire Engine Co. Ltd, Vulcan Foundry, Avonside Engine Co. Ltd, and others.

The Steam Railcar designed by Robert Francis Fairlie was completed at the Hatcham Works in July 1869. The power bogie, fitted with an all-over cab had a vertical boiler. The two 8 in. × 12 in. inside cylinders drove directly on to one of the axles and the 4 ft diameter wheels were coupled. The rest of the design consisted of a main frame of long deep girders carrying the coach body on an inside framed bogie with 2 ft 8 in. dia. wheels at the rear and apparently supported by some kind of pivot at the engine end. The coachwork was of the ordinary compartment type with side doors, and a cambered roof, with the addition of a raised guard's compartment at the front. The vehicle was 43 ft long with two 1st class compartments carrying 16 passengers and five 2nd class compartments seating 50. The weight was 13½ tons.

Public trials took place on a "circle" of 200 yards circumference on ground adjoining the Works where a speed of 18 mph was attained. Whether there was a customer is not known.

References

Illustrated London News 14th August, 1869 (engraving of Railcar)
The Fairlie Locomotive by R.A.S. Abbott

A.R. ETHERINGTON
WOODVILLE
NEAR BURTON-ON-TRENT

Although the conversions to vertical boiler locomotives undertaken by Mr Etherington were of limited commercial application, they are included for completeness of the history of these locomotives.

The first conversion at Newbold Verdon was undertaken in 1969 and was based on a 2 ft gauge Lister four-wheel internal combustion locomotive (Works No. 14005 built 1940) obtained from the Northampton Sewage Works. The

Plate 25 A.R. Etherington's 1969 rebuild of Lister petrol locomotive with a vertical boiler. Photographed at Newbold Verdon in 1970. *A.R. Etherington*

seized-up JAP petrol engine was replaced by a single cylinder horizontal steam engine by E. Green of Wakefield which had previously operated soot scrapers on a stationary boiler plant. This was non-reversing and drove via the original gearbox and roller chains. The vertical boiler was a Merryweather firepump type which was ex Government Surplus from World War II. The locomotive is illustrated in *Plate 25*. It ran a few trials at the Cadeby Light Railway before sale to Mr R.P. Morris in Kent, being later transferred to The Narrow Gauge Railway Centre of North Wales at Blaenau Ffestiniog where it is named STEAM TRAM.

The second conversion was a standard gauge locomotive undertaken in 1983 at the Shackerstone Railway Society. This was based on a Ruston & Hornsby class 48DS four-wheel diesel locomotive, Works No. 235513 built in 1945. The locomotive was fitted with a vertical cross-tube boiler by Hartley & Sugden which had previously been used for soil sterilizing at an agricultural college. The drive was through a small vertical single cylinder engine by Reader of Nottingham connected by cardan shaft to the original gearbox. This engine previously drove an air compressor supplying braking air to a steam winding engine at Bagworth Colliery. The main purpose of this conversion was to use its boiler to provide steam to pre-heat coaching stock used for winter special trains. Although able to do this more cheaply than a larger locomotive, it was another boiler to insure and maintain; on balance it was not a commercial success and was soon out of use.

References

A.R. Etherington

FALCON ENGINE & CAR WORKS LTD
LOUGHBOROUGH

This business was acquired by Henry Hughes about 1855, becoming Hughes Locomotive & Tramway Engine Works Ltd in 1877. The firm changed its title in 1882 to the Falcon Engine & Car Works Ltd and traded under the name until 1899 when it became Brush Electrical Engineering Ltd.

Locomotive building commenced in the early 1860s most examples of which were small four- and six-coupled tanks. Tram engines were built in large numbers from 1876 to 1904, the boilers being conventional horizontal types.

Two vertical boiler locomotives were attributed to this firm: 0–4–0 VBTVC c.1883 purchased second-hand by Caernarvon Granite Quarries Ltd. It bore a plate at some time "Falcon Engine & Car Works Ltd". According to J.I.C. Boyd it was rebuilt by Falcon, and it is certainly a de Winton type locomotive.

The second was also a 0–4–0 VBTVC built 1884 for the Oakeley Slate Quarries Co. Ltd and named MARY OAKELEY. This is also a typical de Winton design. Both were probably repaired/rebuilt by Falcon.

The conclusion is that both were originally built by de Winton.

References

The Festiniog Railway by J.I.C. Boyd
G. Toms

FLETCHER, JENNINGS & CO.
LOWCA WORKS
PARTON, NEAR WHITEHAVEN

The Lowca Works, at Parton near Whitehaven, was founded in 1763 by Thomas Heslop, and his brothers Thomas and Crosby with William Stead and was successively occupied by Millward & Co. (1808), Tulk and Ley (1830), Fletcher, Jennings & Co. (1857), Lowca Engineering Co. Ltd (1884) and finally New Lowca Engineering Co. Ltd in 1905. Between the years 1840 and 1912 some 250 locomotives, mostly of the four- and six-coupled industrial type were built, and of these, only three had vertical boilers and were constructed during the period when the works were owned by Fletcher, Jennings & Co.

The first of these bore Works No. 91 of 1869 and was supplied to the 2 ft 10 in. gauge line of the Barrow Haematite Steel Company. The second appeared in 1872, Works No. 100, and was delivered to the 2 ft 11 in. plateway of the Tredegar Iron Company, whilst the third bearing Works No. 103, was built in March 1872, and went to the Cumberland Iron Mining and Smelting Company Ltd. All these locomotives had 2 ft diameter wheels, and inside cylinders 6 in. in diameter by 10 in. stroke; no photograph or drawing has been found, but Fletcher, Jennings' successors included a sectional illustration in their catalogue.

As shown in *Fig. 13*, there was a water tank at one end of the frame and a guard rail at the other, the coal boxes being apparently at the sides, and the locomotive was mounted on volute springs. These vertical boilers were con-

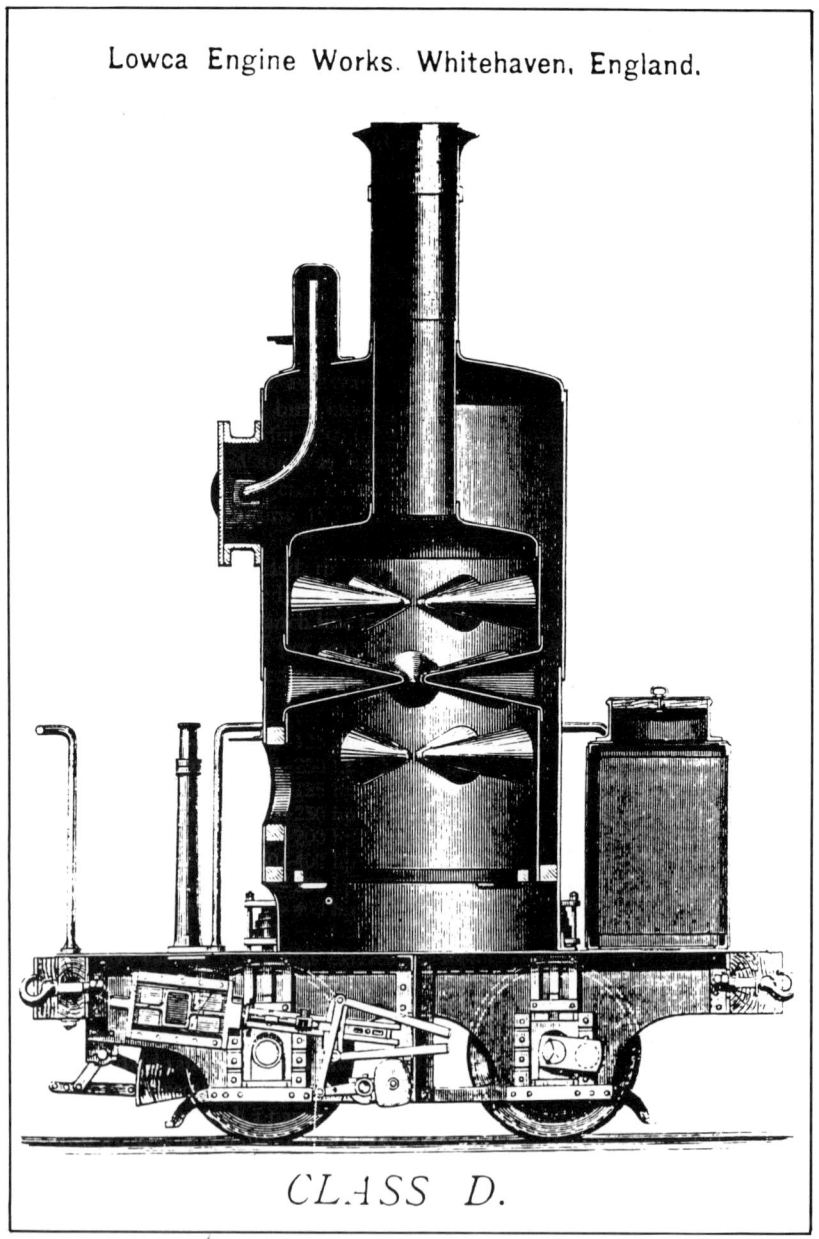

Fig. 13 Vertical boiler locomotive as built by Fletcher Jennings Ltd 1869–1872.
E.W. Taylerson

structed under the patent of Henry Allason Fletcher (No. 998 of 2nd April, 1869). This patent consisted of attaching round the sides of the firebox a series of conical water pockets or thimbles, closed at their converging ends and opening at their outer or expanded ends through apertures made into the water space surrounding the firebox. The heated gases and products of combustion were thus caused to circulate round these water pockets and, owing to the greatly increased heating surface thereby presented, the generation of steam was greatly facilitated.

Although reputed to be a good steamer, this kind of boiler was very costly to make as it involved a large amount of skilled labour; each thimble was formed out of a flat plate of the proper shape, being rolled up, welded and flanged by hand so as to be readily riveted to the firebox. These thimbles were about 9 in. in diameter at their large end. Incidentally, the "thimble" boiler has been re-invented several times since Henry Fletcher first took out his patent.

The Lowca Works closed down in 1926.

FODENS LIMITED
ELWORTH WORKS
SANDBACH

A small country agricultural engineering works was purchased by Edwin Foden in 1856, and traction engines were built from 1884 until 1919. The first steam wagon was marketed in 1899 and from that date up to 1934 several thousands were produced, but Fodens, having the foresight to realise that the heavy transport vehicle of the future was the diesel, had commenced the manufacture of the new type in 1932.

It is not known under what circumstances Fodens Ltd came to design one

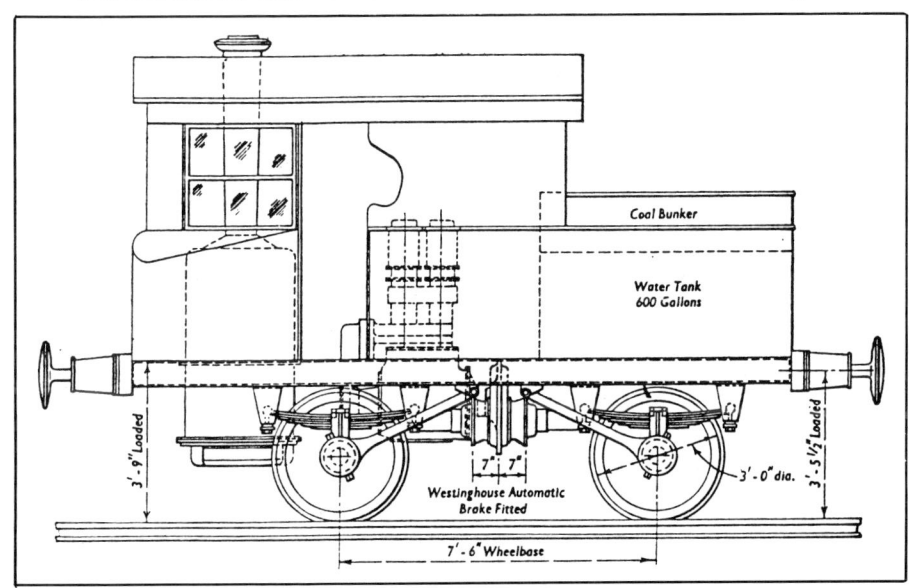

Fig. 14   The Foden locomotive as originally designed in 1927.   *Fodens Ltd*

Plate 26 The only locomotive built by Fodens Ltd, and supplied in 1930 to Palmer Mann & Co. *Fodens Ltd*

vertical boiler locomotive, but the general arrangement drawing, reproduced here in *Fig. 14*, is dated 17th October, 1927, and from it the layout of the boiler, engine and water tank will be clearly seen. The engine was of the Foden Type 'E.2', with two high-pressure cylinders having a bore of 7 in. with a stroke of 10 in. giving a maximum bhp of 75, the motion being totally enclosed in a crankcase with crankshaft mounted on roller bearings. The drive from the crankshaft to carden shafts was by double helical gearing, thence by worm and worm-wheel to each axle; the wheels, 3 ft in diameter, were on a wheelbase of 7 ft 6 in., the axles being located by radius rods.

The boiler, of the water-tube type, working at 250 lb. psi had a heating surface of 62.25 sq.ft and a grate area of 3.66 sq.ft, being fed by one pump and one injector, while the superheater in the smokebox was of the standard pattern as fitted to Foden Type 'E' road vehicles. A coal consumption of 6 lb. per mile was claimed. The tank capacity being 600 gallons, with a large space for coal, it would have been possible to undertake a continuous journey of 220 miles without refuelling, and a speed of 40 mph could be maintained.

Although designed in 1927, this locomotive was not built until 1930, Works No. 13292, and by that time, as illustrated in the photograph (*Plate 26*), the shape of the bodywork and tank had been re-designed, together with several chassis details. It was supplied to a local firm of salt refiners, Messrs Palmer, Mann and Co. Rookery Bridge, Sandbach, whose works were situated about 1½ miles away, alongside the Manchester to Crewe main line. The trade name SIFTA was painted on the side panels at the boiler end.

GLENGARNOCK IRON & STEEL CO.
KILBURNIE
AYRSHIRE

According to the I.R.S. Handbook N *Industrial Locomotives of Scotland* it is probable that this firm built for its own use a 0–4–0 VBT c.1916, although this is not confirmed. That they built at least ten 0–4–0 ST and one 0–4–0 CT from 1902 onwards is known, but no details have been unearthed to establish that a vertical boiler locomotive was actually built.

GREAT CENTRAL RAILWAY COMPANY
GORTON WORKS
MANCHESTER

To improve the local services between New Holland and Barton; Wrexham and Seacombe; and Wrexham and Brymbo, three railmotors were built at the Gorton Works of the Great Central Railway during 1904 and 1905 to the designs of Mr J.G. Robinson.

The length over bodywork was 61 ft 6 in. and this was divided into engine-room, baggage compartment, first class compartment seating twelve, a vestibule with lattice iron gates, and a third class compartment seating forty-four, and finally a driver's compartment for reverse running. The power-bogie carried a vertical boiler, with 450 tubes of 1¼ in. diameter, and fitted with a copper firebox. The cylinders were horizontal and the valves were operated by Walschaerts gear. Coal was carried in the engine room, and the water tanks were fixed under the frame of the coach; it is recorded that the trailing bogie had "cushioned" wheels.

One of these vehicles was later tried on the Marylebone to South Harrow service.

References

The Locomotive 15th October, 1904: drawing p. 180
The Locomotive 15th March, 1905: photograph p. 45
Great Central Vol 3 by Geo. Dow p. 140 & p. 421: illustration of No. 1

GREAT NORTHERN RAILWAY COMPANY
DONCASTER WORKS

The small locomotive illustrated by the drawing *Fig. 15*, was originally constructed at Doncaster in 1892 as the power plant of a carriage traverser, but was replaced in 1906 and some of the parts used to build the vehicle shown, after which it was sent to Peterborough in 1908 for use by the Engineer's Department.

The engine had two cylinders 7 in. in diameter with a stroke of 8 in. and was geared 3⅔ to 1 to wheels 2 ft 6 in. in diameter, set on a wheelbase of 6 ft. The boiler was 3 ft 6 in. in diameter by 6 ft 10½ in. high, with a firebox 4 ft 4 in. high containing two cross water-tubes of 6 in. diameter. The overall length was 16 ft.

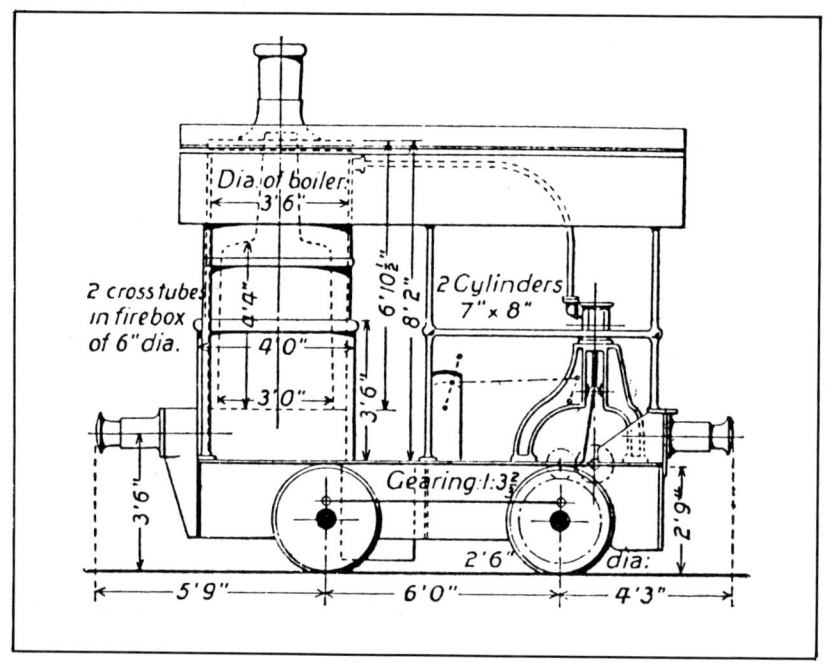

Fig. 15 Locomotive built by the Great Northern Railway at Doncaster in 1906. *Ian Allan*

GREAT SOUTHERN AND WESTERN RAILWAY
INCHICORE WORKS
DUBLIN

For shunting wagons on the coal gantry at Cork, a vertical boiler locomotive named PAT was built at Inchicore Works in 1884, and is illustrated here by *Plate 27*. Many second-hand components were incorporated in its construction, and the underframe was clearly that from an old Wakefield tender of the 1858–63 period, the wheels of which were an exceptionally large 4ft 6in. in diameter. No details are available of the boiler, but the engine was probably a vertical one set at the opposite end of the frame and driving on to the large spur-wheel seen in the photograph.

The first Irish steam railmotor was built at the Inchicore Works in 1904, to the designs of Mr R. Coey. This vehicle, *Plate 28*, had a main channel section frame 50 ft long, and the two bogies each had a wheelbase of 8 ft, the diameter of all wheels being 2 ft 9 in. The power-bogie carried a vertical multitubular boiler with a heating surface of 393 sq.ft, and a working pressure of 130 lb. psi. The

GREAT SOUTHERN AND WESTERN RAILWAY 63

Plate 27 Great Southern & Western Railway of Ireland locomotive *Pat* built in 1884 for the Cork Coal Gantry. *Irish Railway Record Society*

Plate 28 Great Southern & Western Railway of Ireland railmotor built in 1904. *Ian Allan*

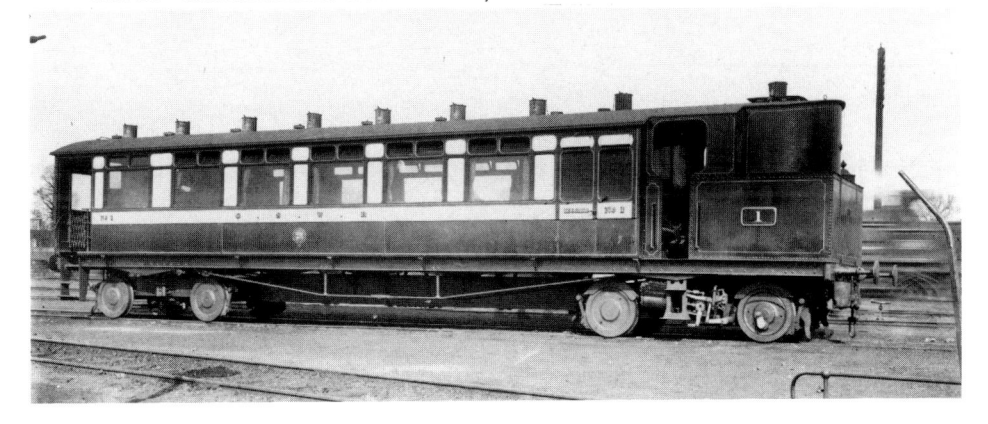

cylinders, with a diameter of 8½ in. and a stroke of 12 in. had valves actuated by Walschaerts gear, and the drive was on to the leading wheels only.

The coach body consisted of a first class compartment, seating six passengers, at the rear, access to which was obtained from the rear platform with fixed steps. A corridor alongside this small compartment led into the main third class saloon with seats for forty passengers. Finally, there was a luggage compartment immediately behind the engine-room.

This railmotor was built mainly for use on the 8 mile branch from Gould's Cross to Cashel, with a service of five journeys in each direction. It was scrapped in 1912.

GREAT WESTERN RAILWAY COMPANY
SWINDON AND WOLVERHAMPTON WORKS

The first two Great Western Railway steam railmotors were built at Swindon to the designs of Mr G.J. Churchward, and placed in service between Stonehouse and Chalford in October 1903, and by February 1908 no less than 85 such railmotors had been constructed, of which 5 were produced at Wolverhampton.

The power-bogie numbers, 0801–0863 and 0878–0912, were part of a series allotted to various machines, and the following table gives details of their construction:

Numbers	Date	Where built
0801–0802	1903	Swindon
0803–0831	1904	Swindon
0851–0852	1904	Swindon
0832–0850	1905	Swindon
0853–0858	1905	Wolverhampton
0859–0863	1905	Swindon
0878–0887	1906	Swindon
0888–0905	1907	Swindon
0906–0912	1908	Swindon

Of these, Nos. 0851, 0852, 0854, 0858, 0863, 0886 to 0888 and 0891 to 0896 were originally the spare units.

When built Nos. 0878 to 0885 had boilers supplied by Abbott and Co. of Newark, and coachwork by the Gloucester Railway Carriage and Wagon Co. (Carriage Nos. 73 to 80); the remaining bodies all came from Swindon. The coach bodies were all numbered separately from 1 to 14, 17 to 60, and 73 to 99, but even the initial allocation of power-bogies was in no orderly numerical sequence, and bodies were interchanged repeatedly often at every repair.

The power-bogies, *Plate 29*, had four-coupled wheels and two cylinders 12 in. in diameter with a stroke of 16 in. and with valves operated by Walschaerts gear, the wheelbase being 8 ft. The wheels of Nos. 0801 and 0802 were 3 ft 8 in. in diameter; those of Nos. 0803 to 0836 had a diameter of 3 ft 6½ in., and all the rest were 4 ft in diameter.

The coned vertical boilers were all 9 ft 6 in. high with a minimum diameter of 4 ft 6 in. and a maximum of 6 ft. The number of 1⅛ in. diameter tubes varied

Plate 29 Great Western Railway power bogies as built at Swindon & Wolverhampton.
R. Wheeler

from 333 to 477, giving a heating surface varying from 436.62 sq.ft to 625.58 sq.ft; the firebox heating surface also varied from 38.82 sq.ft to 46.75 sq.ft. The grate area also varied from 8.4 sq.ft to 11.54 sq.ft; the working pressure was 160 lb. psi.

Water tanks, holding 450 gallons, were located under the coach body, and coal was carried in a bunker in the bow end of the boiler compartment; coal capacity varied from 10 cwt. to 30 cwt. The railmotors with 3 ft 6 in. diameter wheels were 59 ft 6 in. long and were regarded as for suburban work, while all those with 4 ft diameter wheels (except Nos. 73 to 83) were built 70 ft long over mouldings and were intended for country branches, being provided with a luggage compartment. The early vehicles, Nos. 1 and 2, were different from all the others, and were entered only via the driving compartment at the rear by means of a fixed flight of steps. They had flat ends to the coachwork, but all later cars had bow ends. The sides of Nos. 1 to 14 and 17 to 28 were of vertical matchboard, but Nos. 29 to 60 and 73 to 99 all had panel sides and retractable steps.

All Great Western railmotors were third class, with seating capacities varying from forty-nine to sixty-four, and all had gas lighting. Weights were from 34 tons to 45 tons 11 cwt. These railmotors were withdrawn from service between 1914 and 1935.

References

Locomotives of the G.W.R. (R.C.T.S.) Part 11 pp. L.4–L.11
Part 12 pp. M120–M129
Part 13 pp. N16 & N35

T. GREEN AND SON LTD
SMITHFIELD IRONWORKS
NORTH STREET, LEEDS

Established in 1848 as manufacturers of agricultural machinery, the design and construction of steam rollers was taken up in 1874 and these continued to be made up to 1937. In addition, locomotive building was added to the products of the Smithfield Ironworks, and 37 orthodox railway locomotives were made between 1888 and 1920, and 157 tramway locomotives with horizontal boilers between 1885 and 1898.

The firm's first venture into the locomotive field was in 1882, when as explained elsewhere, a licence was granted by William Wilkinson to build his patent vertical boiler type tram locomotives, and 39 of these were supplied to eight customers, as under:

Date	Tramway	No.	Gauge
1881	Manchester, Bury, Rochdale & Oldham St. Tr. Co.	3	Std
1882	Leeds Tramways Co. Ltd	2	Std
1882	Mr Lee, Australia	1	
1883	Manchester, Bury, Rochdale & Oldham St. Tr. Co.	12	3 ft 6 in.
1883	North Shields and Tynemouth District Tramway	2	3 ft 0 in.
1883	South Staffordshire Tramways	4	3 ft 6 in.
1883	Bradford Tramways and Omnibus Co. Ltd	1	4 ft 0 in.
1884	Bradford and Shelf Tramways Co. Ltd	4	4 ft 0 in.
1884	South Staffordshire Tramways	8	3 ft 6 in.
1884	Coventry and District Tramways	2	3 ft 6 in.

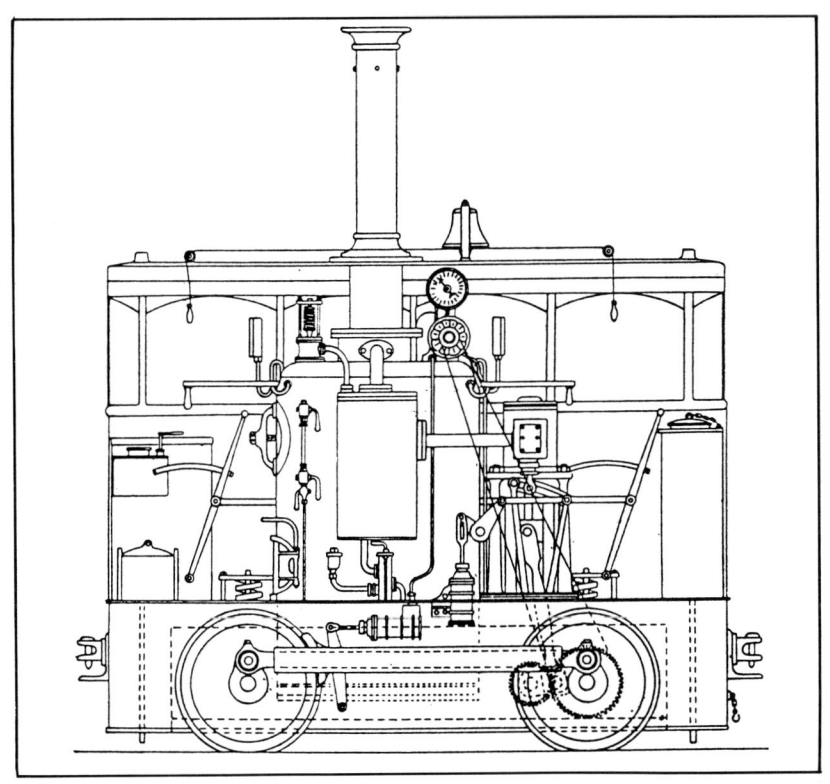

Fig. 16 T. Green & Son Ltd's Wilkinson type tram locomotive built in 1882.   *Ian Allan*

The drawing (*Fig. 16*) which illustrates one of these Green locomotives built in 1882, and used on the Headingley section of the Leeds tramways, also shows the peculiarity about the reversing gear in that the levers had neither catches or quadrants for "notching-up", there being only the forward and backward positions. The governor was of the "Allen" paddle-wheel type, which by forcing oil to the valve of a small steam cylinder (connected to the link motion) reversed the engine when the speed rose above the specified limited. As this was the only brake provided when new, all normal stopping was achieved with the reversing lever, hardly an ideal method on a service demanding frequent and unexpected halts, and very soon a steam brake cylinder, acting on the driving wheels, was added.

Whether all the early series of Wilkinson type locomotives by the patentee, Beyer Peacock Green and Black, Hawthorn, were similar in detail to the drawing shown here, is not known.

Reference

S.L.S. Journal, February 1954—Article by R.T. Russell

GREENWOOD AND BATLEY LTD
ALBION WORKS
LEEDS

In 1878, Greenwood and Batley Ltd constructed for Loftus Perkins a somewhat larger vertical boiler tramway locomotive of a similar design to that sent to Brussels by the Yorkshire Engine Co. in 1874. The engine and boiler were placed side by side in the middle of the frame, *Fig. 17* and *Plate 30*, and the engine was arranged for triple expansion, the high-pressure cylinder having a diameter of 3⅛ in., the intermediate cylinder a diameter of 5½ in., while the low-pressure cylinder was 7½ in. in diameter. There were only two cranks, the high and intermediate cylinders being arranged in tandem with the two pistons on the same rod. The steam acted on the top of the high-pressure piston and then passed to the underside of the intermediate piston, finally passing to the low-pressure cylinder, which was double-acting; the common stroke was 9 in.

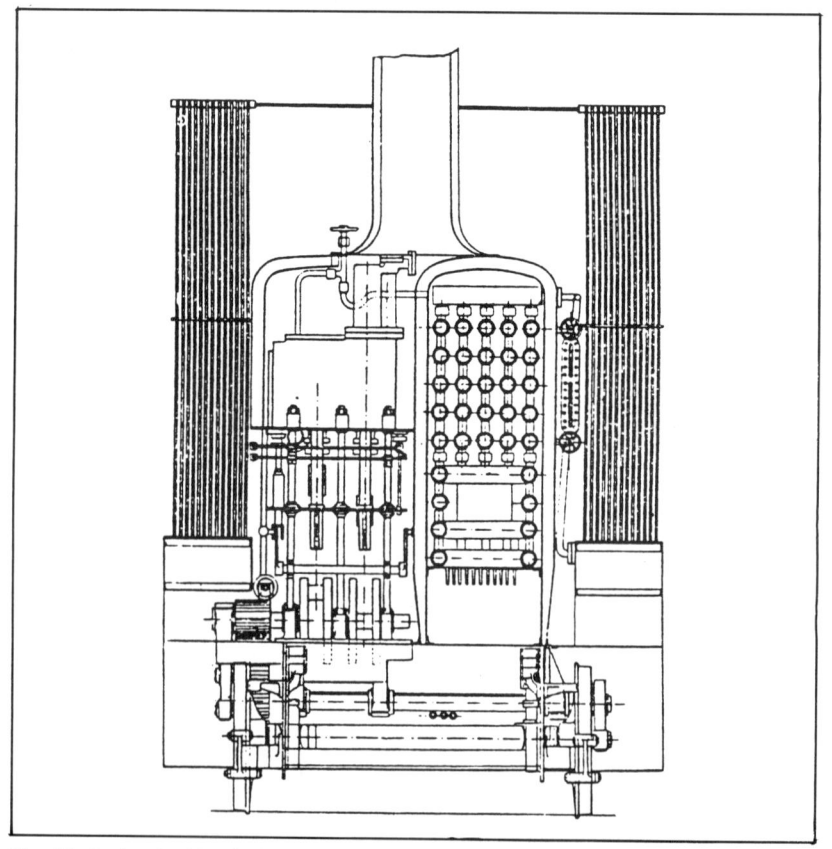

Fig. 17 Loftus Perkins high pressure locomotive built by Greenwood & Batley Ltd in 1878. *Granada Pub. Co.*

GREENWOOD AND BATLEY LTD

Plate 30 The same Loftus Perkins locomotive; note centre drive and air condenser.

Greenwood & Batley Ltd

The object of combining the high-pressure and the intermediate-pressure cylinder in tandem and working them as single action, was to prevent the exposure of the packing round the piston rod to the extreme temperature of the steam as first admitted. The steam was cut off in the high-pressure cylinder at three-quarters of the stroke, its initial temperature at 400 lb. psi being about 450°F. The pressure fell by expansion to something like 300 lb. psi effective pressure before entering the intermediate cylinder where the initial temperature did not exceed 420°F. The cylinders were jacketed with steam direct from the boiler; the jackets consisted of coils of pipes of small bore, wrapped round the cylinders and embedded in the castings.

The gear ratio between the crankshaft and the countershaft was 4 to 1, with the final drive by coupling rods to the 2 ft diameter wheels set on a wheelbase of 4 ft 3 in. The play of the springs was allowed for by the crank pins of the intermediate shaft carrying a block which worked in a slotted stirrup in each coupling rod. The engine's gauge was 4 ft 8½ in.

The Perkins boiler provided a heating surface of 90 sq.ft, with a grate area of 3 sq.ft, and carried a working pressure of 500 lb. psi. The boiler feed water was supplied by one steam donkey pump and one mechanically driven pump. The brass tubes forming the condenser were 6 ft high and ½ in. in diameter and altogether had a cooling surface of 1500 sq.ft. This locomotive was 10 ft long, 7 ft wide and 9 ft 8 in. high excluding the chimney; it weighed, in working order, 6 tons. It was tried on the Leeds Tramways but does not seem to have done any useful work.

The drawing reproduced here is from *Tramways: their construction and working* by D.K. Clark, 1894, but official Greenwood and Batley photographs appeared in *The Engineer* for 10th June, 1955, page 800, and in the *Model Engineer* for 20th June, 1967, page 73, both illustrating articles by the present writer. These show a side view, and a front view respectively, but unfortunately, the negatives are no longer available at the Albion Works.

HARRISON AND SON (HANLEY) LTD
VICTORIA MILL
STANLEY
ENDON, STOKE ON TRENT

This firm, which was an old established business engaged in the manufacture of ceramic colours and other potters' materials, owned a private railway which, after leaving the factory, crossed several fields and a swing bridge to finally terminate in a siding at Endon Station, on the main line between Stoke and Leek.

To work the traffic on this railway a small vertical boiler locomotive was built in the company's workshops during the period 1885–86, but apart from the fact that it was mounted on four wheels, no details of its construction are now available. The only known illustration of this locomotive is in a small photograph showing a general view of the factory; it is understood that this was reproduced in the journal *The Potteries* around the turn of the century.

HEAD WRIGHTSON & CO.
TEESDALE IRONWORKS
THORNABY-on-TEES

Head Wrightson & Co. (formerly Head, Ashley & Co.) are well known engineers, ironfounders, bridge builders and makers of hydraulic machinery. In the latter half of the 19th century (between 1870–1880) a number of vertical

HEAD WRIGHTSON & CO.

Plate 31 Head Wrightson & Co: the 1871 locomotive at Betchworth showing arrangement of cylinders, crankshaft, and centre pinion. *F. Bruton*

Plate 32 Head, Wrightson & Co: detail of the crankshaft of the 1871 Betchworth locomotive.
F. Bruton

boiler locomotives were built. There were two distinct designs, one with a vertical engine and geared drive while the other had normal locomotive framing and sloping outside cylinders although at least one was built with inside cylinders.

The geared type was remarkable in that the frames, axlebox horns, buffers and cokebox were cast in one piece and the two vertical cylinders complete with regulator were bolted directly on to the boiler, while the fork-ended connecting rods were fitted to a crankshaft whose main bearings were held in another casting bolted to the bottom of the firebox.

The 1871 locomotive was rebuilt from the original outside cylinder pattern to a geared drive. No eccentrics were fitted, the link motion being operated by two small return cranks offset from each main crank on either side with the reversing lever on the right hand.

Plate 31 illustrates the widely spaced cylinders of the vertical engine and the casting carrying the crankshaft bearings while *Plate 32* shows the intricate crankshaft forging with its two main and four return cranks. *Plate 33* shows Works No. 21 with inside cylinders working at the Seaham harbour, retaining the conical smokebox. The direct drive design is illustrated by *Plate 34* (Works No. 33) with outside cylinders. Unfortunately no records have survived, so little is known about this series of locomotives or how many were built.

According to an advertisement in *The Engineer* for 24th June, 1869 an inside cylinder saddle tank locomotive is shown as an "improved tank locomotive" for

Plate 33 Head, Wrightson & Co's locomotive for Londonderry Railway Co, Durham: geared type built 1876.
F. Jones

Plate 34 Head, Wrightson & Co's locomotive built 1873 for Londonderry Railway Co. Durham: direct drive type.
F. Bruton

HEAD WRIGHTSON & CO. LOCOMOTIVES (ALL STANDARD GAUGE)

Works No.	Built	Cyls	D.W.	Type	Gear Ratio	WB	Boiler Dia.	Boiler Ht	F'box Height	Tubes Dia.×No.	Tubes Length	Grate Dia.	Overall Length	Customer	Notes
21	1870	6¼"×14"	2'6"	0-4-0VBT	2:1	5'6"	3'6"	6'6½"		2"×70	3'9¼"		2'10¼"	11'7"	Londonderry Estates Co. Durham. Later Seaham Harbour Dock Co. 16	(a)
	1871	OC 6"×12"		0-4-0VBT	3:1 (b)	5'6"	3'6"		2'10"	2"×36					Dorking Greystone Lime Co. Betchworth 1	(c)
32	1872			0-4-0											Hannoversche Maschienen Fabrik Coy. Hanomag Works yard loco.	
33	1873	OC 9"×14"	2'5½"	0-4-0VBT		5'4"	3'4"	7'4"		1¾"×99	3'11½"		2'9½"	13'6"	Seaham Harbour Dock Co. 17	(d)
35	1876	OC		0-4-0VBT											Chell Colliery Co. Stoke-on-Trent	(g)
				0-4-0VBTG											Weardale Iron & Coal Co. Ltd 10	(e)
				0-4-0VBTG											Gjers, Mills & Co. Middlesbrough	(f)
				0-4-0VBTG											Gjers, Mills & Co. Middlesbrough	(g)

(a) Preserved by Head Wrightson. Thornaby pressure 100 lb. psi. Weight 10 tons
(b) Rebuilt at Betchworth
(c) Preserved at Beamish Museum Co. Durham
(d) Preserved at Preston Park & Museum nr Eaglescliffe, Tees-side. Pressure 120 lb. psi. Weight over 10 tons
(e) Original owner unknown
(f) B.L.C. pocket book K *Industrial Locomotives of the North Riding of Yorkshire* p. K.36
(g) Sold to New Haden Colliery and subsequently purchased by Stephen Offer, Contractor

Ironworks, Collieries, Mines, Sidings and Contractors' purposes. In an 1866 advertisement it stated that three engines of that type were now ready for delivery and others to be finished shortly.

References

C.J. Ashford, London
The Locomotive 15th September, 1931 p. 303 illustration
The Cheadle Collieries and their Railways by A.C. Baker (Trent Valley Publications, 1986) p. 9 illustration of No. 35

HETTON COAL COMPANY
HETTON LYONS
CO. DURHAM

The Hetton Coal Company operated the railway originally laid out and completed by George Stephenson in the autumn of 1822, between the colliery and the river Wear at Sunderland. To work the level sections of this line five locomotives were built in the colliery workshops between 1820 and 1822.

Many years later, about 1900, two vertical boiler locomotives were built for shunting the sidings at the colliery. One of these, named LYONS, (which according to a *Railway Magazine* report was built in 1899) was powered by a two-cylinder Tangye donkey engine which had formerly been coupled to a small dynamo, and this had cylinders 6½ in. in diameter by 8 in. stroke, and with the valves of both cylinders operated by only one eccentric. The boiler pressure was only 80 lb. psi, and the weight in working order about 11 tons. The transmission was by chains, the sprocket on the crankshaft having nine teeth and that on the driving axle twenty-five, while the second axle was coupled by an external chain outside the wheels. At 214 rpm the speed was 8 mph.

The second locomotive was named EPPLETON, but whether it was identical as regards the power-unit is not known. A photograph of LYONS appeared on page 72 of *The Locomotive* for April 1901.

BENJAMIN HICK,
SOHO IRONWORKS
BOLTON

Since the establishment of the Soho Ironworks, Bolton in 1833, the firm of Hick, Hargreaves and Co. Ltd has maintained a world-wide reputation as engineers and manufacturers of large steam engines for all purposes, mill gearing and rolling mill drives, engine room equipment, condensing plant and industrial steam turbines, but it should not be overlooked that from as early as 1833 until 1850 approximately 95 locomotives were built for service in Great Britain, France and America.

The first locomotive produced was a four-wheeled vertical boiler steam carriage supplied to the order of a Mr Thomas Lever Rushton in 1833. The most

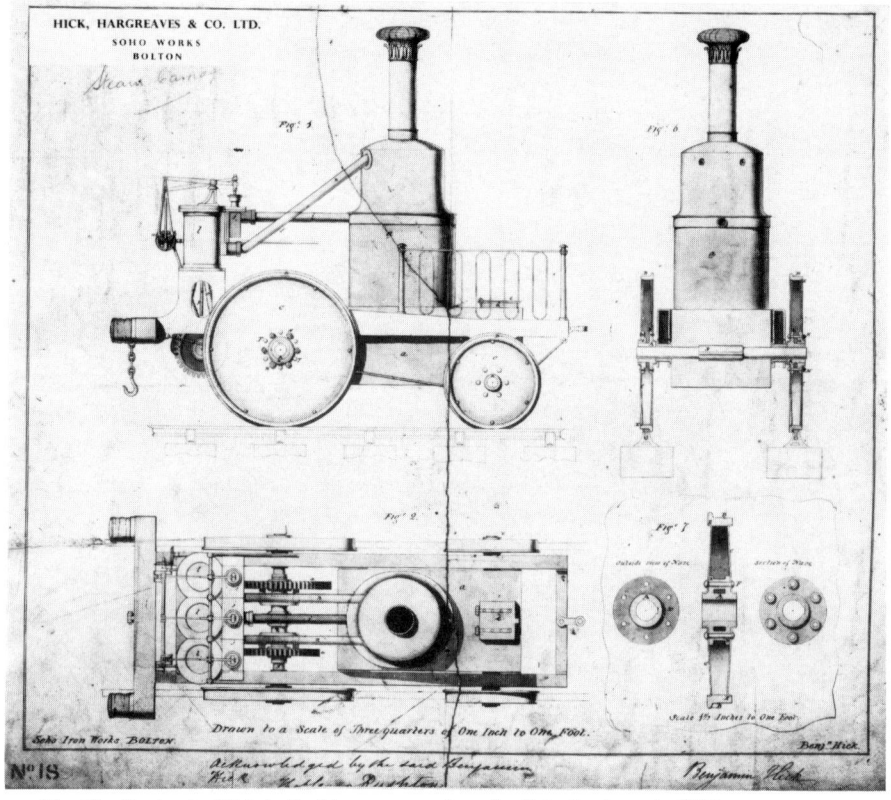

Fig. 18 Benjamin Hick built this steam carriage for T.L. Rushton in 1833.
Hick Hargreaves & Co. Ltd

interesting feature of this locomotive, *Fig. 18*, was the three cylinder vertical engine unit with steam distribution effected by a shaft with three small cranks operating the valves by means of vertical connecting rods and rocking levers. This shaft was driven from the engine crankshaft by slanting shaft and two sets of bevel wheels; the drawing does not indicate how the engine was reversed. The crankshaft carried two gear wheels which engaged with two spur-wheels, the low gear one having a diameter over teeth of 3 ft 4 in., and the high speed one a diameter of 2 ft 6 in. These wheels ran loose on the driving axle and were locked in turn by the central sliding dog-clutch splined to the axle. The high speed pinion on the crankshaft was 1 ft 8 in. in diameter over teeth, but the low speed one is not visible on the drawing and cannot be measured.

The engine's wheelbase was 6 ft 5 in. and each wheel was built up of two wrought iron plates secured by six bolts at the nave to two flanged collars keyed to the axle. Some other dimensions were:

Diameter of driving wheels, 4 ft 7 in.
Diameter of trailing wheels, 2 ft 9 in.
Overall length, 14 ft
Extreme width over buffer beam, 6 ft 2 in.
Height to top of chimney, 12 ft

OWEN HUGHES
VALLEY FOUNDRY
HOLYHEAD, ANGLESEY

One does not usually regard the agricultural island of Anglesey as a district where locomotives have been built, but there is evidence extant which makes it reasonable to conclude that at least two vertical boiler locomotives were constructed by the general engineering firm of Owen Hughes, Valley Foundry, Holyhead.

Before the amalgamation of the two granite quarrying companies at Penmaenmawr with the Welsh Granite Company, of Trevor, to form the Penmaenmawr and Welsh Granite Company, the Penmaenmawr quarries were worked by Darbishires Ltd, at the Graiglwyd quarries (the eastern section), and Brundrit and Company Ltd on the actual Penmaenmawr mountain itself (the western section).

The first locomotive to be used in the quarries was ordered by Brundrit and Co. Ltd and was supplied by Hughes: he made the boiler and frame, and purchased the cylinders and motion from Dublin. This locomotive, named the MONA, did not give satisfaction and had been in use only a short while when an order was placed with de Winton and Co. of Caernarvon, for one of their vertical boiler locomotives. This arrived in 1878 and some kind of a bargain was made with de Winton's to take the MONA in part exchange; this was agreed to and after being rebuilt at Caernarvon it was sold to the company operating the limestone quarry on the Little Orme.

The second 2 ft gauge vertical boiler locomotive attributed to Owen Hughes is referred to by C.E. Lee in his book *Narrow Gauge Railways in North Wales*. It was built in the early 1870s and used by Parry and Co. the contractors who built the Penrhyn Railway from the Penrhyn Quarries at Bethesda to Port Penrhyn on the Menai Straits. Originally named the COETMOR it was sold to Lord Penrhyn's Slate Quarries in 1876 and renamed by its new owners the BRONLLWYD; in later years it was withdrawn from railway service and put to work as a stationary engine to drive some slate-sawing tables in the dressing sheds, being finally broken up in 1906.

THE HUNSLET ENGINE COMPANY LTD
JACK LANE
LEEDS

This company, established in 1864, completed their first vertical boiler locomotive in the year 1871; it carried Works No. 52 and was a 2-2-0 well-tank inspection locomotive for the Oudh and Rohilkund Railway in India. Built to the 5 ft 6 in. gauge, it had two outside cylinders, 5½ in. in diameter, with a stroke of 12 in., while the driving wheels had a diameter of 3 ft 9 in., the carrying wheels being 2 ft in diameter. Although the original general arrangement drawing of this locomotive still exists in a very torn condition it is not suitable for reproduction here, but the photograph, *Plate 35*, gives a much better idea of its appearance and layout.

After a gap of twenty years the company supplied a very small vertical boiler locomotive for a 2 ft 2¾ in. gauge line in Spain. This was Works No. 551 of 1891 and is illustrated in *Fig. 19*. The leading dimensions were as follows: cylinders, 4 in. in diameter with a 6 in. stroke; wheels 1 ft 6 in. in diameter; wheelbase, 2 ft 8 in.; overall height, 7 ft, overall length, 6 ft 5¼ in.

Plate 35 Hunslet Engine Co. Ltd's inspection locomotive for the Oudh and Rohilkund Railway, built 1871. *Hunslet Engine Co. Ltd*

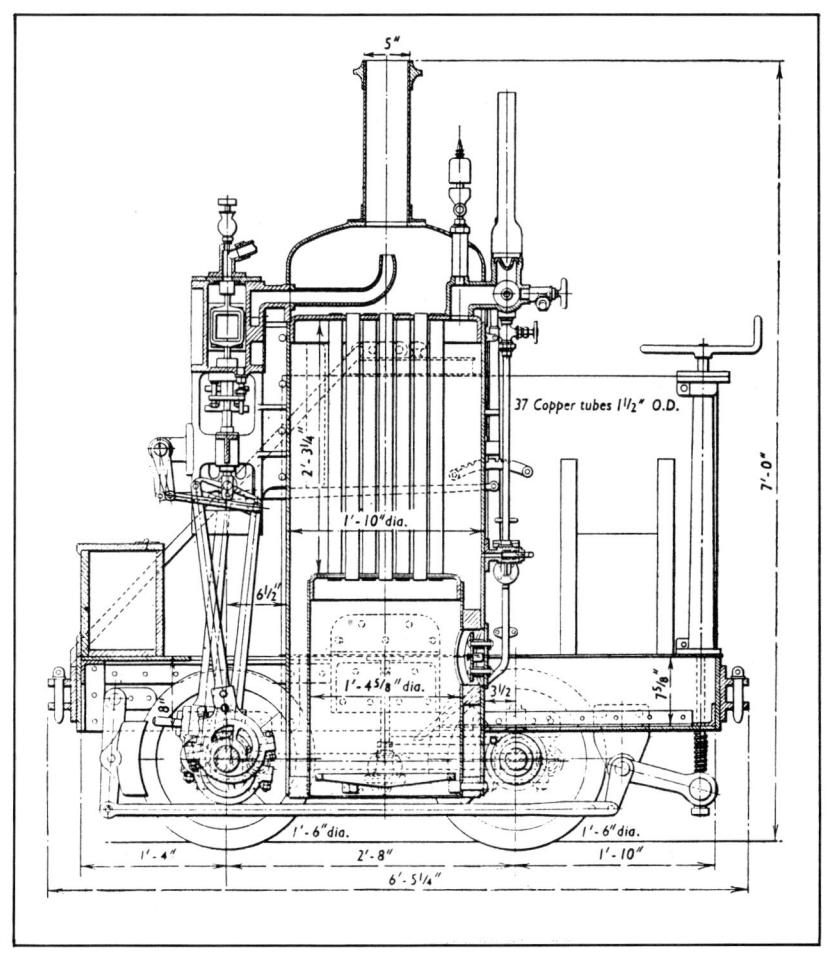

Fig. 19 A narrow gauge locomotive built by the Hunslet Engine Co. Ltd for Spain in 1891. *Hunslet Engine Co. Ltd*

The boiler contained thirty-seven tubes of 1½ in. diameter with a length between tube plates of 2 ft 3¾ in., while the outside diameter of the boiler was 1 ft 10 in. and that of the firebox 1 ft 5¼ in. The heating surface was made up of 21.5 sq.ft of tube surface and 8.5 sq.ft in the firebox. The grate area was 1.5 sq.ft. The water tank capacity was 80 gallons and the bunkers held 8 cubic feet of fuel. It should be noticed that this locomotive had outside frames and cranks for the coupling rods, and was unsprung.

A third vertical boiler locomotive appeared in 1893, Works No. 600, and was

Fig. 20 This locomotive was built by Hunslet in 1893 for a 3 ft gauge line near Novorossisk in Russia. *Hunslet Engine Co. Ltd*

Plate 36 Inspection locomotive supplied by Hunslet in 1909 to the Buenos Ayres & Pacific Railway. *Hunslet Engine Co. Ltd*

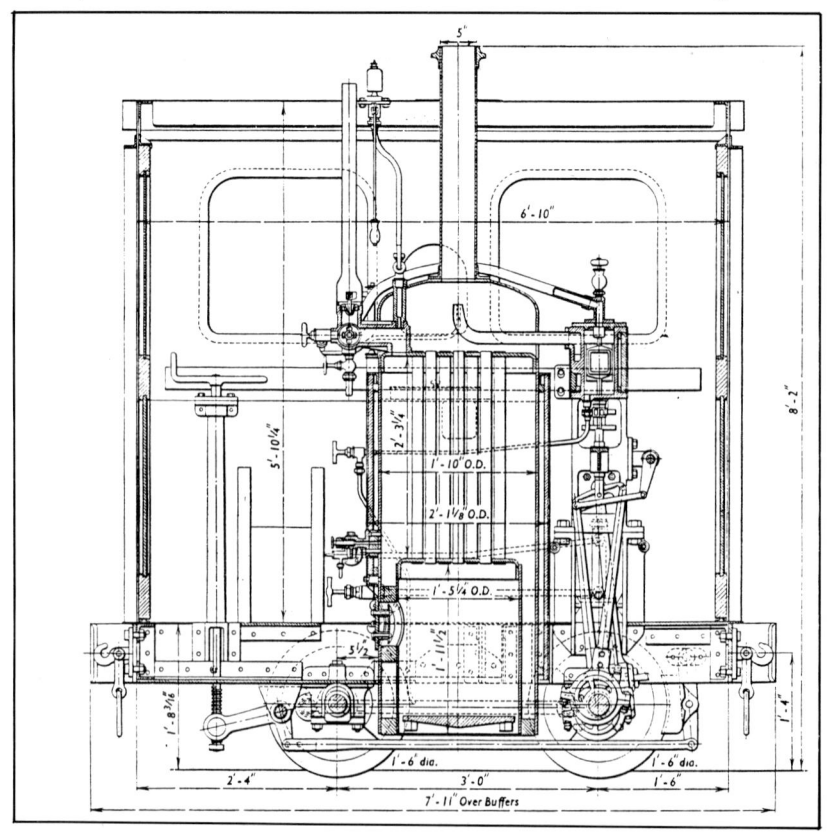

for a 3 ft gauge line near Novorossisk, Russia, *Fig. 20*. This locomotive had the same size cylinders, wheels and boiler as the one built in 1891, but the firebox was ⅝ in. larger in internal diameter. The wheelbase was 3 ft; the overall length 7 ft 11 in.; total height 8 ft 2 in. and it had an overall closed-in cab. The water tank capacity was 80 gallons, and the bunkers held 11 cubic feet of fuel. This locomotive was also unsprung, but had inside frames, and the weight in working order was 2 tons, 14 cwt., 2 qrs.

The locomotive shown in *Plate 36*, maker's No. 999, was a steam inspection trolley supplied in August 1909 to the 5 ft 6 in. gauge Buenos Ayres and Pacific Railway, in conjunction with Clarkson Steam Motors Ltd, Moulsham Street, Chelmsford. It was fitted with an enclosed Clarkson Duplex "Chelmsford" engine believed to have been of the type used at this period in steam buses, and also a vertical oil-fired boiler of Clarkson manufacture. The drive was through two Renold's chains, and there were clutches for disconnecting the drive so that the vehicle could be hauled in a train.

HUTCHINSON, HOLLINGSWORTH & CO. LTD
DOBCROSS LOOM WORKS
DOBCROSS, NEAR DIGGLE
YORKSHIRE

In 1928 the 3 ft gauge Clogher Valley Railway in Ireland was taken over by a joint Committee of Management of Tyrone and Fermanagh County Councils and in an attempt to cut operating costs an Atkinson-Walker locomotive was purchased, (Works No. 114 of 1928). The cylinders were 7 in. × 12 in. driving 2 ft 6 in. wheels on a wheelbase of 6 ft 6 in.; the vertical boiler worked at a pressure of 280 lb. psi, with a heating surface of 60 sq. ft, and a grate area of 3.3 sq. ft, while the total weight was 12 tons. The original boiler proved too small and was replaced by one having a heating surface of 90 sq. ft, but even with this the power output proved insufficient and eventually the engine and boiler were returned to the makers, and the chassis and body sold to the County Donegal Railways Joint Committee in 1932.

About 1934 the firm of Hutchinson, Hollingsworth & Co. Ltd, Dobcross Loom Works, Dobcross, were considering replacing the use of horses for siding haulage by a petrol locomotive, but owing to a slack period in the textile trade the firm had fitters available and it was decided to build a steam locomotive in their own workshops. This decision followed someone discovering that the engine and boiler from the Clogher Valley Railway was then in the possession of a firm named Titus Thorpe and Ainsworth of Preston, and these were subsequently purchased. The locomotive, *Plate 37*, was built in 1935 round this second-hand material, certain drawings being borrowed from some source and afterwards returned.

According to a letter received from Messrs Hutchinson, Hollingsworth in 1951 the total cost of building this locomotive was about £400.

Plate 37 Hutchinson, Hollingsworth & Co. Ltd's geared locomotive built 1935 for their own use in the Dobcross Loom Works. *F. Jones*

KERR, STUART AND CO. LTD
CALIFORNIA WORKS
STOKE-ON-TRENT

In 1892, Kerr, Stuart and Co. Ltd, railway plant factors late of Glasgow, acquired the general engineering business of Hartley, Arnoux and Fanning at the California Works, Stoke-on-Trent. In addition to millwrighting and supplying machinery for the pottery industry, these works had built about 21 steam locomotives during 1891-92.

Under the new organization the firm soon acquired a high reputation for industrial locomotives, and in later years, main line locomotives for home and overseas railways; the total number built amounted to approximately 1500, up to the year 1930 when the California Works closed down.

When the Great Western Railway was engaged in introducing the railmotor in such large numbers between the years 1903 and 1908, its enthusiasm was apparently so great that it was thought necessary to order twelve units from a private builder, the contract being awarded to Kerr, Stuart and Co. This firm built the power-bogies in 1906 as Works Nos. 931 to 942, (GWR Nos. 0866 to

0877), and sub-contracted the coachwork to Hurst, Nelson and Co. of Motherwell (GWR Nos. 61 to 72).

These bogies were similar to those built at Swindon and Wolverhampton with 12 in. diameter cylinders having a 16 in. stroke, and with 3 ft 7½ in. wheels set on a wheelbase of 8 ft. The weight carried by them was 26 tons 18 cwt. out of a total of 43 tons 3 cwt. Like the rest of the Great Western Railway railmotors these units were withdrawn between 1914 and 1935 as follows: two in 1914, two in 1926, four in 1928, three in 1934, and one in 1935.

In an attempt to improve the passenger services on branch lines, the Victoria Government Railways, Australia purchased a vertical boiler power-bogie in 1912 from Kerr, Stuart and Co. This unit, Works No. 1270, had four-coupled wheels and outside cylinders 12 in. in diameter with a stroke of 16 in., operated by Walschaerts valve gear, and was installed in an eight-wheeled coach, built at the Newport Workshops. This vehicle, No. 3, had a seating capacity of 54, but ceased work after 50,000 miles service.

Before describing the two types of Willans-Kerr geared locomotives designed at the California Works, it is necessary to outline the circumstances that had a direct bearing on their eventual construction.

In 1922, Mr Kyrle Willans, the son of Peter William Willans (1851–1892), of compound engine fame, was connected with the general engineering business of Blackwells in Northampton, a firm well known in the area for the repair of locomotives from the local ironstone industry. During 1922 Mr Willans converted a Manning, Wardle 0-4-0 saddle tank locomotive, belonging to the Isham ironstone quarries, to a geared locomotive by fitting the chassis with a second-hand Sentinel wagon boiler and engine. This proved a very successful experiment, and probably had some bearing on the decision of the Sentinel Waggon Works to engage in the manufacture of geared steam locomotives and railmotors.

Mr Willans moved to Shrewsbury in 1923 and was placed in charge of the new department, remaining there until 1927, when he joined Kerr, Stuart and Co. as general manager. Shortly after this appointment the new Willans-Kerr narrow gauge steam locomotive was designed and built, (Works No. 4412) and supplied to Balfour, Beatty for the Fort Williams Hydro-Electric contract in 1928.

In this locomotive, *Plate 38*, the boiler, of vertical rectangular section mounted in the cab, had much in common with the Loftus Perkins boiler, but was modified drastically in the method of connecting the components to facilitate the cleaning of every part of the boiler. The firebox was as nearly surrounded by water as possible, with a small amount of firebrick around the door, and a slab at the far end. There were 50 horizontal cross water-tubes arranged in 5 vertical rows, each tube being accessible for cleaning by removing a plug in the outer firebox. The heating surface was 125 sq. ft, with a grate area of 5.76 sq. ft, and the working pressure was 300 lb. psi. The boiler feed was by a double-acting pump and a high pressure self-acting injector. This boiler was suitable for burning any fuel from anthracite to sugar cane refuse.

The totally enclosed vertical engine, located at the extreme end of the frames, in front of the water tank, had two 6 in. diameter cylinders with a stroke of 8 in., with separate inlet and exhaust piston valves operated by a modified form of Hackworth gear. The engine was supported on a fixed round bar attached to the

Plate 38 Kerr Stuart & Co's high pressure geared locomotive (Willans-Kerr patent) built 1928.
Hunslet Engine Co. Ltd

main framing and steadied by a stay fastened to the top of the crankcase. The drive from the crankshaft was by a pinion which meshed with a spur-wheel mounted on a sleeve which rotated on the fixed round bar. From this countershaft to the front axle the drive was a 2½ in. pitch chain, adjusted by radius rods; a similar roller chain connected the two axles. With 24 in. diameter wheels, and a gear ratio of 2 to 1, the rail speed was 9 mph at 500 rpm.

A second and somewhat larger locomotive embodying the above features was built in 1929 to the order of R. Hudson and Sons Ltd for export. This was a six-coupled narrow gauge design in which the engine was located in the rear of the cab, and the boiler incorporated additional sections at the front, consisting of a superheater and a feed-water heater, with the water tank beneath; the coal bunkers were arranged on each side of the boiler. This locomotive is illustrated in *The Locomotive* for 1929, page 316. Any future development of these geared designs of steam locomotive was brought to an abrupt halt by the sudden and totally unexpected liquidation of Kerr, Stuart and Co. Ltd in 1930.

KITSON AND COMPANY
AIREDALE FOUNDRY
LEEDS

This Works, established in 1834, completed its first locomotive in 1838 and the last in 1938, the total being about 4525. In its earlier years the firm also built ploughing engines for John Fowler (during 1860 to 1862), and large blowing and rolling mill engines until about 1875; in addition a range of machine tools was also offered. Only twelve locomotives with vertical boilers were built, and these were for both street tramways and railways.

Messrs Kitson, with their wide experience of railway locomotive construction, did not seriously consider the manufacture of tram locomotives until 1877, but before this, in 1876, a combined steam tramcar, to the designs of Mr W.R. Rowan, had been built for the street tramways of Copenhagen. This had a vertical boiler mounted on a four-coupled bogie at the front end, with sloping outside cylinders, the rear of the car being carried on a second bogie. Between 1879 and 1882 eight similar power-bogies were built and these, together with the original one of 1876 are listed below:

Works No.	Date	To whom supplied
T.1	1876	Copenhagen Tramways
T.5	1879	To Adelaide, for Glenelg and South Coast Tramway
T.6	1881	To Sydney, for New South Wales Gov. Tramways
T.13	1879	Gribskov Railway, Denmark
T.14	1879	Gribskov Railway, Denmark
T.61	1882	Pontiloff Railway, Russia
T.62	1882	Pontiloff Railway, Russia
T.69	1882	Melbourne, for Victoria Government Railways, No. 1
T.70	1882	Melbourne, for Victoria Government Railways, No. 2

All Kitson tram locomotives were numbered in a separate list, Nos T.1 to T.302 (1876 to 1901).

Fortunately an official works photograph of one of these power-bogies has survived, (T.69 of 1882), and is reproduced here in *Plate 39*. Kitson and Co. supplied the power-bogies only and the coachwork and main frames for these railmotors appear to have been built locally. For instance those on the Gribskov Railway were completed by the Danish firm of Scandia of Randers, while the Victoria Gov. Rlys No. 1 had a body built in the Government Workshops, with a capacity for 40 passengers, and in this case was carried at the rear on a single axle. Bogie No. T.70, was ordered as a spare by the V.G.Rys. and about 1890 this was fitted into a small passenger carriage body and coupled to a four-wheeled trailer.

Plate 40 is very likely the motor portion of the Glenelg & South Coast Tramway 0-4-0 VBT (No. T.5 of 1879) supplied to this 5ft 3in. gauge South Australian tramway. However, if this is so, it only remained in the tramway company's ownership for a very limited time as the locomotive depicted in the photograph was sold to the Wallaroo & Moonta Mining & Smelting Co., South Australia in 1880.

Plate 39 Kitson & Co's power bogie for Rowan type tramcars and railmotors (Works No. T69/1882). *D. Stoyel*

Plate 40 Kitson & Co's motor portion of 0–4–0 VBT believed to be Works No. T5/1879 at Wallaroo & Moonta Mining & Smelting Co. South Australia.
Collection Wallaroo Branch, Nat. Trust

PATENT TRAM CAR ENGINE.

Fig. 21 Experimental tram locomotive built 1877 by Kitson & Co.   *Leeds Central Library*

Kitsons first three tram locomotives were built in 1877–78 (Nos T.2–T.4). They were fitted with a vertical boiler and a multi-tubular condenser on the roof, with a cooling surface of 452 sq.ft (*Fig. 21*). Although not built to any specific order, the first, Works No. T.2, went to the street tramways of Hamburg; the second, Works No. T.3, to the street tramways of Rouen, while the third, Works No. T.4, was sold in 1878 to the Great Eastern Railway for use on its Millwall Extension line.

This latter locomotive had two cylinders placed vertically on either side of the boiler and drove a shaft placed transversely between the axles, from where the drive was taken to the running wheels by coupling rods. These cylinders, 6 in. in diameter by 10 in. stroke, were visible through the side windows of the coachwork. The four-coupled wheels were 2 ft in diameter on a wheelbase of 4 ft 6 in. The regulator was operated by a lever attached to the footplate, and this was also controlled by an automatic brake, which was worked by a governor driven from one of the axles.

The boiler, fitted with 130 cross water-tubes, provided a heating surface of 80 sq.ft, while the grate area was 317 sq.ft. It was designed for working pressure of 150 lb. psi and had a diameter of 2 ft 5 in. with an extreme height of 5 ft 6 in., while the outer shell was made in two parts, so that the top part could be lifted for inspection and repairs. The overall height to top of chimney was 12 ft 8½ in. and the total length of the locomotive over the body was 10 ft 8 in., with an extreme width of 7 ft 1¾ in.

These three locomotives were definitely experiments, designed to test in a practical manner the basic requirements of a serviceable tramway locomotive, but were evidentally not considered to be satisfactory, and the result was the abandonment of the vertical boiler in future. The firm closed down in 1938 through lack of orders. The patterns, drawings and goodwill were taken over by Robert Stephenson & Hawthorns Ltd, and in 1960 all drawings relating to industrial locomotives were acquired by the Hunslet Engine Co. Ltd.

Reference

R.T. Horne
R.D. Grant

THE LIQUID FUEL ENGINEERING CO. LTD
EAST COWES
ISLE OF WIGHT

This company, whose trade mark was "LIFU" and which had registered offices in Abchurch Lane, London, were builders of steam yachts, steam lorries, wagonettes, buses and charabancs, but production ceased during 1901–2 and after laying empty for several years the works were eventually purchased by Saunders-Roe Ltd.

A double-decked steam tramcar, with a vertical boiler and the engine in a central compartment, was built by this company in 1896 and ran a service on the Portsmouth Corporation Tramways, chiefly between North End and Cosham up to 1901, when it was laid aside in the North End Depot.

This vehicle was illustrated in E. Harrison's *Tramways of Portsmouth* (1955), and the photograph shows it as having ten equal-sized window spaces on each side, of which the four at each end were glazed to suit the two independent passenger compartments, while the two central spaces had twelve horizontal louvres, to provide ventilation to the boiler compartment. The upper deck had knife-board seating and full length roof, but no side or end windows. Presumably the engine and boiler were of the type used in the LIFU steam road wagons, and illustrations of these will be found in *Motor Vehicles for Business Purposes* by Wallis-Taylor (1905), pages 108–112 and in *The Development of the English Steam Wagon* by R.H. Clark, pages 160 and 161, published in 1963.

When the roadside tramway known as the Portsdown and Horndean Light Railway was opened in 1903, the car was transferred to this line and used occasionally when there was trouble with the electricity supply to the system. Just how long it remained in working order is not recorded, but it served in later years as a ticket office at the company's Cowplain Depot, until the abandonment of the undertaking in February 1935.

LONDON AND SOUTH WESTERN RAILWAY COMPANY
NINE ELMS WORKS
LONDON

In 1903 two steam railmotors were designed by Mr Dugald Drummond and built at the Nine Elms Works of the London and South Western Railway. They were placed in traffic during June of that year for service between Fratton and Southsea on the joint line of the London and South Western, and London, Brighton and South Coast Railways, the coach bodies being lettered "SW & LBSC JOINT".

This pioneer design was the first of its kind to be constructed in Britain, *Plate 41*, and had accommodation for ten first class and thirty-two third class passengers. There was a central gangway with partition and sliding door between the first and third class; in the former compartment the seats were placed longitudinally, and in the latter in pairs transversely. A luggage compartment holding about 1 ton was placed between the engine room and front platform.

These two vehicles received the numbers 1 and 2 as joint stock. The total length of the frame was 56 ft and the wheelbase of both bogies was 8 ft and all the wheels were 2 ft 9 in. in diameter. There was a separate handbrake on each bogie, in addition to the usual brake on the power-bogie. The inclined outside cylinders, 7 in. in diameter with a 10 in. stroke, drove on to the leading pair of wheels only, the valve gear being of the Walschaerts pattern. The boiler was of the vertical type, with both cross and vertical water tubes, of which there were 88, giving a heating surface of 213 sq.ft, with a working pressure of 150 lb. psi. This boiler rested on a casting on the bogie frames, so that the only flexible pipes necessary were those conveying the feedwater from the tank, on the left-hand side of the boiler, to the injectors; coal was carried on the right-hand side.

The calculated performance of these railmotors was that they should reach a speed of 30 mph within thirty second of starting. The original boilers apparently failed to steam satisfactorily, and by December, 1903, railmotor No. 1, had been fitted with a new design of boiler of unusual proportions, which contained both vertical and horizontal elements. Railmotor No. 2, was similarly reboilered during the early part of 1904, and when seventeen further railmotors were built at Nine Elms during 1904 to 1906, for service on the LSWR as distinct from the Joint lines, this modified type of boiler was fitted.

Both railmotors were withdrawn in September 1919.

Plate 41 L&SWR railmotor for use between Fratton and Southsea. *British Rail*

MANLOVE, ALLIOTT AND FRYER
BLOOMSGROVE WORKS
ILKESTONE ROAD, NOTTINGHAM

A Mr Edward Perrett designed an experimental combined steam tramcar in which two small vertical boilers were used, one at each end of the main frame and connected together, with the centrally placed engine (having two horizontal cylinders of 5 in. diameter by 8 in. stroke) situated under the floor of the vehicle.

This tramcar was built at the Bloomsgrove Works in 1876, and tried on the Nottingham and District Tramways, the gauge of which was 4 ft 8½ in. It was double-decked, and mounted on eight wheels: four central coupled driving wheels of 2 ft 3 in. diameter on a short wheelbase of 4 ft and a Bissell truck at each end with 1 ft 6 in. diameter wheels; the total wheelbase was 14 ft. In this first tramcar, *Fig. 22*, the Bissell trucks could be "steered" from the driving platforms, although the idea behind this refinement seems obscure.

The steam boilers, constructed on Broadbent's system, each had a grate area of 1.60 sq. ft, and the working pressure was only 90 lb. psi. The total weight amounted to 8 tons, of which 5 tons rested on the four coupled wheels.

Manlove, Alliott and Fryer built two similar cars, one for the 3 ft gauge Dublin and Lucan Tramway in 1881, *Fig. 23*, and one for the Burnley and District Tramways in 1882, this latter line being laid to the standard gauge. The dimensions of these somewhat larger cars were: cylinders 7 in. in diameter with a stroke of 9 in.; coupled wheels 2 ft 3 in. in diameter; diameter of Bissell truck

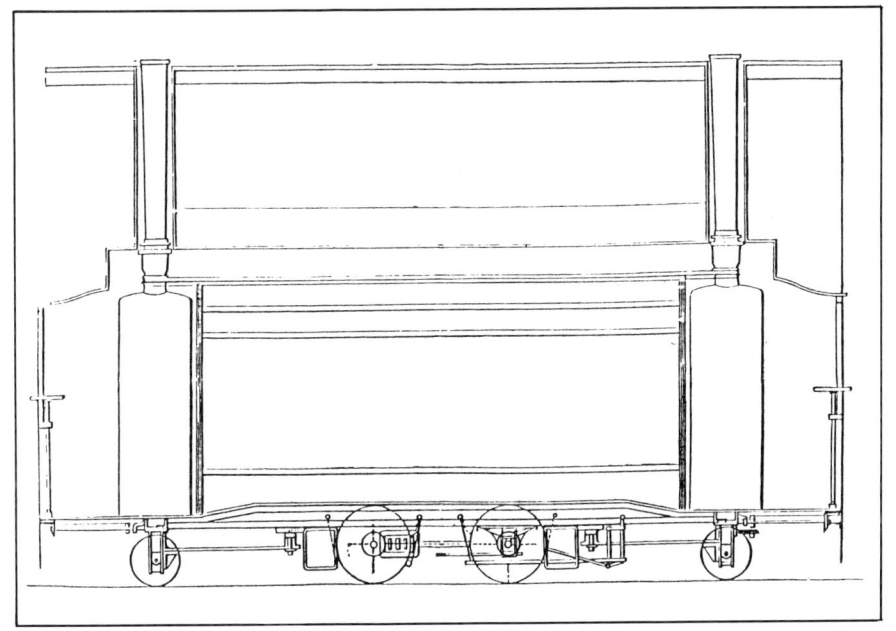

Fig. 22 Manlove, Alliott & Fryer twin boiler tramcar built 1876.   *Granada Pub. Co.*

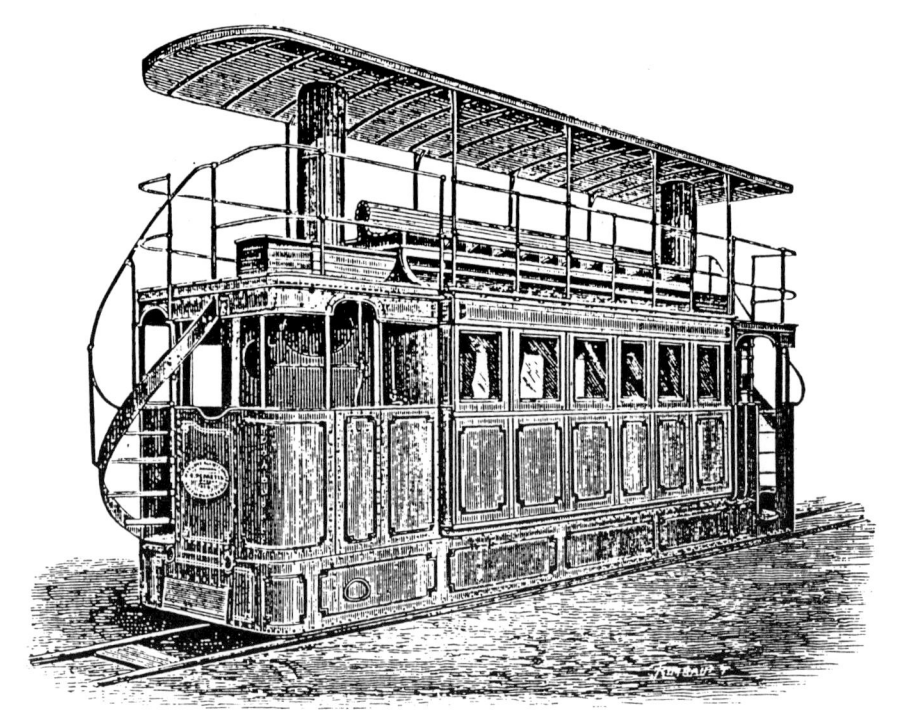

Fig. 23 Twin boiler tramcar built by Manlove, Alliott & Fryer in 1881 for the Dublin & Lucan tramway. *Granada Pub. Co.*

wheels 1 ft 6 in.; coupled wheelbase 4 ft 6 in.; total wheelbase 17 ft 6 in. The boilers were 2 ft 3½ in. in diameter and 6 ft high; the firebox was 20½ in. in diameter and there was a grate area of 2.27 sq.ft for each boiler. The weight without passengers was 9 tons.

The tramcar sent to the Dublin and Lucan Tramway started to work between Dublin and Chapelizod in June 1881, the distance being about 1¾ miles. As the schedule only provided for one double journey each hour, the coke consumption proved very high, for the trip occupied only 10 minutes each way, resulting in the car being at rest for 40 minutes in each hour. It is thought to have been withdrawn after about a year's service, and the fate of this steam tramcar and the other two is not recorded. The two illustrations are taken from *Tramways: their Construction and Working* by D.K. Clark, 1894.

MANNING, WARDLE AND COMPANY
BOYNE ENGINE WORKS
HUNSLET, LEEDS

The firm of Manning, Wardle and Company, Leeds, was established in 1858, and the first locomotive was built in 1859. At that period attention was being directed to the possible application of steam power to street tramways, and a number of experimental vehicles were constructed in America, while in Britain the first independent "dummy" engine was made by Manning, Wardle in 1867, who built two locomotives for the Pernambuco tramways in Brazil, followed by five more in 1870.

Three years after their pioneer contribution to mechanical traction on street tramways, the Boyne Engine Works produced in 1870 three combined steam cars for Murrietta and Company, for service on the Ferrocarril de la Provincia de Buenos Ayres, Works Nos. 295, 296 and 297, named LA PLATA, PARAQUAY and URUGUAY respectively.

They were very unusual articulated machines, (*Fig. 24*), with a centrally placed power-bogie consisting of a vertical boiler 4 ft in diameter over lagging and constructed under Fidler's Patent, supplying steam to two outside cylinders of 7 in. bore acting on four coupled wheels of 3 ft diameter, on a wheelbase of 4 ft. The gauge was 5 ft 6 in. and the height from rails to top of chimney 11 ft 9 in. To each end of this bogie was articulated a single-deck passenger carrying unit supported at the outer ends by a single pair of 3 ft diameter wheels. The total wheelbase was 41 ft 6 in., the overall length 55 ft 6 in., and the height to the roof of the carriages was 10 ft 6 in.

These vehicles were dispatched from Leeds on 8th July, 1870, and it is presumed that the coachwork was built locally on arrival in South America. They were used for a shuttle service between Parque, Once and Central Stations in Buenos Aires, and were scrapped in 1890.

Apart from building 13 orthodox tram locomotives with normal horizontal boilers during 1881–3, Manning, Wardle did not participate in the lucrative trade that developed in steam tram locomotives. When the Great Northern Railway of Ireland placed four additional steam railmotors in service in 1906 the construction of the power-bogies was entrusted to Manning, Wardle and Co. and these were given Works Nos. 1684 to 1687. The illustration *Plate 42*, is a front view of one of these units which had four coupled wheels of 3 ft 9 in. diameter on a wheelbase of 8 ft, with outside cylinders 12 in. in diameter by 16 in. stroke and steam distribution by Walschaert's gear. The vertical multi-tubular boiler had a heating surface of 655 sq. ft and a grate area of 115 sq. ft, while the working pressure was 175 lb. psi.

The coach bodies came from the Brush Electrical Engineering Co. of Loughborough, and were supported at the rear on a four-wheeled Fox's pressed steel carriage bogie. The water tank, 18 ft 4 in. long was suspended below the floor; the first coach was 58 ft long over the bodywork, but the remainder measured 61 ft 6 in. in length, the seating capacity being 59. All were withdrawn in 1913.

In 1927 the firm went into voluntary liquidation due to the trade depression at that time. The goodwill was purchased by Kitson & Co., who themselves closed in 1938 (q.v.).

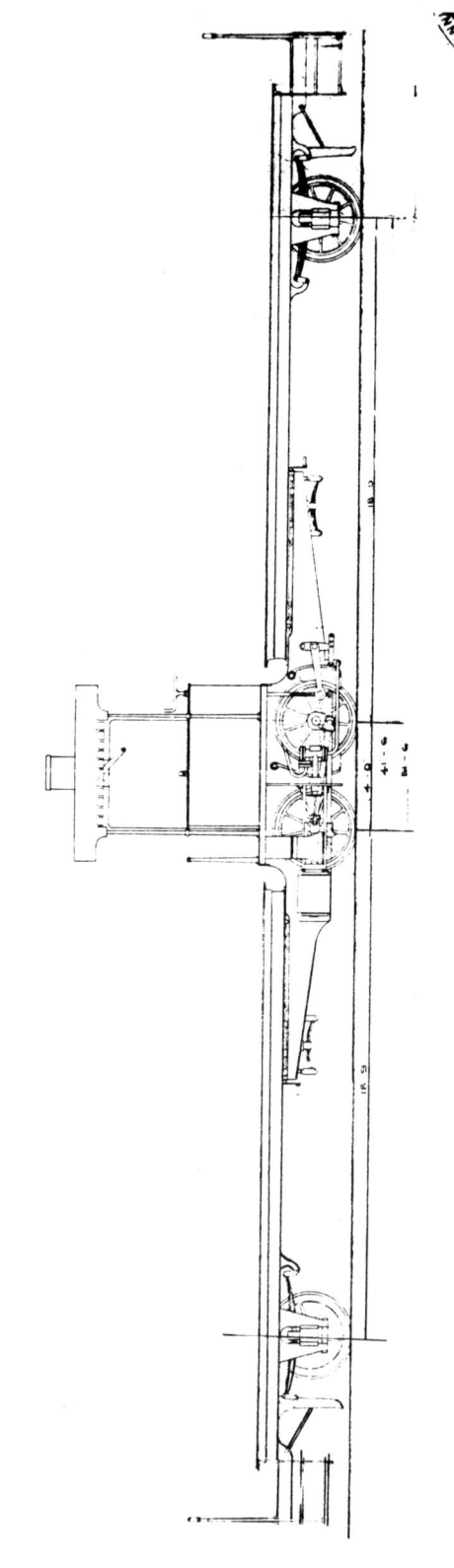

Fig. 24 Manning, Wardle & Co's articulated steam tramcar built 1870 for the Buenos Ayres tramways. (*The original diagram very fragile.*)

Hunslet Engine Co. Ltd

Plate 42 Power bogie of railmotor for the Great Northern Railway of Ireland constructed by Manning, Wardle & Co. in 1906. *Hunslet Engine Co. Ltd*

MARSHALL, FLEMING & CO. LTD
DELLBURN WORKS
MOTHERWELL

Established in 1890, this firm of crane builders was originally known as Marshall, Fleming & Jack. The firm became Marshall, Fleming & Co. Ltd when Jack resigned in 1907.

From 1896 a number of locomotive type cranes were produced with outside cylinders driving four-coupled wheels. Vertical cross-tube boilers were fitted. Three were supplied in 1921 to the Consett Iron Co.; running numbers were E.No.16 and E.No.17.

Cranes and charging machines for steelworks are the main output at the present time.

JAMES IRVING McCONNELL
FOULDHEAD COLLIERY
KIRKCONNEL
DUMFRIESSHIRE

Two standard gauge vertical boiler locomotives were built in the colliery workshops, one c.1886, and the second one c.1903. After 1903 the colliery was owned by Sanquhar and Kirkconnel Collieries Ltd, and from October 1931 passed to Bairds and Dalmellington Ltd.

MERRYWEATHER AND SONS LTD
GREENWICH HIGH ROAD
LONDON

As one of the oldest established engineering concerns in Britain, with a continuous existence dating back to 1690, the name of Merryweather is so intimately associated with the history and manufacture of fire fighting equipment that their work in the field of locomotive construction is apt to be overlooked. Yet during the last quarter of the 19th century the firm was held in high repute as builders of steam locomotives for the world's street tramways, their products going to some 13 countries. However, the full story of their locomotive building activities will probably never be written due to the very serious destruction of records in the air raids on London during World War II.

The first steam tramcar in England was designed by John Grantham under patent No. 1991 of 1871, and the bodywork and chassis was built by the Oldbury Carriage and Wagon Works, while the boilers and engine came from Merryweather and Sons. This firm was chosen because of its experience with quick-steaming boilers and light engine construction as used in their steam fire-engines. The vehicle was completed in 1872 or early 1873, and what is probably the finest and best known illustration is that reproduced as Plate 24 in *The Wantage Tramway* by S.H. Pearce Higgins, 1958.

A felted and lagged boiler chamber was built into each side of the body, in the centre, to hold two small upright boilers constructed on the "Field" system, with pendent water-tubes having internal circulating tubes. The diameter of these boilers was only 18 in. with a height of 4 ft 4 in., and a firegrate of 15 in. diameter; the working pressure was 90 lb. psi. Two horizontal cylinders, 4 in. in diameter with a stroke of 10 in. were placed under the floor and drove on to one axle fitted with steel disc wheels of 30 in. diameter; the other axle had one wheel loose on a sleeve.

When tried on the London Tramways between Victoria Station and Vauxhall Bridge it was found that the boilers were really too small and there was difficulty in access for firing. In 1875 the car was transferred to the Wantage Tramway in Berkshire, but here again the boilers failed to maintain sufficient steam for the inclines and curves of this line, the steepest gradient on which was 1 in 47 for 350 yards and the sharpest curve was of only 75 feet radius. Finally the boilers were removed and a single large vertical water-tube boiler, constructed by Shand, Mason was then fitted, again in the central position of the frames, but to one side. This left more room for firing purposes and for access between the 1st and 2nd class ends of the car, and at the same time new wheels of 24 in. diameter were fitted.

The vehicle was 27 ft 3 in. long, 6 ft 6 in. wide and 11 ft 1 in. high, with an unladen weight of 6½ tons. It ceased to work the traffic at Wantage in 1887.

A second "Grantham" steam tramcar was built in 1876 by the Starbuck Carriage and Wagon Co. of Birmingham to the designs of a Mr Edward Woods, for service on the tramways of Vienna, and in one of the surviving notebooks among the archives at the Greenwich Road Works of Merryweather and Sons, there is a statement which reads "Grantham cars built 1872 and 1876, one sent to Vienna." Just what mechanical parts were made by Merryweather is in some dispute, for on the authority of the late D.K. Clark, the engine and boiler were made by Shand, Mason and Co.

This vehicle was mounted on a four-wheeled bogie at one end, while at the other the boiler and machinery were placed over a single pair of wheels, driven by a two-cylinder engine secured below the platform. The vertical water-tube boiler was of the type used by the makers in their steam fire engines, but although a rapid generator of steam, it was eventually proved to be too limited in water capacity for the working conditions demanded by tramway service.

The leading dimensions were:

> Cylinders 6 in. in diameter with a stroke of 9 in.
> Driving wheels 2 ft in diameter
> Diameter of bogie wheels 1 ft 8 in.
> Total length of car 28 ft 6 in.
> Length of boiler room 9 ft 6 in.
> Total weight with passengers 7 tons

It may not be generally known that John Grantham planned a series of steam tramcars of various standard patterns, and these designs appeared in a printed book, a copy of which is in the Library of the Institution of Civil Engineers.

An Englishman, G.P. Harding, obtained a concession to work the Southern Tramways of Paris by steam and he placed the order for the construction of the motive power with Merryweather who eventually supplied 46 locomotives between 1875 and 1877, although only the first three had vertical boilers.

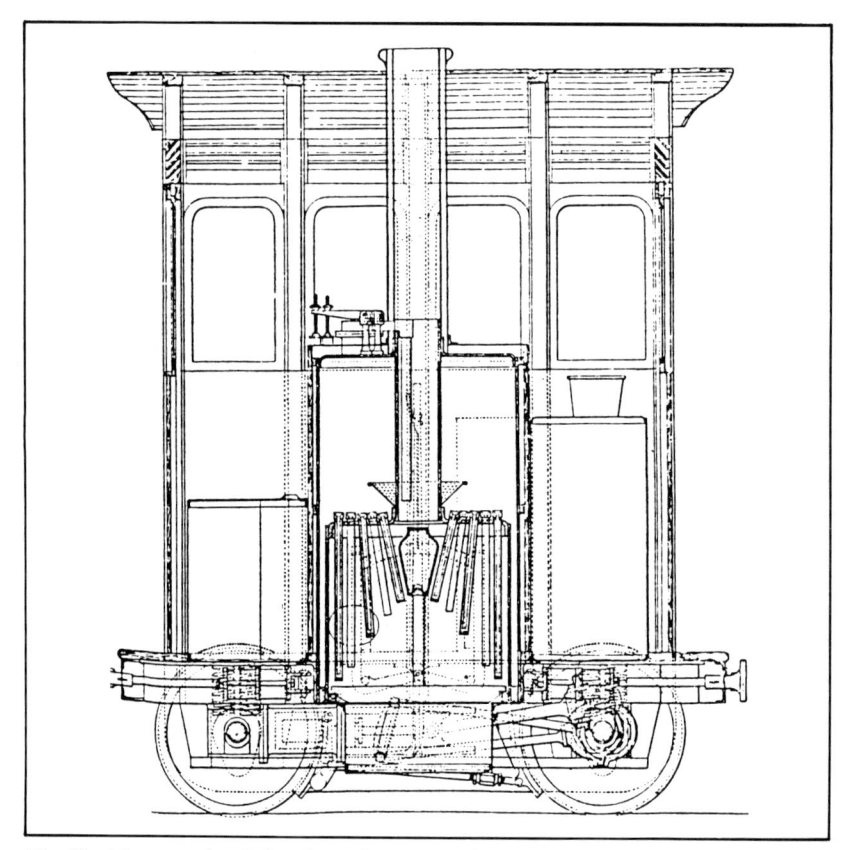

Fig. 25 Merryweather & Sons' tram locomotive built in 1876 for the Southern Tramways of Paris.
Engineering

In order to undertake the manufacture of locomotives in addition to fire-engines and ancillary equipment, the business was transferred in 1876 from Lambeth to Greenwich High Road. These new works were referred to as the Light Locomotive Works; the Lambeth works closed in 1879.

The first locomotive for Paris was a small experimental unit delivered in November, 1875, and had a vertical boiler with "Field" tubes similar in construction to those the firm had used on their fire-engines since 1861. It was a very small machine, only 5 ft 3 in. in length over buffers, and weighing only 2 tons; the horizontal cylinders, 5 in. in diameter with a stroke of 9 in., were placed inside the frames.

The second locomotive, *Fig. 25*, delivered in the early part of 1876 had a similar boiler and the two cylinders, 6 in. in diameter by 9 in. stroke, were placed horizontally on the centre-line of the axles so that the vertical motion of

Fig. 26 Power bogie of combined steam tramcar built 1876 by Merryweather & Sons.
Engineering

the bearing springs, of the coil type, should not affect the action of the valve gear. A sheet iron box protected the motion from the dust. A water tank was fitted at one end and a coke bunker at the other, leaving a clear gangway on each side of the boiler. The exhaust steam was superheated in a box arranged at the bottom of the chimney uptake, being conducted thence by pipes, passing through the ashpan and inside the firebox. This arrangement was found to heat the steam sufficiently to render it invisible. An iron dish surrounding the uptake was placed there to catch the dislodged scale and prevent it from falling into the Field tubes.

The overall height was about 9 ft 6 in. and the length of the bodywork only 6 ft 6 in.; the weight of this locomotive with fuel and water was under 4 tons.

The power-bogie illustrated in *Fig. 26* has not been identified satisfactorily, but it is described on page 221 of *Engineering* for 9th March, 1883 as having been built by Merryweather for Paris, and delivered in 1876. The chief point of interest here is that the boiler and engine were enclosed in a cab on the front bogie and were free to radiate while at the same time being quite independent of the passenger part of the car. The vehicle was intended to run engine first at all times.

This machine had a Field boiler, with superheating apparatus and scale catcher as in the previous locomotive, and the power unit comprised a vertical steam cylinder placed on either side of the boiler, driving through suitable gearing to one axle, the wheels being coupled by rods; the total weight was only 5 tons.

A design for a small single-driver 0–2–2 inspection locomotive was introduced in the early 1880s, and only a few were built, mostly for South America. They were primarily intended for the railway Civil Engineering staff for surveying and inspecting the permanent way, and were designed for speeds up to 40 mph. The earliest example known was built in 1886 with seating arranged for two passengers; the gauge is not known but as the seats were set between the driving wheels, it was presumably not a narrow gauge design. The canopy was supported on six iron columns.

Another locomotive built in 1890 (Works No. 1065) for the Chilian-Transandine Railway is illustrated in *Plate 43*. This metre gauge line forms a short but important link in the great trans-continental route between Buenos Ayres and Valparaiso (895½ miles). The total length of the Chilian-Transandine Railway is 43.84 miles. Fortunately particulars of most of the dimensions of this locomotive have survived: the cylinders, with single slide bars of round section, were 5½ in. in diameter by 6 in. stroke; driving wheels were 2 ft 6 in. in diameter; trailing wheels were 2 ft in diameter and overall length was 9 ft 6 in. The boiler barrel was 2 ft 3 in. in height with a diameter of 2 ft; the grate area was 4.2 sq.ft and the boiler had a working pressure of boiler 120 lb. psi. The locomotive had a water capacity of 35 gallons; its weight on the driving wheels was 1 ton 6 cwt., while weight on the trailing wheels was 14 cwt.

Intended to carry three passengers on the narrow gauge, it was necessary to raise the seating about a foot higher to allow it to clear the driving wheels. The canopy, supported on four columns, had a rather ungainly-looking forward extension.

As late as 1907 a larger design of inspection locomotive was built for the Buenos Ayres and Pacific Railway which had a 5 ft 6 in. gauge. The outside cylinders were 6 in. in diameter, with link motion arranged inside the frames operating the slide valves through rocking shafts, and with double slide bars and crosshead, but here the wheels appear to have been of equal size, see *Plate 44*.

The boiler was lagged with hair felt and planished steel sheeting, and the chimney outer casing was of large diameter with polished brass cap so characteristic of the steam fire engine in its heyday. The brakes, which were quite adequate for such a machine, could be applied not only by the driver, but also from either the front or rear passenger seat.

Water tanks of large capacity were fitted at each end under the seats the total capacity being 300 gallons, which was sufficient for running long distances, and there was ample accommodation for coal and tools. The powerful headlamp, with parabolic reflector, was fitted to one side of the boiler top, on a turntable, so as to be reversible to suit the direction of travelling. The Merryweather New Patent Quick Steam Raising Boiler (Patent No. 1855 of 6th May, 1880) was used on these locomotives.

Plate 43 Merryweather & Sons' inspection locomotive built c.1890 for the Chilean-Transandine Railway. *Merryweather & Sons*

Plate 44 This inspection locomotive was built in 1907 by Merryweather & Sons for the Buenos Ayres & Pacific Railway. *Merryweather & Sons*

MIDLAND RAILWAY COMPANY
DERBY WORKS

The Midland Railway Co. built two railmotor coaches at the Derby locomotive works during 1904, and these were intended to work the service on the Morecambe and Heysham branch in Lancashire.

The four-coupled power-bogie, *Plate 45*, was designed by Mr R.M. Deeley, and had a vertical multi-tubular boiler, carrying a working pressure of 160 lb. psi, and the cylinders had a diameter of 11 in. with a 15 in. stroke. The coachwork had an overall length of 60 ft and was divided into four sections, made up of engine-room, passenger and baggage compartments, and a vestibule.

In running order the vehicle weighed 36 tons, and was designed to operate at a speed of 30 mph although in service it proved to be capable of 50 mph. These railmotors were numbered in the carriage stock.

Plate 45 Power bogie for a Midland Railway railmotor built at Derby Works in 1904.
British Rail

NEILSON AND COMPANY
HYDE PARK STREET
GLASGOW

The firm was founded by Walter Neilson and James Mitchell c.1836–7. It was known as Neilson & Mitchell in 1845 and Neilson & Co., in 1855.

The first section of the Morayshire Railway was that between Lossiemouth and Elgin, opened on 10th August, 1852. Two locomotives, designed by the company's Engineer, Mr James Samuel who had previously been with the Eastern Counties Railway, were built by Neilson and Co. and delivered in 1852 (Works Nos. 51 and 52). These were 2-2-0 type vertical boiler well-tank locomotives named LOSSIEMOUTH and ELGIN and had two vertical cylinders of 10 in. diameter with a stroke of 16 in. driving on the rear axle. The weight was 14 tons and the cost is said to have been £1311 3s. 10¼d. each.

The *Illustrated London News* published an engraving of Lossiemouth terminus on the opening day, and although the locomotive is shown very small in the far distance it is represented correctly as of the vertical boiler type.

In 1898 the firm became Neilson Reid & Co., and became part of the North British Locomotive Co. Ltd in 1903 as their Hyde Park Works.

NORTH BRITISH LOCOMOTIVE COMPANY LTD
GLASGOW

The company was founded in 1903 by the amalgamation of Neilson Reid & Co. (Hyde Park Works), Dübs & Co. (Queens Park Works) and Sharp Stewart & Co. (Atlas Works), all located in Glasgow.

The Barry Railway Company experimented with steam railmotors at an early date and two of these were constructed for them by the North British Locomotive Co. in 1905 (Works Nos. 16466 and 16467). They were originally intended for the service from Cardiff to Pontypridd via St Fagans but were only used on this route for a year or so and were then transferred to the Vale of Glamorgan line in 1906. Their working life in regular service was short and about 1910 they were stored at Barry for emergency relief workings to Barry Island. Both railmotors ceased work at the end of 1913.

Plate 46 illustrates the power-bogie of one of these vehicles which had a wheelbase of 8 ft and wheels of 3 ft 7½ in. diameter. The cylinders were 12 in. in diameter with a stroke of 16 in. and the piston valves were operated by Walschaerts gear. A large vertical boiler 8 ft 1 in. high and 4 ft 11 in. in diameter contained 462 copper tubes of 1½ in. diameter and 4 ft 11 in. between tubeplates, providing 552 sq.ft of heating surface. The copper firebox with a grate area of 11.5 sq.ft, had a heating surface of 45 sq.ft, making a total of 597 sq.ft. The working steam pressure was 160 lb. psi. The coal bunker held 15 cwt. and the tank capacity was 500 gallons.

The coach portion of these railmotors was supported on a trailing bogie having a wheelbase of 8 ft 6 in. and 3 ft 7½ in. diameter wheels, and had accommodation

Plate 46 North British Locomotive Co's power bogie built 1905 for a Barry Railway railmotor. *Mitchell Library, Glasgow*

Plate 47 North British Locomotive Co's power bogie built 1905 for GNR (I).
Mitchell Library, Glasgow

for ten first class, and forty third class passengers. The vehicle had a wheel base of 48 ft 3 in. and an overall length of 64 ft 10 in., the total weight in working order being 50 tons 15 cwt. An illustration of one of these vehicles appeared in *The Locomotive* for 1923, page 170.

Following the contract for the Barry Railway and in the same year, the North British Locomotive Co. supplied three railmotors to the Great Northern Railway of Ireland, built to the designs of Mr Charles Clifford. They were introduced on the local services between Belfast and Lisburn (7½ miles) and Dublin and Howth (8¼ miles). The power-bogies, seen in *Plate 47*, Works Nos. 16607, 16608 and 16609, had 3 ft 7½ in. diameter coupled wheels on a wheelbase of 8 ft driven by cylinders 12 in. in diameter by 16 in. stroke and slide valves operated by Walschaerts gear. The boiler had a tube heating surface of 623 sq. ft. The coach bodies came from R. and T. Pickering of Wishaw, and were suspension hung from the power-bogie frames, the other end being carried on a four-wheeled Fox's pressed steel carriage bogie. A water tank, suspended below the car was 18 ft 4 in. long by 2 ft 7¾ in. wide and 1 ft 10½ in. deep, made of ⅛ in. mild steel plates with flanged ends and surge plates. All three railmotors were withdrawn in 1913. A photograph of a complete railmotor appeared on page 226 of *The Engineer* for 9th August, 1963.

Severe competition in the diesel locomotive field led to the liquidation of this famous firm in 1963, Andrew Barclay Sons & Co. Ltd of Kilmarnock acquiring the goodwill and drawings.

OLIVER & CO. LTD
BROAD OAKS WORKS
CHESTERFIELD

The output of this old established company has been chiefly notable for its tremendous variety, which included winding engines, rolling mill engines, ships' engines, rolling mills, presses, furnace plant, bridges, water turbines, landing craft, midget submarines, radio telescopes and locomotives. Established in the mid-1840s by John Oliver and his son William, and after occupying two previous sites, the firm moved to new premises which were completed in 1877 alongside the Midland Railway, the name Broad Oaks Works originating from the meadow on which it was built.

On 1st October, 1889 Charles Paxton Markham purchased the business which continued to grow and prosper. In 1926 Mr Markham formally made over the Works to the Staveley Coal & Iron Co. Ltd, who carried on manufacturing until the company was again sold to John Brown & Co. Ltd, Coalmasters, Steel Makers and Shipbuilders in July 1937.

Between 1888 and 1914 nineteen orthodox steam locomotives were built, but in addition it has recently been discovered that at least three vertical locomotives were built, two in 1888 under the aegis of Oliver & Co. Ltd, and one in 1890 by Markham & Co. Ltd (*Plate 48*).

The first was built for their own use, as a works shunter, and the second was supplied to Edward Eastwood, the Chairman of Oliver & Co. Ltd, who at that

Plate 48 Oliver & Co's vertical boiler geared locomotive built at the Broad Oaks Works, Chesterfield.   *Markham & Co. Ltd*

time had his own railway wagon building and repair works in Chesterfield. One of these was eventually sold to the Stanton Iron Works, Ilkeston for £350. The third vertical boiler locomotive has the more interesting history. It was supplied to T.W. & J. Walker, Railway Contractors, and was for the 3 ft 6 in. gauge; designed to burn wood it had inside cylinders 6 in. × 12 in. Walkers may have undertaken work in Tasmania as, according to the records of the Tasmania Department of Labour and Industry in Hobart, there are notes to the effect that a locomotive by Markham & Co. was inspected on 22nd November, 1901. In 1914 a new boiler was fitted and at that time it was owned by Hay & Chopping of Hastings.

During the 1970s a vertical boiler locomotive was found abandoned in the bush in the vicinity of Sharp's Siding in the Derwent Valley and it has since been donated to the Tasmanian Transport Museum Society at Glenorchy. On examining the locomotive it was found that the boiler was numbered 1818 and the Department of Labour & Industry records revealed that it was supplied by Cowley, England in 1911 for Huon Timber Company. This firm operated an extensive system of 3 ft 6 in. gauge rail network out of Geeveston in Southern Tasmania.

Plate 49 Vertical boiler locomotive built by Oliver & Co. rescued from the bush and now being refurbished at Derwent Valley by the Tasmanian Transport Museum Society Inc., Hobart. *Tasmanian Transport Museum Society Inc.*

Plate 50 This view shows the cylinders at the opposite end of the locomotive from that pictured in *Plate 49*. This locomotive is probably Works No. 1467/1890.
Tasmanian Transport Museum Society Inc.

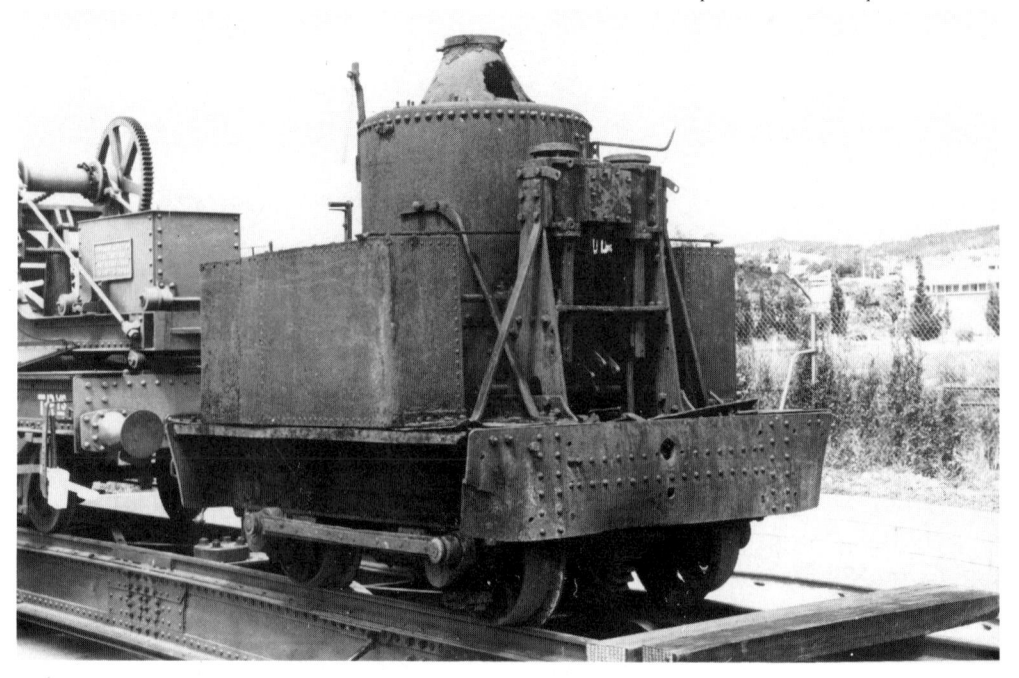

Plate 51 Probably the same locomotive shown in *Plates 49* and *50* working for Huon Timber Co.(?) Tasmania. There is a plate on the tank, either bearing a name or maker's details.

Tasmanian Transport Museum Society Inc.

The previous paragraph contains information kindly supplied by the Museum Society in 1985. If there was only one of these vertical boiler locomotives in Tasmania, the statement that a new boiler was fitted in 1914 under Hay & Chopping's ownership, does not agree with the second statement unless the Huon Timber Company sold it to Hay & Chopping before fitting the new boiler (*Plates 49, 50, 51*).

Order No.	Built	Customer	Gauge
688	1/1882	For own use	Std
689	1/1882	Edward Eastwood, Chesterfield	Std
1467	3/1890	T.W. & J. Walker, Contractor	3ft 6in.*

*Sold for £360 (new); cost of building £425 17s. 0d.

References

Mr D.H. Jones, Tasmanian Transport Museum Society, Inc. Hobart
Dr J. Kramer, Woolgoolga, N.S.W., Australia

MESSRS PARSONS AND MAY
CROSSWAYS WORKSHOPS
JAYWICK, NEAR CLACTON

The Jaywick Light Railway, laid to a gauge of 18 inches, connected the Bungalow Estate at Jaywick, near Clacton, with the sea front. The length was about a mile, following the course of an old sea wall across marshy land.

In 1939 a vertical boiler locomotive was completed in the company's workshops at Crossways. This was a most interesting design, based on a Sentinel geared industrial locomotive, and the power unit was a double-acting two-cylinder enclosed Stanley steam car engine, with cylinders 3¼ in. in diameter with a stroke of 4½ in., mounted horizontally. The oil-fired vertical water-tube boiler worked at 250 lb. psi, being equipped with a superheater and an exhaust steam feed-water heater. There were two water pumps and an oil pump all driven by a rocking shaft from one of the eccentrics. The transmission was by gears from the crankshaft and then by a 1 in. pitch Renolds chain to the axles.

The Stanley engine had ball-bearings on the crankshaft, big and little ends, while the main axleboxes also had ball-bearings. With 20 gallons of oil fuel, and 50 gallons of water, the total weight was 2½ tons.

R.Y. PICKERING AND COMPANY
WISHAW
LANARKSHIRE

As early as 1905, an experimental four-wheeled geared railmotor was designed by Mr Holman F. Stevens for the Rother Valley Railway, (later the Kent and East Sussex Railway) and was unique for the period in that it had no affinity with contemporary railmotors on other railways in Britain.

Built by R.Y. Pickering and Co. Ltd of Wishaw, a firm that had been concerned with the construction of railway carriages and wagons since 1864, this vehicle had a two-cylinder engine with a bore of 5½ in. and a stroke of 6 in., with link reversing gear, supplied with steam from a vertical multi-tubular boiler.

The drive was transmitted via an intermediate shaft and pitch chain to the axle nearest the engine-room. All four wheels had a diameter of 3 ft 6 in. The maker of the engine and boiler is not known. Adjoining the engine-room was a smoking compartment with eleven seats, then a non-smoking compartment for twenty passengers. The guard's compartment at the rear was designed to take fourteen milk churns and some luggage, and, in addition, had seats for a further six passengers.

Very few photographs of this railmotor have survived, but a very good one of it when new appeared in *The Locomotive* for 1905, page 47. It was never a success, and did not remain long in service; it stood for many years as a wreck in Rolvendon Works Yard, and was finally sold as scrap in 1941.

RANSOMES AND RAPIER LTD
WATERSIDE WORKS
IPSWICH

Ransomes and Rapier Ltd was established in 1868 for the manufacture of general railway plant, such as chairs, rails and points. But a few years later the firm commenced building various kinds of narrow gauge locomotives, among which was a series of vertical boiler inspection locomotives, the prototype of which had originally been designed and built for export to one of the Colonies.

The illustration, *Plate 52*, is from Ransomes and Rapier's official photograph No. 1876/61, and it is understood that a woodcut of another photograph No. 90, appeared in a catalogue of 1880, which gives some indication of the date when these locomotives were being built. As very little appears to be known about these locomotives, and the writer has as yet found no other contemporary account, it will be convenient here to quote from the maker's catalogue:

> Steam Carriage suitable for rails of 18–20 lb. per yard . . . This engine has since done exceedingly good service, both as an auxiliary on ordinary railways and as principal Engine on light railways. It is practically a combination of Engine, Tender, Brake and Carriage, all in one; and it is the least expensive contrivance for travelling 20 miles an hour which has yet been produced. For economy of space, the boiler is made of the vertical type, with grate surface and heating surface so ample as to enable a good supply

Plate 52 Ransomes & Rapier Ltd's inspection locomotive, customer not known.
Ransomes & Rapier Ltd

of steam to be easily maintained, even when burning wood or refuse fuel. The Engine has two cylinders, and is fitted with reversing gear, and all other fittings usual in the best locomotive work. It can be made of any gauge from 2 ft to 5 ft 6 in., according to the gauge of the railway in the locality. If there are no railways, the best gauge will be 3 ft or 3 ft 6 in. We build these Engines on stock, and can finish them at short notice to any of the following gauges, viz. 3 ft, metre, or 3 ft 6 in. The example here given has the following leading features and dimensions:

> Maintained speed 20 miles per hour, with light loads.
> Maximum train load at 8 mph on level, 80 tons
> Maximum train load at 5 mph on 1 in 100, 40 tons
> Maximum train load at 3 mph on 1 in 35, 20 tons
> Supply of coal and water for 30 miles
> Weight in working order 6 tons
> Cylinders 7 inches in diameter by 10 inches stroke; wheels 1 ft 8 in. diameter
> Length overall 11 feet
> Room for six or eight passengers
> Fitted with locker to contain mails and parcels.

> Price of the machine, fitted with roof, £480, price for enclosing with glass windows, £40 . . .

These locomotives were spring mounted, and all appear to have had disc wheels, but not always of the same pattern, some being solid, while others had the four circular holes as shown in the illustration. An engraving was published in Ransomes and Rapier's Catalogue No. 151, illustrating an alternative design of Inspection Locomotive in which the wheels were coupled and the cylinders attached to the end of the frame nearest the boiler. Normal type crossheads and twin slide-bars were used, and the valve gear was inside. The position of the boiler and the layout of the seats was similar to *Plate 52*, with the addition of a canopy.

The firm was a branch of Ransomes Sims & Head, later changed to Ransomes Sims & Jefferies, who were principally manufacturers of agricultural machinery at their Orwell Works. The branch factory was situated on the opposite side of the river and was built to cope with the demand for railway equipment.

THOMAS ROBINSON AND SON, LTD
RAILWAY WORKS
ROCHDALE

Established in 1838, this firm, which is well-known as a producer of woodworking and flourmilling machinery, was at one time involved in the production of stationary steam engines, railway material and some locomotives.

The first locomotive was built for their own use in 1881, and was named MARY, *Plate 53*. This was a well-built machine with vertical boiler and a two cylinder compound engine, with disc cranks and a centre driving pinion gearing with a spur wheel on the axle.

Only two other locomotives are thought to have been built by the company: one in 1884 for New Zealand, and a later one for Brazil, neither of these was of the vertical boiler type.

Plate 53   Compound locomotive *Mary* built by Thomas Robinson & Son Ltd in 1884 for their own use.   *Thomas Robinson & Son Ltd*

ROTHWELL, HICK AND ROTHWELL
UNION FOUNDRY
BOLTON

This firm started in business at the Union Foundry, Bolton, a short while before 1830, one of the partners being Benjamin Hick, who left in 1832 and set up in business with his two sons at the Soho Iron Works, Bolton. The Union Foundry was then operated under the name of Rothwell and Co. who built about 200 locomotives up to 1864, when construction ceased.

The first locomotive built at the Union Foundry, and the only one which qualifies for inclusion in this book, was produced in 1830 for the Bolton and Leigh Railway which had been opened in 1828. Named the UNION, this loco-

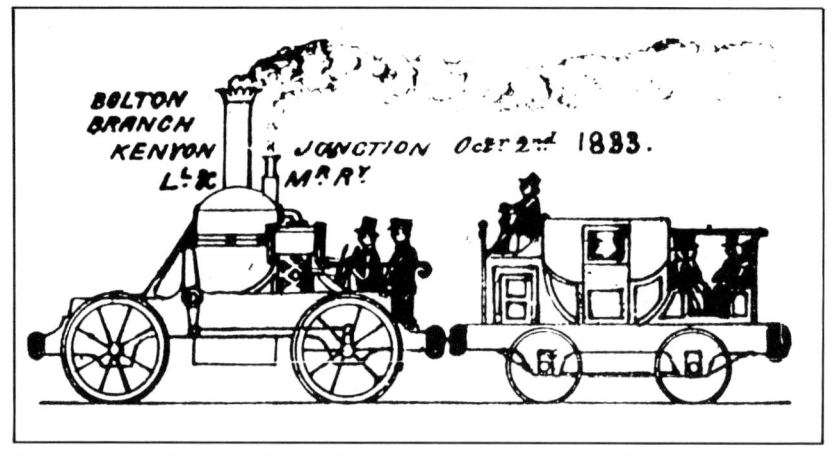

Fig. 27 Rothwell, Hick & Rothwell's locomotive *Union* built 1830 for the Bolton & Leigh Railway. *Cleveland Soc. of Engineers*

motive in addition to having a vertical boiler with a spiral flue, had the cylinders and motion arranged in a rather unorthodox position even for that date. There was a horizontal cylinder high up on either side of the boiler, but not fixed to it, and driving forward on to a rocking level from the lower end of which a connecting rod drove a crank on the rear wheel. According to Whishaw, the cylinders were 9 in. in diameter with a stroke of 18 in. and the driving wheels were 5 ft in diameter while the leading wheels are stated to have been only 3 ft in diameter.

The only known illustration of this locomotive, *Fig. 27*, is taken from Theodore West's paper "An Outline History of the Locomotive Engine" read before the Cleveland Society of Engineers on 1st March, 1886. This drawing is generally considered to be substantially correct, although the leading wheels are shown as approximately the same size as the driving wheels.

Before final delivery to the Bolton and Leigh Railway the UNION was subjected to several experimental runs on the railway during December 1830, and according to the *Bolton Chronicle* for 4th December, these trials were very successful. When running light without any other load than the tender, the locomotive attained a speed of 30 mph, and with a heavy train of loaded coal wagons a speed of 12 mph was maintained.

GEORGE RUSSELL AND COMPANY
ALPHA STEAM CRANE AND ENGINE WORKS
PARK STREET, MOTHERWELL JUNCTION

Established in 1865 for the construction of steam engines and boilers, steam and hand cranes, winches and hoisting engines, this firm remained a private concern until 1958 when it became a subsidiary of Joseph Adamson and Co. Ltd of Hyde, Cheshire. According to John S. Brownlie in *Railway Steam Cranes* the

Fig. 28 George Russell & Co's design of vertical boiler locomotive built c.1875.
George Russell & Co.

control of the company was acquired by Messrs The Adamson Alliance Co. Ltd, of Horsehay who withdrew in 1967.

In addition to the above range of machinery, a small number of vertical boiler contractors' type locomotives, *Fig. 28*, were built and offered in six sizes, as follows:

Diameter of cylinders	Diameter of wheels
4 inches	2 ft 3 in.
4½ inches	2 ft 3 in.
5½ inches	2 ft 6 in.
6½ inches	2 ft 6 in.
7 inches	2 ft 9 in.
8 inches	2 ft 9 in.

The gear ratio was varied to suit customers' requirements as to speed and haulage capacity, and the locomotives could be supplied for any gauge from 2 ft onwards.

In the maker's description the boiler is said to have been of best iron, tested to 200 lb. psi, and fitted with a Bourdon pressure gauge, and Salter safety valve.

The boiler feed was by pump and the tank had a water heater.

These locomotives are thought to have been in production about the period 1875 or so, but the maker is unable to confirm this as a large number of records were destroyed at the change of ownership in 1958. A point of interest is that George Russell was Alexander Chaplin's designer (1858–1863) and in 1865 set up his own business.

SARA AND COMPANY
PLYMOUTH

To work the Sutton Harbour branch, the broad gauge South Devon Railway purchased from Sara and Co. the small vertical boiler locomotive illustrated in *Plate 54* and this was delivered in January 1868. This locomotive had a wheelbase 1 ft 3¼ in. shorter than the gauge, at 5 ft 9 in.; wheels were 3 ft in diameter and the two vertical cylinders, 9 in. in diameter with a stroke of 12 in. were attached to the boiler. The boiler was tubeless, with a central flue, and had a height of 6 ft 3 in. and a diameter of 2 ft 8½ in., while the firebox was 2 ft 4½ in. in diameter, with a grate area of 6.137 sq.ft.

Plate 54 Broad gauge locomotive *Tiny* built by Sara & Co. in 1868 for the South Devon Railway.   *British Rail*

A well-tank, formed in the framing, held 80 gallons, and coal was carried in a small bunker at one corner of the driver's platform on which there was also a vertical brake column. The overall height of the locomotive was 11 ft 10½ in. Named TINY by the South Devon Railway, it became Great Western Railway No. 2180, and in June 1883 was withdrawn from service and used as a stationary engine to work the pumps in the boiler house of Newton Abbot locomotive shops.

It remained on this duty until 1927 when it was overhauled and placed on exhibition on the down platform of the new station. As far back as 1927 reports were circulating that Sara and Co. had built other vertical boiler locomotives for local china clay works, but over the intervening years no further information has come to light.

SARA AND BURGESS
PENRYN, NEAR FALMOUTH

At Penryn, near Falmouth, a foundry was started in 1857 by Nicholas Sara, at one time a foreman at the famous Perran Foundry; in 1887 the owners were his son, E.B. Sara, and John Burgess, also an old Perran man. This firm was responsible for building at least four vertical boiler locomotives, although the dates are not known; three were supplied to the Falmouth Docks and Engineering Co. during the 1860s and were known as No. 1 BLACKBIRD, No. 2

Plate 55 Sara & Burgess' geared locomotive built c.1860 for Falmouth Docks.

TORBAY, and No.3 BILLY. They were originally built to the broad gauge, but about 1892 were converted to the standard gauge; all were withdrawn in the mid-1920s.

In the early years of the present century, c.1910–12, a fourth locomotive was built for the Port of Par Limited, and this seems to have worked until about 1936. The vertical cylinders, 7 in. in diameter by 12 in. stroke, drove the 3 ft diameter wheels by spur gearing to the front axle, and the boiler was 8 ft high by 3 ft in diameter. The water tank was between the frames with the coal bunker at the rear, and like many locomotives of this type the driving position was alongside the boiler. *Plate 55* illustrates these locomotives in the final years of their existence.

The firm of Sara and Burgess closed down sometime before 1918.

THE SAVILE STREET FOUNDRY AND ENGINEERING CO. LTD SHEFFIELD

According to an advertisement in the 1884 edition of the Sheffield Trades Directory, this concern is described as "Colliery, Hydraulic, and General Engineers, Manufacturers of Pumping, Blowing, Winding, Mill, Forge and all kinds of Stationary Engines . . . also all kinds of Castings".

This firm patented a compound tramway locomotive with a vertical boiler, horizontal cylinders, and an air-condenser under the roof. The high-pressure cylinder was 8 in. in diameter, and the low-pressure cylinder is said to have been 21 in. in diameter, but if this latter dimension is correct the ratio was most unusual; the piston stroke was 14 in. The date of construction would be about 1881, and after trials in Sheffield it was transferred to Burnley in 1883. The foundry was also responsible for a combined steam tramcar, again with a vertical

Plate 56 Steam tramcar constructed by the Savile Street Foundry c.1881.
Edgar Allen Eng. Ltd

boiler, and this was tried in Sheffield between 1886 and 1888.

By the courtesy of Edgar Allen Engineering Ltd, Sheffield, it has been possible to illustrate this tramcar in *Plate 56*. Recent research has revealed the possibility of some of the components of both the locomotive and the combined car having been manufactured elsewhere.

J. SCARISBRICK WALKER AND BROTHERS
PAGEFIELD IRONWORKS
WIGAN

Founded in 1870, by John S. Walker as a general engineering business, at least 32 locomotives were built between 1872 and 1888. One is known to have been a four-wheeled vertical boiler machine with a geared drive, and was supplied to the Shap Granite Company, who bestowed on it the name of WASDALE.

The firm was reorganised as Walker Brothers (Wigan) Ltd about 1880, and became well-known as builders of horizontal compressors and fan engines for mines throughout the world, and particularly for their large colliery winding engines. The last of these was built for the Scottish Division of the N.C.B. in 1954 and installed at Easthouses Colliery, Lothians Area.

SENTINEL WAGGON WORKS LTD
SHREWSBURY

One firm—Alley & MacLellan of Polmadie, Glasgow, were makers of all types of valves, later to embrace ship building, marine engineering and stationary steam engines. Their trademark was SENTINEL. In 1915 a new works was built in Shrewsbury, as a result of the introduction of the Sentinel steam waggon at Polmadie in association with David Simpson of Horsehay. The vertical boiler used on these road waggons had an inner and outer shell, the inner having water tubes, above which was a superheater coil. The firebox was within the boiler shell. The boiler pressure was 230 lb. psi. Apart from some modifications this boiler remained the basic design for over forty years for road waggons, locomotives and railcars, varying in size from 100 hp to 200 hp.

Railcars

The first railcar was built in 1923 in co-operation with Cammell Laird & Co., of Nottingham who built the coachwork. It was delivered to the Jersey Railways & Tramways Ltd (3 ft 6 in. gauge). The four-wheeled power unit had a horizontal engine which drove the rear axle by means of a single chain. The front end was similar to that of a Super Sentinel Waggon with a superheated vertical boiler and equipped with a steam brake. Initially it could only be driven from the power unit end but subsequently it was modified for dual control. It was named THE PIONEER and was very successful with good acceleration, low coal consumption and steady running, so successful that two more were ordered and delivered in 1924/5. Orders came from India, Denmark, Australia, South Africa, Sweden, France, Egypt, and other overseas customers. Later models had vertical cylinders and higher pressure boilers at 275 lb. psi. At home the LM & SR ordered thirteen in 1925–7 and the LNER two, all fitted with vacuum brake cylinders on the power units operating expanding brakes on all four wheels fitted with brake drums.

In 1928 a six cylinder 6 in. × 7 in. engine was introduced for future railcars. The engine unit was underslung and in a transverse position driving the front axle using Hardy Spicer universal joint cardan shaft and gearbox. The boiler pressure was increased to 300 lb. psi with twin superheater coils. Railcars continued to be built up to 1953 of various types including compound engines, and articulated coaches.

Of particular interest was the Railbus built in March 1933 for the Southern Railway. A Super Sentinel boiler with a working pressure of 325 lb. psi was fitted with automatic coal feed so dispensing with the services of the fireman. The engine was a two-cylinder compound developing 97 bhp. It worked the Dyke branch which had awkward reverse curves and testing gradients. It acquitted itself efficiently but, having only 44 seats, the increase in passengers made it necessary to transfer it to other branches where it was not so successful, and in 1938 it was laid aside at Ashford and withdrawn in 1940. This was in marked contrast to the general success of the railcars and locomotives. For instance up to and including 1937 the LNER had purchased 80 railcars and one articulated unit.

The railcar was intended to combat the increasing competition by road vehicles, and it was claimed that the cars could be run at less than half the running costs of a conventional branch line train with separate locomotives and carriages, and lower operating costs per seat-mile compared with a road omnibus.

Railcars were constructed to gauges from 2 ft 6 in. to 5 ft 6 in. and the standard designs were:

A	Single engined	100–125 hp	Single car
B	Double engined	200–250 hp	Single car
C	Single engined	100–125 hp	Double car
D	Double engined	200–250 hp	Double car
E	Single engined	175–200 hp	Single car
F	Double engined	350–400 hp	Single car
G	Single engined	175–200 hp	Double car
H	Double engined	350–400 hp	Double car

In the single car the body was carried on two bogies and in the double car on three, the central bogie being arranged on the "Gresley" patent system of articulation. Horsepower shown above for each type indicate the power at early cut-off and intermediate cut-off respectively.

The standard railcars were built around the engine unit and varied according to the customer's requirements. The water feed tank was placed over the driving bogie and filled through a panel on either side of the car. For single-engined units the capacity was 400 gallons and 600 gallons for the double unit. Coal bunkers were fixed at the front left hand side opposite the controls with capacity of 15 cwt. and 30 cwt. for single and double units respectively, which would serve for an average of 120 to 150 miles.

Many boilers were made by Abbott & Co. (Newark) Ltd. Woolnough water tube boilers were fitted to three railcars for the Colombian National Railways and a Doble steam car built to A. Doble's designs but proved far too complicated in maintenance and running.

An interesting car built in 1928 for the Leopoldina Railway was used as an inspection car with a day saloon and pantry at one end, bathroom and sleeping accommodation at the other end, with the boiler in the centre compartment. The coach could be driven from either end. The power unit consisted of a vertical six-cylinder single-acting engine with 6 in. × 7 in. cylinders arranged for working with steam at 300 lb. psi. The cylinder heads were detachable and incorporated the valve chests and ports. The valves were of the mushroom type with cast iron valve guides, camshaft operated with case-hardened steel cam followers. The camshafts were driven by spur gearing from the crankshaft. "Notching up" was done by sliding the camshafts which were connected to the driver's controls by a suitable mechanism. The crankshaft ran in a totally enclosed crankcase. The entire engine unit was suspended from the underframe and the drive transmitted to a gearbox mounted on the driving axle, by means of a Hardy-Spicer Cardan shaft with a disc joint at the engine end and a universal joint at the gearbox end. A spur gear on the layshaft meshed with the final drive pinion pressed on the axle. The standard gear ratios were arranged to give a speed of 30 or 38 mph at 500 rpm of the engine, with a maximum speed of 40 to 45 or 50 to 55 mph respectively. The controls were arranged at both ends of the car dispensing with turntable requirements.

The standard 100 hp boiler consisted of two cylindrical shells (outer and inner), the inner shell was provided with a series of diagonally disposed corrugations forming landings for three banks of tubes arranged spirally round a central "chute", through which the fuel was fed into the grate below. The superheater consisted of two coils of solid drawn steel piping lying in the space round the stoking chute between the top tubes and the boiler top. One end connected with the collector steam pipe round the top of the steam space in the boiler and the other with the main stop valve. The heating surface of the tubes excluding the superheater was 73 sq.ft and the grate area 5.1 sq.ft and on good coal would evaporate 2300 to 2400 lb. of water per hour at a pressure of 300 lb. psi and a steam temperature of 700°–750°F.

Other boilers were designed for various conditions; the 'Bengal' boiler which was adapted for burning inferior coal in India, also oil fired boilers and for the larger applications for the double-engined cars, a 200 hp boiler of water tube type with a 27 in. diameter steam drum and tubular superheater elements could be coal or oil fired.

Shunting & Goods Locomotives

The first locomotive came out in the same year as the railcar; the unit was practically the same with four wheels, a vertical water tube boiler from the Super Sentinel range, the main modification to the boiler was the disposition of the water tubes which had a much steeper angle than the standard boiler and also had a double coil superheater (*Figs 29 & 30*). The feed water from the tank was preheated. As previously stated the engine was underslung, the crankshaft protruding at each side and fitted with sprocket wheels providing a double chain drive, usually one to each axle. Later vertical cylinders became standard.

Fig. 29 Diagram of 100hp and 200hp boilers.

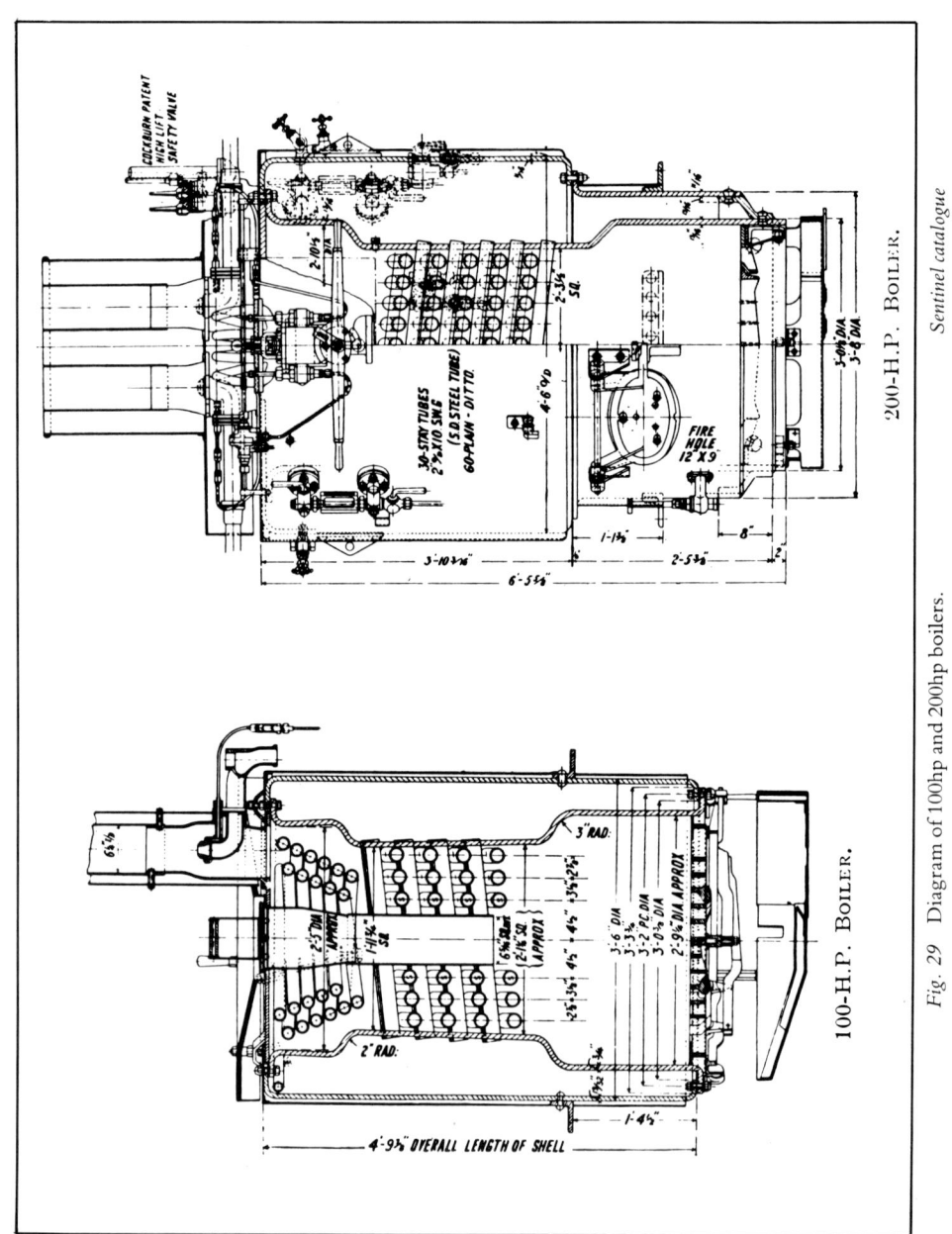

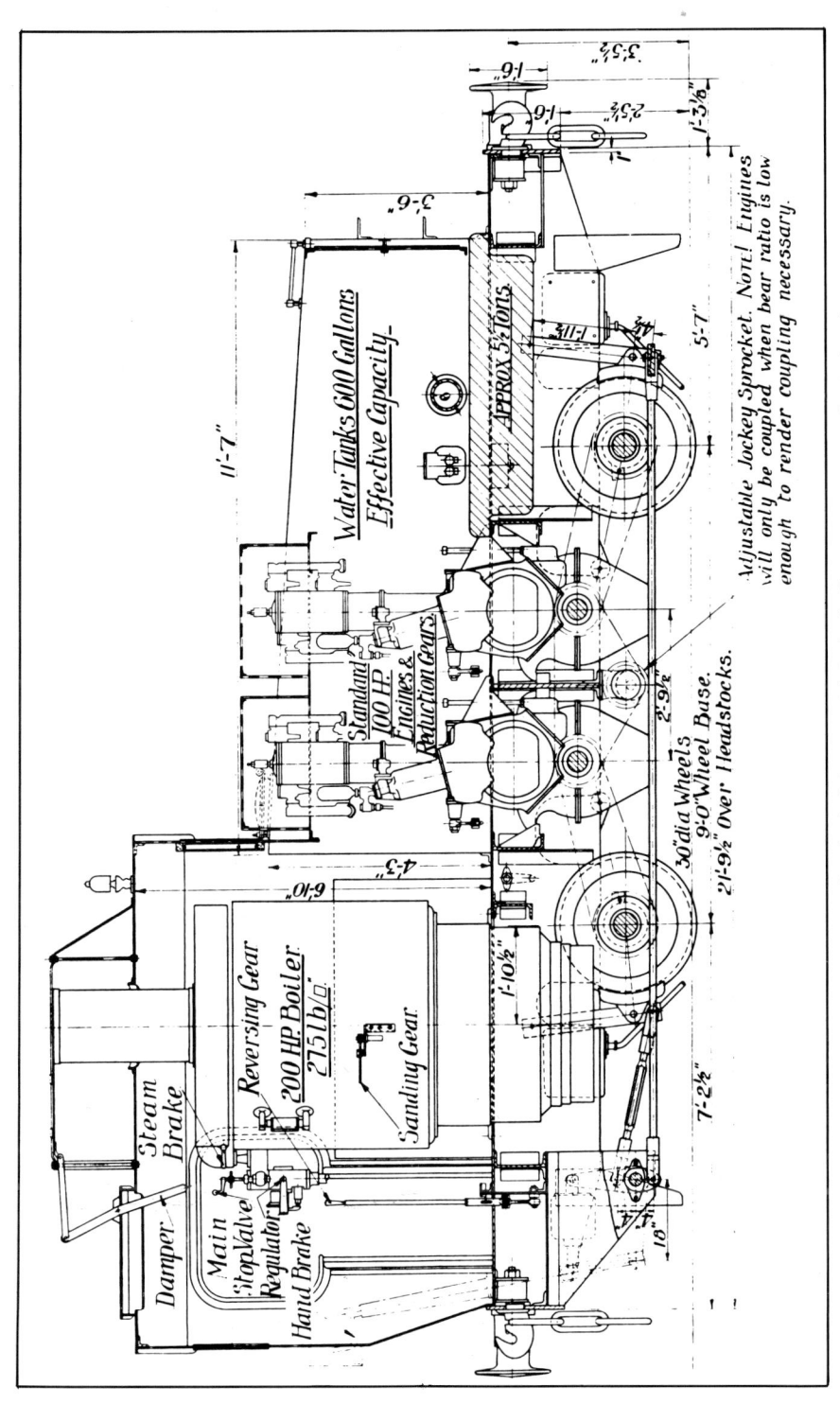

Fig. 30 Diagram of 4 wheeled shunter with 200hp boiler.   *Sentinel catalogue*

Plate 57 Sentinel Waggon Works Ltd narrow gauge 80 hp Sentinel locomotive working at Macclesfield Reservoir (Works No.6894 or 6900/1927) designed by R.W. Willan. *D. Stoyel*

The initial 'BE' type engine (balanced engine) was arranged at the rear end of the frames to counterbalance the boiler at the front end and to provide ease of access. The second type 'CE' was a centrally placed engine, still in the vertical position and to balance the axle weights the water tank was placed at the rear. The two cylinders were 6¾ in. × 9 in. and both steam and exhaust valves were operated by camshafts to give cut-offs of 30 per cent and 80 per cent. The sprocket ratios were varied according to the duty required. Larger models were built with boiler pressure at 275 lb. psi which gave an evaporation of 1900 lb./hour—this from a boiler 3 ft 6in. diameter × 4 ft 9in. high.

A double engine (DE) locomotive was produced, one engine driving the front axle and one the rear. In this case the front (boiler) end was counterbalanced by means of a cast iron weight at the rear adding to the weight of the water tank above it. To provide more versatility in speed and tractive effort double gearing was introduced (type BEDG and DEDG).

In 1926 a unique articulated locomotive was built for the Kettering Coal & Iron

Co. Ltd, in effect two standard four-wheeled vehicles back to back, which was expected to provide considerable economies but did not come up to those expectations.

In this Country the LNER were the biggest customer (as for Railcars) having bought 58 of three types:

(1) 100 hp 2ft 6in. wheels, 1 speed
(2) 100 hp 2ft 6in. wheels, 2 speeds and larger boiler
(3) Double ended with 3ft 2in. wheels specially designed for the Wisbech & Upwell Tramway with two 100 hp engines, two were built in 1930.

Sentinel Industrial/Shunting locomotives were built with two, four or six cylinders 6 in. × 7 in, 6¾ in. × 9 in. or 7 in. × 9 in. Altogether approximately 830 units were built of which over 30 per cent were Railcars. Undoubtedly the Sentinel Vertical Boiler Units were the most successful of this type of locomotive. The quantity produced far exceeded that of any other maker. Their success was mainly due to a very efficient boiler which gave free steaming, careful attention to accessibility, weight distribution, and prompt spares service. Another advantage was the arrangement of the ashpan which was clear of the front axle so that the fire and ash could be dropped easily, when necessary the firebox could be dealt with in the same way.

Change of Title
1917 Sentinel Waggon Works Ltd
1920 Sentinel Waggon Works (1920) Ltd
1936 The Sentinel Waggon Works (1936) Ltd

References

The Sentinel Vol. 1 1875–1930 by W.J. Hughes & J.L. Thomas
The Locomotive Vol. 29/1923 pp. 140/1, Vol. 31/1925 p. 309, Vol. 32/1926 pp. 8–10, Vol. 33/1927 pp. 149, 281–2, Vol. 34/1928 pp. 183–6, Vol. 36/1930 pp. 183, 229, 368, 401–2, 405–6, Vol. 38/1932 pp. 32, 355, Vol. 40/1934 pp. 198–202, Vol. 41/1935 pp. 110, 273–4, Vol. 56/1950 pp. 172–3, Vol. 58/1952 pp. 172/3, Vol. 62/1956 pp. 61–3
J.F. Ward
D. Stoyel

SENTINEL VERTICAL BOILER LOCOS & RAILCARS

Note: HB = Horizontal Boiler, L = 4wVBTG, RC = Railcar, P = Preserved.

Works No.	Built	Type	Cyls	D.W.	Gauge	Customer	No./Name/Notes
4863	6/1923	RC	H/6¾"×9"	2'6"	3'6"	Jersey Rlys	No.1 THE PIONEER HB
5155	7/1923	RC	H/6¾"×9"	2'6"	M	Orki Div. India	
5156	7/1923	L	H/6¾"×9"	2'6"	2'6"	Richard Thomas, Clydach	
5157	7/1923	L	H/6¾"×9"	2'0"	2'0"	Pathankoj Bajri Stone Supply Co.	
5158	7/1923	RC	H/6¾"×9"	2'6"	M	Orki Div. India	
5159	1/1924	RC	H/6¾"×9"	2'6"	3'6"	Jersey Rlys	No.2 PORTELET
5164	2/1924	L	H/6¾"×9"	1'8"	2'0"	Pathankoj Bajri Stone Supply Co.	
5165	2/1924	L	H/6¾"×9"	1'8"	2'0"	Sutlej Valley Project	
5166	2/1924	L	H/6¾"×9"	1'8"	2'0"	Sutlej Valley Project	
5193	1/1924	L	H/6¾"×9"	1'8"	2'0"	Sutlej & Sukkum Canal Irrigation Schemes	
5198	1924	L	H/6¾"×9"	1'8"	2'0"	Pathankoj Bajri Stone Supply Co.	
5199	1924	L	H/6¾"×9"	1'8"	2'0"	Sutlej Valley Project	
5200	1924	L	H/6¾"×9"	1'8"	2'0"	Sutlej Valley Canal Schemes	
5201	1924	L	H/6¾"×9"	1'8"	2'0"	Sutlej Valley Canal Schemes	
5234	7/1924	RC	H/6¾"×9"	2'6"	3'6"	Commonwealth Rlys, Australia	
5245	8/1924	RC	H/6¾"×9"	2'6"	3'6"	Griffen, S. African Rlys.	
5297	5/1924	L	H/6¾"×9"	1'8"	2'0"	Sutlej & Sukkum Canal Irrigation Schemes	
5298	5/1924	L	H/6¾"×9"	1'8"	2'0"	Sutlej & Sukkum Canal Irrigation Schemes	
5299	5/1924	L	H/6¾"×9"	1'8"	2'0"	Sutlej & Sukkum Canal Irrigation Schemes	
5300	5/1924	L	H/6¾"×9"	1'8"	2'0"	Sutlej & Sukkum Canal Irrigation Schemes	
5308	6/1924	L	H/6¾"×9"	2'4½"	2'5½"	Egyptian Delta Lt Rly	
5384	5/1924	L	H/6¾"×9"	1'8"	2'0"	Sutlej & Sukkum Canal Irrigation Schemes	
5410	5/1924	L	H/6¾"×9"	1'8"	2'0"	Sutlej & Sukkum Canal Irrigation Schemes	
5476	6/1924	RC	H/6¾"×9"	2'6"	Std	Helsingor Rly, Denmark	
5481	8/1924	RC	H/6¾"×9"	2'6"	Std	Gavle Dala Rly, Sweden	
5534	11/1924	RC	H/6¾"×9"	2'6"	Std	Paris Orleans Rly	
5559	6/1924	L	H/6¾"×9"	1'8"	2'0"	Sutlej & Sukkum Canal Irrigation Schemes	
5560	6/1924	L	H/6¾"×9"	1'8"	2'0"	Sutlej & Sukkum Canal Irrigation Schemes	
5561	6/1924	L	H/6¾"×9"	1'8"	2'0"	Sutlej & Sukkum Canal Irrigation Schemes	
5567	11/1924	RC	H/6¾"×9"	2'6"	3'6"	New Zealand Govt	
5586	11/1924	L	H/6¾"×9"	1'8"	2'0"	Sutlej & Sukkum Canal Irrigation Schemes	
5587	11/1924	L	H/6¾"×9"	1'8"	2'0"	Sutlej & Sukkum Canal Irrigation Schemes	

Works No.	Built	Type	Cyls	D.W.	Gauge	Customer	No./Name/Notes
5622	1/1925	RC	H/6¾"×9"	2'6"	5'6"	Ceylon Rlys	301
5623	1/1925	RC	H/6¾"×9"	2'6"	5'6"	Ceylon Rlys	302
5624	1/1925	RC	H/6¾"×9"	2'6"	5'6"	Ceylon Rlys	303
5639	8/1925	RC	H/6¾"×9"	2'6"	Std	Central Argentine Rly	
5640	3/1926	RC	H/6¾"×9"	2'6"	Std	Nitrate Rlys, Chile	'A'
5641	6/1925	RC	H/6¾"×9"	2'6"	3'6"	Newfoundland Rly	
5642	3/1926	RC	H/6¾"×9"	2'6"	Std	Nitrate Rlys, Chile	
5654	3/1925	RC	H/6¾"×9"	3'1"	Std	LNER	13E
5655	1925	RC	H/6¾"×9"	2'6"	Std	Jersey Eastern Rly	NORMANDIE HB
5656	3/1926	RC	H/6¾"×9"	2'6"	Std	Nitrate Rlys, Chile	
5657	3/1926	RC	H/6¾"×9"	3'1"	Std	LNER	12E
5705	1925	L	H/6¾"×9"	1'8"	2'0"	Sutlej Valley Project	
5706	1925	L	H/6¾"×9"	1'8"	2'0"	Sutlej Valley Project	
5707	1925	L	H/6¾"×9"	1'8"	2'0"	Sutlej Valley Project	
5708	1/1925	L	H/6¾"×9"	2'6"	Std	Entre Rios Rly	
5709	3/1925	L	H/6¾"×9"	2'6"	Std	Harnosand Rly, Sweden	
5710	7/1925	L	H/6¾"×9"	2'6"	Std	Czechoslovakian Rly	
5711	6/1925	L	H/6¾"×9"	2'6"	3'6"	Newfoundland Rly	'B'
5733	6/1925	CE/L	H/6¾"×9"	2'6"	Std	Leys Malleable Castings Co. Ltd, Derby	2
5734	1925	CE/L	V/6¾"×9"	2'6"	Std	J.C. Edwards Ltd, Ruabon	
5735	1926	CE/L	V/6¾"×9"	2'6"	Std	S. Williams & Son, Dagenham	5
5738	1926	CE/L	V/6¾"×9"	2'6"	Std	Glaenzeret Pereand, Paris	
5750	4/1925	CE/L	V/6¾"×9"	2'6"	5'3"	LMS (NCC) Belfast	91
5751	5/1925	CE/L	V/6¾"×9"	2'6"	5'3"	LMS (NCC) Belfast	40
5752	3/1925	CE/L	V/6¾"×9"	2'6"	2'6"	Baroda State Rly	
5833	3/1925	RC	H/6¾"×9"	2'6"	3'6"	Jersey Rly	No.3 LA MOYE
5906	2/1925	L	V/6¾"×9"	1'8"	2'0"	Rosehaugh Co. Tanganyika Kingolwira Sisal Estate	
5907	2/1925	L	V/6¾"×9"	1'8"	2'0"	Wigglesworth Coll. Barnard Castle	
5989	1925	L	V/6¾"×9"	1'8"	2'0"	Northumberland Whinstone Co.	4
5990	1925	L	V/6¾"×9"	1'8"	2'0"	Northumberland Whinstone Co.	3
6007	1926	L	V/6¾"×9"	2'6"	Std	Aitken & Morcom, Craig-yr-Hesg	
6009	4/1926	RC	V/6¾"×9"	2'6"	5'6"	Bengal Nagpur Rly	
6020	c.1926	L	V/6¾"×9"	2'6"	Std	APCM, Dunstable	
6061	5/1926	L	V/6¾"×9"	2'6"	5'6"	Indian Irrigation Schemes	
6075	1926	L	V/6¾"×9"	1'8"	60cm	Gas, Light & Coke Co., Kensal Green	2
6076	4/1926	L	V/6¾"×9"	2'6"	Std	Derwent Valley Lt Rly	
6090	1925	L	V/6¾"×9"	2'6"	Std	Mendip Mountain Quarries	

VERTICAL BOILER LOCOMOTIVES

Works No.	Built	Type	Cyls	D.W.	Gauge	Customer	No./Name/Notes
6104	4/1926	RC	V/6¾"×9"	2'6"	2'6"	Bengal Nagpur (Satpura Rly)	
6106	5/1925	L	V/6¾"×9"	2'6"	5'6"	Indian Irrigation Schemes	
6126	4/1926	RC	V/6¾"×9"	2'6"	5'6"	Bengal Nagpur (Satpura Rly)	
6127	4/1926	RC	V/6¾"×9"	2'6"	5'6"	Bengal Nagpur (Satpura Rly)	
6128	4/1926	RC	V/6¾"×9"	2'6"	5'6"	Bengal Nagpur (Satpura Rly)	
6130	7/1925	L	V/6¾"×9"	2'6"	2'5½"	Egyptian Delta Lt Rly	211
6131	1925	L	V/6¾"×9"	2'6"	2'5½"	Egyptian Delta Lt Rly	208
6132	1925	L	V/6¾"×9"	2'6"	2'5½"	Egyptian Delta Lt Rly	207
6133	1925	L	V/6¾"×9"	2'6"	2'5½"	Egyptian Delta Lt Rly	210
6134	1925	L	V/6¾"×9"	2'6"	2'5½"	Egyptian Delta Lt Rly	212
6135	1925	L	V/6¾"×9"	2'6"	2'5½"	Egyptian Delta Lt Rly	
6136	1925	L	V/6¾"×9"	2'6"	2'5½"	Egyptian Delta Lt Rly	201
6137	1925	L	V/6¾"×9"	2'6"	2'5½"	Egyptian Delta Lt Rly	205
6138	1925	L	V/6¾"×9"	2'6"	2'5½"	Egyptian Delta Lt Rly	203
6139	1925	L	V/6¾"×9"	2'6"	2'5½"	Egyptian Delta Lt Rly	204
6140	1925	L	V/6¾"×9"	2'6"	2'5½"	Egyptian Delta Lt Rly	
6141	1925	L	V/6¾"×9"	2'6"	2'5½"	Egyptian Delta Lt Rly	202
6170	9/1925	CE/L	V/6¾"×9"	2'6"	Std	LNER class 'Y1'	8400
6177	8/1927	RC	V/6¾"×9"	2'6"	Std	Jersey Eastern Rly (ex LMS No.2)	BRITANNIE
6185	1927	L	V/6¾"×9"	2'6"	Std	Coalbrookdale Co.	Chassis P
6197	1927	L	V/6¾"×9"	2'6"	3'6"	Sudan Govt Rlys	54
6222	1926	L	V/6¾"×9"	2'6"	3'0"	Field & Mackay Titterstone, Clee Hill	LILIAN
6224	1926	L	V/6¾"×9"	2'6"	Std	Argentine N.E.R.	
6238	11/1926	RC	V/6¾"×9"	2'6"	3'0"	Pachitea Rly, Peru	
6240	10/1926	RC	V/6¾"×9"	2'6"	5'6"	North Western Rly, India	
6241	1926	RC	V/6¾"×9"	2'6"	5'6"	North Western Rly, India	
6242	1926	RC	V/6¾"×9"	2'6"	5'6"	North Western Rly, India	
6251	1927	L	V/6¾"×9"	2'6"	Std	North Thames Gas Board	
6255	1926	L	V/6¾"×9"	2'6"	3'0"	Little Orme Limestone Quarry	2
6256	1926	L	V/6¾"×9"	2'6"	3'0"	Little Orme Limestone Quarry	1
6257	1926	L	V/6¾"×9"	2'6"	3'0"	Little Orme Limestone Quarry	3
6273	1/1926	L	V/6¾"×9"	2'6"	5'6"	Indian Irrigation Schemes	
6276		L	V/6¾"×9"	2'6"	3'0"	Balfour Beatty & Co. Ltd	Preserved. Delhi
6277		L	V/6¾"×9"	2'6"	3'0"	A.H. Carmichael, Perth (Contractor)	
6289	1/1927	RC	V/6¾"×9"	2'6"		North Western Rly, Peru	HB
6301		L			Std	Clay Cross Co., Grin Quarry	
6341	2/1927	RC	V/6¾"×9"	2'6"	2'6"	Barsi Lt Rly	28 HB
6342	1927	RC	V/6¾"×9"	2'6"	2'6"	Barsi Lt Rly	27 HB
6359	1926	L	V/6¾"×9"	2'6"	Std	Cammell Laird Birkenhead	1

Works No.	Built	Type	Cyls	D.W.	Gauge	Customer	No./Name/Notes
6366	1926	L	V/6¾"×9"	2'6"	2'6"	Barsi Lt Rly	24
6367	1926	L	V/6¾"×9"	2'6"	2'6"	Barsi Lt Rly	25
6368	1926	L	V/6¾"×9"	2'6"	2'6"	Barsi Lt Rly	26
6375	11/1926	L	V/6¾"×9"	2'6"	M	British N. Borneo Co.	13 Sentinel HB Preserved Kota Kinabalu
6387	5/1927	RC	V/6¾"×9"	2'6"	5'6"	Ceylon Rlys class 'R1'	304
6388	1927	RC	V/6¾"×9"	2'6"	5'6"	Ceylon Rlys class 'R1'	305
6389	1927	RC	V/6¾"×9"	2'6"	5'6"	Ceylon Rlys class 'R1'	306
6390	1927	RC	V/6¾"×9"	2'6"	5'6"	Ceylon Rlys class 'R1'	307
6391	3/1927	RC	V/6¾"×9"	2'6"	2'6"	Ceylon Rlys class 'V1'	328
6392	1927	RC	V/6¾"×9"	2'6"	2'6"	Ceylon Rlys class 'V1'	329
6393	1927	RC	V/6¾"×9"	2'6"	2'6"	Ceylon Rlys class 'V1'	330
6410	10/1926	L	V/6¾"×9"	2'6"	3'0"	Chimbote Rly Peru (oil fired)	
6412	1926	L†	V/6¾"×9"	1'8"	3'0"	Kettering Coal & Iron Co. Ltd (oil fired)	(13)
6416	7/1926	L	V/6¾"×9"	2'6"	3'6"	Anglo Newfoundland Dev. Co.	
6425	3/1926	L	V/6¾"×9"	2'6"	5'6"	Indian Irrigation Schemes	
6462	6/1927	L	V/6¾"×9"	1'8"	M	Iraq Rlys	
6463	1926	L	V/6¾"×9"	2'6"	2'0"	Rochdale Corp. Waterworks Wardle	ALICE
6464	6/1926	L	V/6¾"×9"	2'6"	5'6"	Indian Irrigation Schemes	
6484	8/1927	RC	V/6¾"×9"	2'6"	3'0"	Salvador Rlys	2
6499	1926	L	V/6¾"×9"	2'6"	Std	Cammell Laird Birkenhead	
6500	9/1927	RC	V/6¾"×9"	2'6"	5'6"	B.A. Pacific Rly	
6514	7/1926	L	V/6¾"×9"	2'6"	Std	Great Western Rly	13
6515	1926	L	V/6¾"×9"	2'6"	Std	Great Western Rly	12
6516	1926	L	V/6¾"×9"	2'6"	Std	Cammell Laird Nottingham	2
6517	10/1926	L	V/6¾"×9"	2'6"	Std	LNER class 'Y1'	4801
6518	1926	L	V/6¾"×9"	2'6"	Std	LNER class 'Y1'	4802
6519	1926	L	V/6¾"×9"	2'6"	Std	LNER class 'Y1'	4803
6520	1927	L/BE	V/6¾"×9"	2'6"	Std	Treffrey Estates, Par harbour	(TOBY)
6523	4/1927	RC	V/6¾"×9"	2'6"	Std	LNER 2 cyl chain drive	VALIANT 21
6524	4/1927	RC	V/6¾"×9"	2'6"	Std	LNER 2 cyl chain drive	BRILLIANT 22
6526	6/1926	L	V/6¾"×9"	2'6"	2'0"	Indian Irrigation Schemes	
6533	1927	L	V/6¾"×9"	2'6"	2'0"	Rochdale Corp. Waterworks, Wardle	JUMBO
6564	1926	L	V/6¾"×9"	2'2¼"	2'5½"	Egyptian Delta L.R.	215 HB
6565	1926	L	V/6¾"×9"	2'2¼"	2'5½"	Egyptian Delta L.R.	227 HB
6566	1926	L	V/6¾"×9"	2'2¼"	2'5½"	Egyptian Delta L.R.	213 HB
6567	1926	L	V/6¾"×9"	2'2¼"	2'5½"	Egyptian Delta L.R.	228 HB
6568	1926	L	V/6¾"×9"	2'2¼"	2'5½"	Egyptian Delta L.R.	HB

VERTICAL BOILER LOCOMOTIVES

Works No.	Built	Type	Cyls	D.W.	Gauge	Customer	No./Name/Notes
6569	1926	L	V/6¾"×9"	2'2¼"	2'5½"	Egyptian Delta L.R.	214 HB
6570	1926	L	V/6¾"×9"	2'2¼"	2'5½"	Egyptian Delta L.R.	225 HB
6571	1926	L	V/6¾"×9"	2'2¼"	2'5½"	Egyptian Delta L.R.	218 HB
6572	1926	L	V/6¾"×9"	2'2¼"	2'5½"	Egyptian Delta L.R.	226 HB
6573	1926	L	V/6¾"×9"	2'2¼"	2'5½"	Egyptian Delta L.R.	220 HB
6574	1926	L	V/6¾"×9"	2'2¼"	2'5½"	Egyptian Delta L.R.	222 HB
6575	1926	L	V/6¾"×9"	2'2¼"	2'5½"	Egyptian Delta L.R.	HB
6576	1926	L	V/6¾"×9"	2'2¼"	2'5½"	Egyptian Delta L.R.	219 HB
6577	1926	L	V/6¾"×9"	2'2¼"	2'5½"	Egyptian Delta L.R.	235 HB
6578	1926	L	V/6¾"×9"	2'2¼"	2'5½"	Egyptian Delta L.R.	230 HB
6579	1926	L	V/6¾"×9"	2'2¼"	2'5½"	Egyptian Delta L.R.	HB
6580	1926	L	V/6¾"×9"	2'2¼"	2'5½"	Egyptian Delta L.R.	232 HB
6581	1926	L	V/6¾"×9"	2'2¼"	2'5½"	Egyptian Delta L.R.	HB
6582	1926	L	V/6¾"×9"	2'2¼"	2'5½"	Egyptian Delta L.R.	231 HB
6583	1926	L	V/6¾"×9"	2'2¼"	2'5½"	Egyptian Delta L.R.	217 HB
6584	1926	L	V/6¾"×9"	2'2¼"	2'5½"	Egyptian Delta L.R.	221 HB
6585	1926	L	V/6¾"×9"	2'2¼"	2'5½"	Egyptian Delta L.R.	223 HB
6586	1926	L	V/6¾"×9"	2'2¼"	2'5½"	Egyptian Delta L.R.	224 HB
6587	1926	L	V/6¾"×9"	2'2¼"	2'5½"	Egyptian Delta L.R.	HB
6588	10/1926	L	V/6¾"×9"	2'6"	M	Eastern Bengal Rly	
6589	10/1926	L	V/6¾"×9"	2'6"	M	Eastern Bengal Rly	
6635	8/1926	L	V/6¾"×9"	2'6"	5'6"	Indian Irrigation Schemes	
6636	2/1927	L	V/6¾"×9"	2'6"	5'6"	Indian Irrigation Schemes	
6638	12/1926	L	V/6¾"×9"	2'6"	5'3"	Adelaide Gas Co.	
6642	2/1927	L/DE	V/6¾"×9"	2'6"	3'6"	Springs Mines Ltd, Transvaal S.A.	No. 2
6643	9/1926	L	V/6¾"×9"	1'8"	2'0"	Indian Stores Dept, Madras	
6644	9/1926	L	V/6¾"×9"	1'8"	2'0"	Indian Stores Dept, Madras	
6645	9/1926	L	V/6¾"×9"	1'8"	2'0"	Indian Stores Dept, Madras	
6646	9/1926	L	V/6¾"×9"	1'8"	2'0"	Indian Stores Dept, Madras	
6647	9/1926	L	V/6¾"×9"	1'8"	2'0"	Indian Stores Dept, Madras	
6648	9/1926	L	V/6¾"×9"	1'8"	2'0"	Indian Stores Dept, Madras	
6687	11/1926	L	V/6¾"×9"	1'8"	M	Bhavnagar S.R.	
6710	12/1926	L	V/6¾"×9"	1'8"	Std	LNER class 'Y1/1'	8401
6711		L	V/6¾"×9"	1'8"	Std	London Brick Co., Stewartby	
6713	11/1926	L	V/6¾"×9"	1'8"	M	Indian Irrigation Schemes	
6735	11/1926	L	V/6¾"×9"	1'8"	Std	LNER class 'Y1/3'	19
6742	1926	L	V/6¾"×9"	1'8"	2'0"	Woodside Brickworks (Croydon) Ltd	
6751		L	V/6¾"×9"	1'8"	2'0"	Northumberland Whinstone Co.	

Works No.	Built	Type	Cyls	D.W.	Gauge	Customer	No./Name/Notes
6754	1929	L	V/6¾"×9"	1'8"	2'11"	London Brick Co., Fletton	S5 HB
6770	1926	L	V/6¾"×9"	1'8"	2'0"	Cliffe Hill Granite	4
6776	1927	L	V/6¾"×9"	2'6"	Std	Dunlop Rubber Co. Ltd (on loan)	4145
6777	6/1927	RC	V/6¾"×9"	2'6"	Std	LMSR	4148
6778	1927	RC	V/6¾"×9"	2'6"	Std	LMSR	4147
6779	1927	RC	V/6¾"×9"	2'6"	Std	LMSR	4144
6780	1927	RC	V/6¾"×9"	2'6"	Std	LMSR	4143
6781	1927	RC	V/6¾"×9"	2'6"	Std	LMSR	4146
6782	1927	RC	V/6¾"×9"	2'6"	Std	LMSR	4154
6783	1927	RC	V/6¾"×9"	2'6"	Std	LMSR	4152
6784	1927	RC	V/6¾"×9"	2'6"	Std	LMSR	4153
6785	1927	RC	V/6¾"×9"	2'6"	Std	LMSR	4149
6786	1927	RC	V/6¾"×9"	2'6"	Std	LMSR	4150
6787	1927	RC	V/6¾"×9"	2'6"	Std	LMSR	4151
6788	1927	RC	V/6¾"×9"	2'6"	Std	LMSR	
6802	3/1927	L/DE	V/6¾"×9"	2'6"	5'6"	Marala Div. Indian Irrigation Schemes	
6811	11/1927		V/6¾"×9"	2'6"	M	Nizam's S. Rly	1
6812	11/1927		V/6¾"×9"	2'6"	M	Nizam's S. Rly	2
6817	10/1927		V/6¾"×9"	2'6"	5'6"	GIPR	
6818	1927		V/6¾"×9"	2'6"	5'6"	GIPR	
6819	1927		V/6¾"×9"	2'6"	5'6"	GIPR	
6829	8/1927	RC	V/6¾"×9"	2'6"	5'6"	Ceylon Rlys class 'R1'	308
6830	1927	RC	V/6¾"×9"	2'6"	5'6"	Ceylon Rlys class 'R1'	309
6831	1927	RC	V/6¾"×9"	2'6"	5'6"	Ceylon Rlys class 'R1'	310
6832	1927	RC	V/6¾"×9"	2'6"	5'6"	Ceylon Rlys	311
6833	1927	L	V/6¾"×9"	2'6"	Std	Oxted Greystone Lime Co.	
6834		L	V/6¾"×9"	2'6"	Std	William Evans & Co., Widnes	1 MAUREEN
6844	11/1927		V/6¾"×9"	2'6"	5'3"	G.S. Rly Ireland	354
6845	1927		V/6¾"×9"	2'6"	5'3"	G.S. Rly Ireland	355
6846	5/1927		V/6¾"×9"	2'6"	5'3"	G.S. Rly Ireland	No. 1
6847	1927		V/6¾"×9"	2'6"	5'3"	G.S. Rly Ireland	No. 2
6870	1927	L	V/6¾"×9"	1'8"	2'0"	Rochdale Corp. Waterworks Wardle	
6893	1927	L	V/6¾"×9"	2'6"	Std	Brunner Mond. Sandbach	HASSALL
6894	1927	L	V/6¾"×9"	1'8"	1'11½"	Macclesfield Corp. Trentabank Reservoir	(Plate 57)
6895		L	V/6¾"×9"	1'8"	2'0"	Greenlow Mining Co. Yorks	
6896	1928	L	V/6¾"×9"	1'8"	3'0"	G. & T. Earle Melton Wks nr Hull	
6897	1927	L	V/6¾"×9"	1'8"	3'0"	Hayes & Co. (Stockport) Ltd	BIDDY
6898	1927	L	V/6¾"×9"	1'8"	3'0"	Hayes & Co. (Stockport) Ltd	BARBY

VERTICAL BOILER LOCOMOTIVES

Works No.	Built	Type	Cyls	D.W.	Gauge	Customer	No./Name/Notes
6899	1927	L	V/6¾"×9"	1'8"	3'0"	Hayes & Co. (Stockport) Ltd	JOAN
6900	1927	L	V/6¾"×9"	1'8"	1'11½"	Macclesfield Corp. Trentabank Reservoir	
6901	1927	L	V/6¾"×9"	1'8"	2'11½"	Raynes & Co. Quarries nr Colwyn Bay	
6902	1927	L	V/6¾"×9"	1'8"	2'0"	J.C. Oliver	
6903	1927	L	V/6¾"×9"	1'8"	3'0"	Balfour Beatty	
6904	1927	L	V/6¾"×9"	1'8"	3'0"	Barnsley Corp. Scout Dyke Reservoir	
6905	1927	L	V/6¾"×9"	1'8"	2'0"	New Gorsllan Coll Co. Ltd, Llangyfelach	
6906	9/1927	RC	V/6¾"×9"	2'6"	5'6"	Ceylon Rlys class 'R1'	312
6907	1927	RC	V/6¾"×9"	2'6"	5'6"	Ceylon Rlys class 'R1'	313
6909	4/1927	L	V/6¾"×9"	2'6"	Std	W.D. Tidworth	MOLLY
6912	11/1927		V/6¾"×9"	2'6"	5'3"	G.S. Rly, Ireland	356
6913	1927		V/6¾"×9"	2'6"	5'3"	G.S. Rly, Ireland	357
6915	6/1927		V/6¾"×9"	1'8"	2'6"	Punjab Hydro-Electric Scheme	
6916	12/1927	RC	V/6¾"×9"	2'6"	3'6"	Gold Coast Rly	1
6917	11/1925	RC	V/6¾"×9"	2'6"	Std	Dorman Long & Co. Ltd	
6935	1928	RC	V/6¾"×9"	2'6"	Std	Berry Hill & Stapleford Sand Co.	
6936	1927		V/6¾"×9"	2'6"	Std	Pelaw Main Colly. Birtley Iron Co.	
6971			V/6¾"×9"	2'6"	3'0"	Balfour Beatty	SENTINEL
6994	10/1927	RC	V/6¾"×9"	2'6"	Std	Jersey Eastern Rly (conv. to loco)	BRITTANY P
7017	1/1928	RC	V/6¾"×9"	2'6"	5'6"	Ceylon Rlys class 'R'	317
7018	1928	RC	V/6¾"×9"	2'6"	5'6"	Ceylon Rlys class 'R'	318
7019	1928	RC	V/6¾"×9"	2'6"	5'6"	Ceylon Rlys class 'R'	319
7020	1928	RC	V/6¾"×9"	2'6"	5'6"	Ceylon Rlys class 'R'	320
7024	8/1927	DE	V/6¾"×9"	2'6"	Std	NWR of India	
7026	1926	L	V/6¾"×9"	2'6"	Std	Cerriog Granite Co.	
7034	6/1927	L	V/6¾"×9"	1'8"	2'0"	Equator Sawmills, Kenya	
7048	8/1927	L	V/6¾"×9"	2'6"	Std	LNER class 'Y1/4'	44
7049	8/1927	L	V/6¾"×9"	2'6"	Std	LNER class 'Y1/1'	8402
7060	1927	L	V/6¾"×9"	2'6"	Std	Wm. Cory & Sons, Gallions Jetty	WOOLWICH
7061	1927	L	V/6¾"×9"	2'6"	Std	Yorkshire Amalgamated Products	
7062	1927	L	V/6¾"×9"	2'6"	Std	Hendon Paper Co., Sunderland	HENDON
7088	10/1927	L	V/6¾"×9"	2'6"	Std	Poznan City Council, Poland	
7109	1927	DE	V/6¾"×9"	2'6"	Std	Croydon Gas Co., Waddon	JOYCE
7133	2/1928	RC	V/6¾"×9"	2'6"	5'6"	B.A. Western Rly	RM10
7138	12/1927	L	V/6¾"×9"	2'6"	Std	LNER class 'Y1/2'	79
7139	12/1927	L	V/6¾"×9"	2'6"	Std	LNER class 'Y1/2'	9529
7140	12/1927	L	V/6¾"×9"	2'6"	Std	LNER class 'Y3'	81

SENTINEL WAGGON WORKS LTD 133

Works No.	Built	Type	Cyls	D.W.	Gauge	Customer	No./Name/Notes
7141	12/1927	L	V/6¾"×9"	2'6"	Std	LNER class 'Y3'	90
7142	1/1928	RC	V/6¾"×9"	3'1"	Std	LNER class 'Y3'	26 TALLY HO
7143	1928	RC	V/6¾"×9"	3'1"	Std	LNER class 'Y3'	210 HIGH FLYER
7144	1928	RC	V/6¾"×9"	3'1"	Std	LNER class 'Y3'	212 ECLIPSE
7145	1928	RC	V/6¾"×9"	3'1"	Std	LNER class 'Y3'	29 ROCKINGHAM
7146	1928	RC	V/6¾"×9"	3'1"	Std	LNER class 'Y3'	237 RODNEY
7147	1928	RC	V/6¾"×9"	3'1"	Std	LNER class 'Y3'	220 WATER WITCH
7148	1928	RC	V/6¾"×9"	3'1"	Std	LNER class 'Y3'	225 TRUE BLUE
7149	1928	RC	V/6¾"×9"	3'1"	Std	LNER class 'Y3'	255 PERSEVERANCE
7150	1928	RC	V/6¾"×9"	3'1"	Std	LNER class 'Y3'	238 YORKSHIRE HUSSAR
7151	1928	RC	V/6¾"×9"	3'1"	Std	LNER class 'Y3'	265 NEPTUNE
7152	1928	RC	V/6¾"×9"	3'1"	Std	LNER class 'Y3'	272 HERO
7153	1928	RC	V/6¾"×9"	3'1"	Std	LNER class 'Y3'	250 ROB ROY
7154	1928	RC	V/6¾"×9"	3'1"	Std	LNER class 'Y3'	226 EBOR
7155	1928	RC	V/6¾"×9"	3'1"	Std	LNER class 'Y3'	253 RED ROVER
7156	1928	RC	V/6¾"×9"	3'1"	Std	LNER class 'Y3'	267 LIBERTY
7157	1928	RC	V/6¾"×9"	3'1"	Std	LNER class 'Y3'	263 NORTH STAR
7158	1928	RC	V/6¾"×9"	3'1"	Std	LNER class 'Y3'	244 TRUE BRITON
7159	1928	RC	V/6¾"×9"	3'1"	Std	LNER class 'Y3'	283 TEAZLE
7160	1928	RC	V/6¾"×9"	3'1"	Std	LNER class 'Y3'	254 PHOENIX
7161	1928	RC	V/6¾"×9"	3'1"	Std	LNER class 'Y3'	273 TRAFALGAR
7174	2/1928	RC	V/6¾"×9"	2'6"	Std	Entre Rios Rly	
7199	2/1928	RC	V/6¾"×9"	2'6"	5'6"	East Indian Rly	
7200	2/1928	RC	V/6¾"×9"	2'6"	5'6"	East Indian Rly	
7201	2/1928	RC	V/6¾"×9"	2'6"	5'6"	East Indian Rly	
7214	12/1927	RC	2/7"×9"	3'1"	Std	LNER	2135 INTEGRITY (a)
7232	1927	L	V/6¾"×9"	2'6"	Std	British Tar Products Co. Ltd, Irlam	ANN P
7233	6/1928	DEDG	V/6¾"×9"	2'6"	Std	Palestine Rly	33
7238	1928	L	V/6¾"×9"	1'8"	2'6"	For Donya Sabouk Sugar Est. Kenya	(b)
7239	12/1927	L	V/6¾"×9"	1'8"	M	A.W. Smith, Glasgow	
7240	1928	L	V/6¾"×9"	2'6"	Std	Singapore Garforth-Colls.	
7243	1928	L	H/6¾"×9"	1'8"	2'11"	London Brick Co.	L.66
7250	1/1928	L	V/6¾"×9"	1'8"	80cm	Mauritius	

Works No.	Built	Type	Cyls	D.W.	Gauge	Customer	No./Name/Notes
7255	2/1928	L	V/6¾"×9"	1'8"	1'8"	Indian Stores Dept, Madras	
7256	1928	L	V/6¾"×9"	1'8"	1'8"	Indian Stores Dept, Madras	
7257	1928	L	V/6¾"×9"	1'8"	1'8"	Indian Stores Dept, Madras	
7258	1928	L	V/6¾"×9"	1'8"	1'8"	Indian Stores Dept, Madras	
7259	1928	L	V/6¾"×9"	1'8"	1'8"	Indian Stores Dept, Madras	
7260	1928	L	V/6¾"×9"	1'8"	1'8"	Indian Stores Dept, Madras	
7261	1928	L	V/6¾"×9"	1'8"	1'8"	Indian Stores Dept, Madras	
7262	1928	L	V/6¾"×9"	1'8"	1'8"	Indian Stores Dept, Madras	
7263	1928	L	V/6¾"×9"	1'8"	1'8"	Indian Stores Dept, Madras	
7264	1928	L	V/6¾"×9"	1'8"	1'8"	Indian Stores Dept, Madras	
7265	1928	L	V/6¾"×9"	1'8"	1'8"	Indian Stores Dept, Madras	
7266	1928	L	V/6¾"×9"	1'8"	1'8"	Indian Stores Dept, Madras	
7272	1927	L	V/6¾"×9"	2'6"	Std	Cammell Laird, Birkenhead	3
7274	6/1928	L	V/6¾"×9"	2'6"	5'6"	Union Cold Storage Co., Buenos Ayres	
7275	5/1928	RC	6/6"×7"	3'1"	2'6"	LNER	2133 NETTLE
7276	2/1928	L	V/6¾"×9"	1'8"	1'8"	Punjab Hydro-Electric Scheme (wood burner)	
7281	6/1928	L	V/6¾"×9"	2'2¼"	2'5½"	Egyptian Delta Lt Rly	243
7282	1928	L	V/6¾"×9"	2'2¼"	2'5½"	Egyptian Delta Lt Rly	244
7283	1928	L	V/6¾"×9"	2'2¼"	2'5½"	Egyptian Delta Lt Rly	245
7284	1928	L	V/6¾"×9"	2'2¼"	2'5½"	Egyptian Delta Lt Rly	237
7285	1928	L	V/6¾"×9"	2'2¼"	2'5½"	Egyptian Delta Lt Rly	246
7286	1928	L	V/6¾"×9"	2'2¼"	2'5½"	Egyptian Delta Lt Rly	248
7287	1928	L	V/6¾"×9"	2'2¼"	2'5½"	Egyptian Delta Lt Rly	247
7288	1928	L	V/6¾"×9"	2'2¼"	2'5½"	Egyptian Delta Lt Rly	242 ?or 241
7289	1928	L	V/6¾"×9"	2'2¼"	2'5½"	Egyptian Delta Lt Rly	238
7290	1928	L	V/6¾"×9"	2'2¼"	2'5½"	Egyptian Delta Lt Rly	242 ?or 241
7291	1928	L	V/6¾"×9"	2'2¼"	2'5½"	Egyptian Delta Lt Rly	239
7292	6/1928	L	V/6¾"×9"	2'2¼"	2'5½"	Egyptian Delta Lt Rly	240
7297	1928	L	V/6¾"×9"	2'6"	Std	Brunner Mond, Sandbach	WHEELOCK
7299	1928	L	V/6¾"×9"	2'6"	Std	John Russell & Co., Walsall	
7303	2/1928	RC	6/6"×7"	2'6"	2'6"	Ceylon Rlys class 'R3'	331
7304	1928	RC	6/6"×7"	2'6"	2'6"	Ceylon Rlys class 'R3'	332
7305	1928	RC	6/6"×7"	2'6"	2'6"	Ceylon Rlys class 'R3'	333
7306	1928	RC	6/6"×7"	2'6"	5'6"	Ceylon Rlys class 'R3'	323
7307	1928	RC	6/6"×7"	2'6"	5'6"	Ceylon Rlys class 'R3'	322
7308	1928	RC	6/6"×7"	2'6"	5'6"	Ceylon Rlys class 'R3'	324
7309	1928	RC	6/6"×7"	2'6"	5'6"	Ceylon Rlys class 'R3'	321
7310	1928	RC	6/6"×7"	2'6"	5'6"	Ceylon Rlys class 'R3'	325

Works No.	Built	Type	Cyls	D.W.	Gauge	Customer	No./Name/Notes
7311	1928	RC	6/6"×7"	2'6"	5'6"	Ceylon Rlys class 'R3'	327
7312	1928	RC	6/6"×7"	2'6"	5'6"	Ceylon Rlys class 'R3'	326
7314	1928		6/6"×7"	2'6"	3'6"	Newfoundland Rly	'C'
7315	1928		6/6"×7"	2'6"	3'6"	Newfoundland Rly	'D'
7316	1928		6/6"×7"	2'6"	3'6"	Newfoundland Rly	'E'
7319	1928	L	V/6¾"×9"	2'6"	Std	Motherwell & Wishaw Corpn. Gas Dept	HB
7362	7/1929	RC	6/6"×7"	2'6"	Std	LMSR	4349
7397	3/1928	RC	6/6"×7"	3'1"	Std	LNER	31 FLOWER OF YARROW
7398	3/1928	RC	6/6"×7"	3'1"	Std	LNER	2140 EAGLE
7399	3/1928	RC	6/6"×7"	3'1"	Std	LNER	45 COMMERCE
7400	3/1928	RC	6/6"×7"	3'1"	Std	LNER	2136 HOPE
7401	1928	RC	6/6"×7"	3'1"	Std	LNER	2139 HARK FORWARD
7402	1928	RC	6/6"×7"	3'1"	Std	LNER	2144 TRAVELLER
7403	1928	RC	6/6"×7"	3'1"	Std	LNER	2145 RUBY
7404	1928	RC	6/6"×7"	3'1"	Std	LNER	2147 WOODPECKER
7405	1928	RC	6/6"×7"	3'1"	Std	LNER	2151 UMPIRE
7406	1928	RC	6/6"×7"	3'1"	Std	LNER	2152 COURIER
7407	1928	RC	6/6"×7"	3'1"	Std	LNER	2133 CLEVELAND
7408	1928	RC	6/6"×7"	3'1"	Std	LNER	51909 EXPEDITION
7409	1929	RC	6/6"×7"	3'1"	Std	LNER	51909 WATERLOO
7410	1929	RC	6/6"×7"	3'1"	Std	LNER	32 FAIR MAID
7411	1929	RC	6/6"×7"	3'1"	Std	LNER	33 HIGHLAND CHIEFTAIN
7412	1929	RC	6/6"×7"	3'1"	Std	LNER	34 TWEEDSIDE
7413	1929	RC	6/6"×7"	3'1"	Std	LNER	36 ROYAL EAGLE
7414	1929	RC	6/6"×7"	3'1"	Std	LNER	37 CLYDESDALE
7420	3/1928	RC	6/6"×7"	3'1"	M	Leopoldina Rly Inspection Car	
7432	3/1928	RC	6/6"×7"	2'6"	Std	Palestine Rly Double articulated	1
7433	3/1928	RC	6/6"×7"	2'6"	Std	Palestine Rly Double articulated	2
7434	3/1928	RC	6/6"×7"	2'6"	105cm	Palestine Rly Double articulated	11
7435	3/1928	RC	6/6"×7"	2'6"	105cm	Palestine Rly Double articulated	12
7436		DEDG	V/6¾"×9"	2'6"	3'6"	Spring Mines S.A.	
7459		L	V/6¾"×9"	1'8"	75cm	R. Hudson for Mauritius	

VERTICAL BOILER LOCOMOTIVES

Works No.	Built	Type	Cyls	D.W.	Gauge	Customer	No./Name/Notes
7492	1928	BE	V/6¾"×9"	2'6"	Std	J.S. Fry & Sons Ltd, Somerdale	P 100hp
7496	1928	BE	V/6¾"×9"	2'6"	Std	Wm. Gossage & Sons, Widnes	4
7500	1928	L	V/6¾"×9"	2'6"	Std	Adams & Benson Ltd, West Bromwich	
7543	11/1928	L	V/6¾"×9"	2'6"	643cm	Stromsnas Bruks (paper wks)	4 May ENGESTROM
7544	1928	L	H/6¾"×9"	1'8"	2'11"	London Brick Co.	L.67
7551	6/1928	RC	V/6¾"×9"	2'6"	2'6"	Barsi S. Rly	
7552	6/1928	RC	V/6¾"×9"	2'6"	2'6"	Barsi S. Rly	
7564	1928	RC	6/6"×7"	2'6"	3'0"	Nor Oeste Peru Rly	
7566	1928	RC	V/6¾"×9"	2'6"	5'3"	Kerang-Koondrook Tramway	
7571	7/1928	RC	V/6¾"×9"	2'6"	M	Iraq Rly	
7572	1928	RC	V/6¾"×9"	2'6"	M	Iraq Rly	
7573	1928	RC	V/6¾"×9"	2'6"	M	Iraq Rly	
7574	1928	RC	V/6¾"×9"	1'8"	2'0"	Jodhpur S. Rly	
7584	7/1928	RC	6/6"×7"	2'6"	M	B.B. & C.I. Rly	
7585	1928	RC	6/6"×7"	2'6"	M	B.B. & C.I. Rly	
7586	1928	RC	6/6"×7"	2'6"	M	B.B. & C.I. Rly	
7587	1928	DE L	V/6¾"×9"	2'6"	Std	S. & D.J.R.	101
7588	1928	DE L	V/6¾"×9"	2'6"	Std	S. & D.J.R.	102
7604	4/1929		6/6"×7"	2'6"	1675m	Zaffra Huelva Rly	
7605	1928	L	V/6¾"×9"	2'6"	2'0"	Standard Bank, Nairobi	2
7606	8/1928	L	V/6¾"×9"	2'6"	3'6"	Gold Coast Rly	
7607	1928	L	V/6¾"×9"	2'6"	3'6"	Nigerian Rlys	
7608	1928	L	V/6¾"×9"	2'6"	Std	Polish State Rly	
7615	8/1928	L	V/6¾"×9"	2'6"	2'6"	B.B. & C.I. Rly	30
7616	1928	L	V/6¾"×9"	2'6"	2'6"	B.B. & C.I. Rly	31
7617	1928	L	V/6¾"×9"	2'6"	2'6"	B.B. & C.I. Rly	32
7634	1928	L	V/6¾"×9"	2'6"	Std	Heenan & Froude Ltd, Worcester	
7638	9/1928	RC	6/6"×7"	2'6"	M	Tanganyika Rly	51
7639	1928	RC	6/6"×7"	2'6"	M	Tanganyika Rly	52
7669	1928	L	V/6¾"×9"	2'6"	Std	Steetley Lime Co., Coxhoe	
7688	11/1928	RC	V/6¾"×9"	1'8"	2'0"	Cauvery Metur Project India	
7689	1928	RC	V/6¾"×9"	1'8"	2'0"	Cauvery Metur Project India	
7696	1929	L	V/6¾"×9"	2'6"	Std	Wm. Cory & Sons Ltd, Gallions Jetty	GREENWICH
7699	1929	L	H/6¾"×9"	1'8"	2'11"	London Brick Co., Stewartby	S.2
7700	1929	L	H/6¾"×9"	1'8"	2'11"	London Brick Co., Stewartby	S.1
7701	1929	L	H/6¾"×9"	1'8"	2'11"	London Brick Co., Stewartby	NUTTY
7704	12/1928	RC	6/6"×7"	2'6"	Std	Shanghai-Nanking Rly	

Works No.	Built	Type	Cyls	D.W.	Gauge	Customer	No./Name/Notes
7705	1928	RC	6/6"×7"	2'6"	Std	Shanghai–Nanking Rly	
7706	1928	RC	6/6"×7"	2'6"	Std	Shanghai–Nanking Rly	
7707	1928	RC	6/6"×7"	2'6"	Std	Shanghai–Nanking Rly	
7708	1928	RC	6/6"×7"	2'6"	Std	Shanghai–Nanking Rly	
7714	12/1928	RC	6/6"×7"	2'6"	Std	Entre Rios Rly	
7715	1928	RC	6/6"×7"	2'6"	Std	Entre Rios Rly	
7716	1928	RC	6/6"×7"	2'6"	Std	Argentine N.E. Rly	
7728		L	V/6¾"×9"	1'8"	2'0"	Jacks (Dealer) Karachi (wood burner)	
7740	1/1929	RC	6/6"×7"	3'1"	Std	LNER	2198 TIMES
7741	1929	RC	6/6"×7"	3'1"	Std	C.L.C.	601
7742	1929	RC	6/6"×7"	3'1"	Std	C.L.C.	600
7743	1929	RC	6/6"×7"	3'1"	Std	C.L.C.	602
7779	2/1929	RC	6/6"×7"	2'6"	Std	Central Rly of Peru	
7781	2/1929	RC	6/6"×7"	2'6"	M	F.M.S. Rly	251.01 LANGHAR
7791	2/1929	RC	6/6"×7"	2'6"	Std	Chusan Rly, Korea	
7792	1929	RC	6/6"×7"	2'6"	Std	Chusan Rly, Korea	
7793	1929	RC	6/6"×7"	2'6"	Std	Chusan Rly, Korea	
7794	2/1929	RC	6/6"×7"	3'1"	Std	CLC	603 100hp
7795	1929	RC	6/6"×7"	3'1"	Std	LNER	38 PEARL
7796	1929	RC	6/6"×7"	3'1"	Std	LNER	39 PROTECTOR
7797	1929	RC	6/6"×7"	3'1"	Std	LNER	51913 RIVAL
7798	1929	RC	6/6"×7"	3'1"	Std	LNER	51912 RISING SUN
7799	1929	RC	6/6"×7"	3'1"	Std	LNER	51914 ROYAL FORRESTER
7800	1929	RC	6/6"×7"	3'1"	Std	LNER	2200 SURPRISE
7801	1929	RC	6/6"×7"	3'1"	Std	LNER	2217 ROYAL CHARLOTTE
7802	1929	RC	6/6"×7"	3'1"	Std	LNER	2218 TELEGRAPH
7803	1929	RC	6/6"×7"	3'1"	Std	LNER	2219 NEW FLY
7804	1929	RC	6/6"×7"	3'1"	Std	LNER	2231 SWIFT
7805	1929	RC	6/6"×7"	3'1"	Std	LNER	2232 ALEXANDER
7806	1929	RC	6/6"×7"	3'1"	Std	LNER	2235 BRITANNIA
7807	1929	RC	6/6"×7"	3'1"	Std	LNER	2236 BRITISH QUEEN
7808	1929	RC	6/6"×7"	3'1"	Std	LNER	2235 CELERITY
7809	1929	RC	6/6"×7"	3'1"	Std	LNER	310 PRINCE REGENT

138 VERTICAL BOILER LOCOMOTIVES

Works No.	Built	Type	Cyls	D.W.	Gauge	Customer	No./Name/Notes
7810	1929	RC	6/6"×7"	3'1"	Std	LNER	311 QUICKSILVER
7811	1929	RC	6/6"×7"	3'1"	Std	LNER	312 RETALIATOR
7812	1929	RC	6/6"×7"	3'1"	Std	LNER	2242 CORNWALLIS
7813	1929	RC	6/6"×7"	3'1"	Std	LNER	2245 CRITERION
7814	1929	RC	6/6"×7"	3'1"	Std	LNER	2257 DEFIANCE
7815	1929	RC	6/6"×7"	3'1"	Std	LNER	2261 DILIGENCE
7816	1929	RC	6/6"×7"	3'1"	Std	LNER	2267 RECOVERY
7817	1929	RC	6/6"×7"	3'1"	Std	LNER	2268 EMERALD
7818	1929	RC	6/6"×7"	3'1"	Std	LNER	2270 INDEPENDENT
7819	1929	RC	6/6"×7"	3'1"	Std	LNER	2271 INDUSTRY
7820	1930	RC	6/6"×7"	3'1"	Std	LNER	2276 NORTH BRITON
7821	1930	RC	6/6"×7"	3'1"	Std	LNER	2279 NORFOLK
7822	1930	RC	12/6"×7"	3'1"	Std	LNER (articulated) Type Ha 200hp	2281 OLD JOHN BULL
7823	1930	RC	12/6"×7"	3'1"	Std	LNER (articulated) Type Ha 200hp	2283 OLD BLUE
7824	1930	RC	12/6"×7"	3'1"	Std	LNER (articulated) Type J 200hp	2291 PHENOMENA
7831	3/1929	L	V/6¾"×9"	1'8"	2'0"	Cauvery Metur Project, India	
7832	1929	L	V/6¾"×9"	1'8"	2'0"	Cauvery Metur Project, India	
7833	1929	L	V/6¾"×9"	1'8"	2'0"	Cauvery Metur Project, India	
7834	1929	L	V/6¾"×9"	1'8"	2'0"	Cauvery Metur Project, India	
7835	1929	L	V/6¾"×9"	1'8"	2'0"	Cauvery Metur Project, India	
7836	1929	L	V/6¾"×9"	1'8"	2'0"	Cauvery Metur Project, India	
7837	3/1929	L	V/6¾"×9"	2'6"	Std	LNER class 'Y1/2' (1 speed)	100
7838	1929	L	V/6¾"×9"	2'6"	Std	LNER class 'Y1/2' (1 speed)	106
7839	1929	L	V/6¾"×9"	2'6"	Std	LNER class 'Y1/2' (1 speed)	108
7840	1929	L	V/6¾"×9"	2'6"	Std	LNER class 'Y1/2' (1 speed)	119
7841	1929	L	V/6¾"×9"	2'6"	Std	LNER class 'Y1/2' (1 speed)	124
7842	1929	L	V/6¾"×9"	2'6"	Std	LNER class 'Y1/2' (1 speed)	142
7843	1929	L	V/6¾"×9"	2'6"	Std	LNER class 'Y1/2' (1 speed)	150
7844	4/1929	L	V/6¾"×9"	2'6"	Std	LNER class 'Y1/2' (1 speed)	171
7845	1929	L	V/6¾"×9"	2'6"	Std	LNER class 'Y1/2' (1 speed)	174
7846	1929	L	V/6¾"×9"	2'6"	Std	LNER class 'Y1/2' (1 speed)	175
7847	1929	L	V/6¾"×9"	2'6"	Std	LNER class 'Y1/2' (1 speed)	183
7848	1929	L	V/6¾"×9"	2'6"	Std	LNER class 'Y1/2' (1 speed)	187
7849	1929	L/CEDG	V/6¾"×9"	2'6"	Std	LNER class 'Y3' (2 speed)	189
7850	1929	L/CEDG	V/6¾"×9"	2'6"	Std	LNER class 'Y3' (2 speed)	192

Works No.	Built	Type	Cyls	D.W.	Gauge	Customer	No./Name/Notes
7851	1929	L/CEDG	V/6¾"×9"	2'6"	Std	LNER class 'Y3' (2 speed)	193
7852	3/1929	L/CEDG	V/6¾"×9"	2'6"	Std	LNER class 'Y3' (2 speed)	196
7853	1929	L	V/6¾"×9"	2'6"	Std	LNER class 'Y3' (2 speed)	197
7854	1929	L	V/6¾"×9"	2'6"	Std	LNER class 'Y3' (2 speed)	198
7924		L	V/6¾"×9"	2'6"	Std	Yorkshire Amalgamated Products, Wakefield	
7925	1929	L	V/6¾"×9"	2'6"	Std	Pilsley Colly Co. Ltd	
7926		L	V/6¾"×9"	1'8"	2'0"	McMillan Estates, Nairobi	
7965	5/1929	L	V/6¾"×9"	2'6"	M	Tanganyika Rly	
7975	6/1929	RC	6/6"×7"	2'6"	M	Gold Coast Rly	3
7976		RC	6/6"×7"	2'6"	M	Gold Coast Rly	4
7997	1929	L	V/6¾"×9"	2'6"	Std	Wm. Gossage & Sons, Widnes	5
8007	1929	L	V/6¾"×9"	2'0"	M	Barsi Lt Rly	2
8012	7/1929	L	V/6¾"×9"	2'6"	Std	Hanomag Loco. Wks, Hanover	
8024	1929	L	V/6¾"×9"	2'6"	Std	Cambridge Gas Co.	P
8056	9/1929	L	V/6¾"×9"	1'8"	2'0"	Cauvery Metur Project, India	
8057	1929	L	V/6¾"×9"	1'8"	2'0"	Cauvery Metur Project, India	
8058	1929	L	V/6¾"×9"	1'8"	2'0"	Cauvery Metur Project, India	
8059	1929	L	V/6¾"×9"	1'8"	2'0"	Cauvery Metur Project, India	
8085	1929	L	V/6¾"×9"	2'6"	3'0"	Minerals Concentration Co. Ltd, Anglesey	
8087	1929	L	V/6¾"×9"	2'6"	Std	Tottenham & District Gas Co.	5
8088	1929	L	V/6¾"×9"	2'6"	3'0"	Dinmor Quarries Ltd, Anglesey	
8097	1929	L	V/6¾"×9"	2'6"	Std	Staveley Coal & Iron Co.	
8098	1929	L	V/6¾"×9"	2'6"	Std	Chatwood Safe Co, Shrewsbury	
8133	11/1929	RC	0–6–0	2'6"	M	Ahmadpur-Katwa Lt Rly, India	8
8134	1929	RC	0–6–0	2'6"	M	Bankura-Damodar Lt Rly, India	
8135	1929	RC		2'6"	M	Kalighat Falta Lt Rly, India	7
8144	1929	RC	6H/6"×7"	2'6"	M	Nigerian Rlys	
8147	6/1929	DEDG/L	2V/6¾"×9"	3'2"	Std	LNER for Wisbech & Upwell Tramway cl. Y10	8403 double cab
8148	6/1929	DEDG/L	2V/6¾"×9"	3'2"	Std	LNER for Wisbech & Upwell Tramway cl. Y10	8404 double cab
8157	12/1929	Crane/L	2H/6¾"×9"	2'6"	Std	LNER Grab Crane Loco.	773044c HB
8168	1930	L	2V/6¾"×9"	2'6"	M	Carthagena-Herrerias Steam Tramway (6wh)	20
8169	1930	L	2V/6¾"×9"	2'6"	M	Carthagena-Herrerias Steam Tramway (6wh)	21
8170	1930	L	2V/6¾"×9"	2'6"	M	Carthagena-Herrerias Steam Tramway (6wh)	22
8171	1930	L	2V/6¾"×9"	2'6"	M	Carthagena-Herrerias Steam Tramway (6wh)	23
8186	1930	L	2V/6¾"×9"	1'8"	M	Cox & Co., Nairobi	
8189	1/1930	RC	6H/6"×7"	2'6"	3'6"	W. Australian G. Rly	
8193	1930	RC	6H/6"×7"	3'1"	Std	Belgian State Rlys	S.1

Works No.	Built	Type	Cyls	D.W.	Gauge	Customer	No./Name/Notes
8194	1930	RC	6H/6"×7"	3'1"	Std	Belgian State Rlys	S.2
8195	1930	RC	6H/6"×7"	3'1"	Std	Belgian State Rlys	S.3
8203	1930	L	2V/6¾"×9"	1'8"	2'6"	Cauvery Metur Project, India	
8204	1930	L	2V/6¾"×9"	1'8"	2'6"	Cauvery Metur Project, India	
8207	1/1930	L	2V/6¾"×9"	2'6"	Std	Cafferata & Co., Newark	
8209	1930	L	2V/6¾"×9"	2'6"	Std	LMSR	7160
8210	1930	L	2V/6¾"×9"	2'6"	Std	LMSR	7161
8211	1/1930	L	2V/6¾"×9"	2'6"	Std	LMSR	7162
8212	1930	L	2V/6¾"×9"	2'6"	Std	LMSR	7163
8228	2/1929	RC	6/6"×7"	3'1"	Std	Axholme Jt. Rly	44
8239	3/1930	L	2V/6¾"×9"	2'6"	3'6"	Tanganyika Rly	71
8240	1930	L	2V/6¾"×9"	2'6"	3'6"	Tanganyika Rly	72
8241	1930	L	2V/6¾"×9"	2'6"	3'6"	Tanganyika Rly	73
8242	1930	L	2V/6¾"×9"	2'6"	3'6"	Tanganyika Rly	74
8243	1930	L	2V/6¾"×9"	2'6"	3'6"	Tanganyika Rly	75
8244	1930	L	2V/6¾"×9"	2'6"	3'6"	Tanganyika Rly	76
8245	1930	L	2V/6¾"×9"	2'6"	3'6"	Tanganyika Rly	77
8253	1930	L	2V/6¾"×9"	2'6"	3'6"	Low Temp. Carbonisation Co.	DARTON
8257	1930	RC	6/6"×7"	3'1"	Std	LNER	314 QUEEN OF BEAUTY
8258	1930	RC	6/6"×7"	3'1"	Std	LNER	313 BANKS OF DON
8276	7/1930	L	2V/6¾"×9"	1'8"	2'6"	Cauvery Metur Project, India	
8277	1930	L	2V/6¾"×9"	1'8"	2'6"	Cauvery Metur Project, India	
8314	9/1930	L	2V/6¾"×9"	2'6"	Std	LNER class 'Y3' 2 speed	18
8315	9/1930	L	2V/6¾"×9"	2'6"	Std	LNER class 'Y3' 2 speed	21
8316	9/1930	L	2V/6¾"×9"	2'6"	Std	LNER class 'Y3' 2 speed	23
8317	9/1930	L	2V/6¾"×9"	2'6"	Std	LNER class 'Y3' 2 speed	35
8318	9/1930	L	2V/6¾"×9"	2'6"	Std	LNER class 'Y3' 2 speed	42
8319	9/1930	L	2V/6¾"×9"	2'6"	Std	LNER class 'Y3' 2 speed	49
8320	9/1930	L	2V/6¾"×9"	2'6"	Std	LNER class 'Y3' 2 speed	55
8321	9/1930	L	2V/6¾"×9"	2'6"	Std	LNER class 'Y3' 2 speed	60
8322	9/1930	L	2V/6¾"×9"	2'6"	Std	LNER class 'Y3' 2 speed	61
8323	10/1930	L	2V/6¾"×9"	2'6"	Std	LNER class 'Y3' 2 speed	62
8324	10/1930	L	2V/6¾"×9"	2'6"	Std	LNER class 'Y3' 2 speed	63
8325	10/1930	L	2V/6¾"×9"	2'6"	Std	LNER class 'Y3' 2 speed	64
8326	10/1930	L	2V/6¾"×9"	2'6"	Std	LNER class 'Y3' 2 speed	65
8327	10/1930	L	2V/6¾"×9"	2'6"	Std	LNER class 'Y3' 2 speed	78

Works No.	Built	Type	Cyls	D.W.	Gauge	Customer	No./Name/Notes
8328	10/1930	L	2V/6¾"×9"	2'6"	Std	LNER class 'Y3' 2 speed	87
8329	10/1930	L	2V/6¾"×9"	2'6"	Std	LNER class 'Y3' 2 speed	94
8330	10/1930	L	2V/6¾"×9"	2'6"	Std	LNER class 'Y3' 2 speed	96
8331	10/1930	L	2V/6¾"×9"	2'6"	Std	LNER class 'Y3' 2 speed	98
8332	9/1930	L	2V/6¾"×9"	2'6"	Std	LNER class 'Y1/2' 2 speed	45
8383	2/1931	RC	6/6"×7"	2'6"	Std	Den Spoorweg Maatschappij Sumatra	
8398	12/1930	L	2V/6¾"×9"	2'6"	5'3"	Sao Paulo Rly, Brazil	201
8399	1930	L	2V/6¾"×9"	2'6"	5'3"	Sao Paulo Rly, Brazil	202
8400	1930	L	2V/6¾"×9"	2'6"	5'3"	Sao Paulo Rly, Brazil	203
8406	1930	L	2V/6¾"×9"	3'0"	M	Ahmadpur Katwa Lt Rly, India	
8407	1930	L	2V/6¾"×9"	3'0"	M	Bankura–Damodar Lt Rly, India	BK10
8408	1930	L	2V/6¾"×9"	3'0"	M	Kalighat Falta Lt Rly, India	
8410	4/1931	RC	6/6"×7"	2'6"	3'6"	Tasmanian G.R.	SP.1
8411	1931	RC	6/6"×7"	2'6"	3'6"	Tasmanian G.R.	SP.2
8421	10/1931	RC	6/6"×7"	2'9"	5'3"	Buenos Ayres Midland Rly cl.J	301
8422	1931	RC	6/6"×7"	2'9"	5'3"	Buenos Ayres Midland Rly cl.J	302
8426	8/1931	RC	6/6"×7"	2'9"	Std	Trinidad Rly	
8459	3/1931	L	2V/6¾"×9"	1'8"	2'6"	Cauvery Metur Project, India	
8460	1931	L	2V/6¾"×9"	1'8"	2'6"	Cauvery Metur Project, India	
8470	2/1932	RC	6/6"×7"	2'6"	5'6"	N.W. State Rly, India Kangra Valley Sec.	
8471	1932	RC	6/6"×7"	2'6"	5'6"	N.W. State Rly, India Kangra Valley Sec.	
8472	1932	RC	6/6"×7"	2'6"	5'6"	N.W. State Rly, India Kangra Valley Sec.	
7476	4/1931	L	2V/6¾"×9"	2'6"	Std	LNER class 'Y3' 2-speed	117
8477	4/1931	L	2V/6¾"×9"	2'6"	Std	LNER class 'Y3' 2-speed	148
8478	4/1931	L	2V/6¾"×9"	2'6"	Std	LNER class 'Y3' 2-speed	154
8479	5/1931	L	2V/6¾"×9"	2'6"	Std	LNER class 'Y3' 2-speed	155
8480	5/1931	L	2V/6¾"×9"	2'6"	Std	LNER class 'Y3' 2-speed	172
8535	7/1931	L	2V/6¾"×9"	1'8"	2'6"	Cauvery Metur Project, India	
8536	1931	L	2V/6¾"×9"	1'8"	2'6"	Cauvery Metur Project, India	
8538	1/1932	RC	6/6"×7"	2'9"	M	FMSR	252.01 RAJAWAU
8539	1932	RC	6/6"×7"	2'9"	M	FMSR	252.02
8540	1932	RC	6/6"×7"	2'9"	M	FMSR	252.03
8541	1932	RC	6/6"×7"	2'9"	M	FMSR	252.04
8542	1932	RC	6/6"×7"	2'9"	M	FMSR	252.05
8565	12/1931	Crane/L	2H/6¾"×9"	2'6"	Std	LNER Grab Crane Loco.	773045c HB
8593	1931	L	2V/6¾"×9"	2'6"	Std	LM&SR	7164
8609	12/1931	L	2V/6¾"×9"	2'6"	Std	LNER class 'Y3' 2 speed	86
8668	12/1931	RC	6/6¾"×9"	2'6"	Std	Roumanian S.R.	

Works No.	Built	Type	Cyls	D.W.	Gauge	Customer	No./Name/Notes
8669	1931	RC	6/6¾"×9"	2'6"	Std	Roumanian S.R.	
8670	1931	RC	6/6¾"×9"	2'6"	Std	Roumanian S.R.	
8671	1931	RC	6/6¾"×9"	2'6"	Std	Roumanian S.R.	
8672	1931	RC	6/6¾"×9"	2'6"	Std	Roumanian S.R.	
8673	1931	RC	6/6¾"×9"	2'6"	Std	Roumanian S.R.	
8674	1931	RC	6/6¾"×9"	2'6"	Std	Roumanian S.R.	200 hp
8675	1931	RC	6/6¾"×9"	2'6"	Std	Roumanian S.R.	200 hp
8689	1931	RC	6/6¾"×9"	2'6"	3'6"	Nyasaland Rlys	1
8690	1931	RC	6/6¾"×9"	2'6"	3'6"	Nyasaland Rlys	2
8740	3/1933	RC	4½/7½"×6"	2'6"	Std	Southern Rly (Rail Bus) 97 hp	6
8796	1933	L	2V/6¾"×9"	2'6"	Std	Wm. Cory & Son, Erith	CHARLTON
8797	1933	L	2V/6¾"×9"	1'8"	Std	Gas Light & Coke Co., Kensal Green	
8805	1933	L	2V/6¾"×9"	2'6"	Std	LM&SR Double acting 200 hp	7192 Compound
8806?	1933	L	2V/6¾"×9"	2'6"	Std	LM&SR	
8808	1933	L	6/4¼"×7¼"×6"	2'11"	M	Colombian National Rlys★	
8809	1933	L	"	2'11"	M	Colombian National Rlys★	600 hp 2-4-4-2T Compound
8810	1933	L	"	2'11"	M	Colombian National Rlys	600 hp 2-4-4-2T
8811	1933	RC	6V/6"×7"	2'9"	3'6"	Tasmanian G.R.	600 hp 2-4-4-2T SP.3
8812	1933	RC	6V/6"×7"	2'9"	3'6"	Tasmanian G.R.	SP.4
8813	1933	RC	6V/4¼"×7¼"×6"	2'6"	5'9"	Sao Paulo Rly, Brazil	Compound
8837	12/1933	L	2V/6¾"×9"	2'6"	5'9"	LNER class 'Y1/2'	59 P
8892	1933	RC	6V/6"×7"	3'3"	5'9"	Northern Rly of France	
8920	1933	L	2V/6¾"×9"	2'6"	M	Egyptian Phosphate Co.	Safaga No.4
8983	1934	RC	6V/6"×7"	2'6"	Std	Peruvian Central Rly 100 hp	Oil fired bus
8986	1935	RC	6V/6"×7"	2'6"	Std	Peruvian Central Rly 100 hp	
9069	1935	RC	6V/6"×7"	2'6"	Std	Belgian National Rly 200 hp	
9070	1935	RC	6V/6"×7"	2'6"	Std	Paraguay Central Rly 250 hp	
9071	1935	RC	6V/6"×7"	2'6"	Std	Paraguay Central Rly 250 hp	
9072	1935	RC	6V/6"×7"	2'6"	Std	Paraguay Central Rly 250 hp	
9098	1935	RC	6V/6"×7"	2'6"	Std	Paraguay Central Rly 250 hp	
9099	1935	RC	6V/6"×7"	2'6"	Std	Paraguay Central Rly 250 hp	
9112	1934	RC	6V/6¾"×9"	2'10"	Std	Egyptian S.R.	Coach No. 5060
9113	1934	RC	6V/6¾"×9"	2'10"	Std	Egyptian S.R.	" 5061
9114	1934	RC	6V/6¾"×9"	2'10"	Std	Egyptian S.R.	" 5062
9115	1934	RC	6V/6¾"×9"	2'10"	Std	Egyptian S.R.	" 5063

Works No.	Built	Type	Cyls	D.W.	Gauge	Customer	No./Name/Notes
9116	1934	RC	6V/6¾"×9"	2'10"	Std	Egyptian S.R.	" 5064
9117	1934	RC	6V/6¾"×9"	2'10"	Std	Egyptian S.R.	" 5065
9118	1934	RC	6V/6¾"×9"	2'10"	Std	Egyptian S.R.	" 5066
9119	1934	RC	6V/6¾"×9"	2'10"	Std	Egyptian S.R.	" 5067
9120	1934	RC	6V/6¾"×9"	2'10"	Std	Egyptian S.R.	" 5068
9121	1934	RC	6V/6¾"×9"	2'10"	Std	Egyptian S.R.	" 5069
9129	not built					LNER	
9135	1935	L	2V/6¾"×9"	2'6"	M	La Guaiya Corp., Venezuela	
9149	1934	L	2V/6¾"×9"	2'6"	2'5½"	Marston Valley Brick Co.	7
9167	1935	L	2V/6¾"×9"	1'8"	Std	Tottenham District Gas Co.	No.24
9179	1935	L	2V/6¾"×9"	1'8"	2'0"	Tata Steel Works, India	
9193	1935	RC	6V/6¾"×9"	2'6"	Std	Eastern Rly of France	
9194	1935	RC	6V/6¾"×9"	2'6"	Std	Eastern Rly of France	
9201	1937	RC	6V/4¼"× 7¼"×6"	2'10"	3'6"	Tasmanian G.R.	SP.5
9202	1937	RC	"	2'10"	3'6"	Tasmanian G.R.	SP.6
9221	1935	L	2V/6¾"×9"	1'8"	2'11"	London Brick Co., Stewartby	S.3
9230	1935	L	2V/6¾"×9"	2'6"	M	La Guaiya Corp., Venezuela	
9234	1937	RC	6V/4¼"× 7¼"×6"	2'10"	3'6"	Tasmanian G.R.	SP.8
9235	1937	RC	"	2'10"	3'6"	Tasmanian G.R.	SP.7
9238	1937	RC	"	2'10"	3'6"	Tasmanian G.R.	SP.9
9259	1936	L	2V/6¾"×9"	1'8"	2'11"	London Brick Co., Arlesley	S.4
9265	1936	RC	6V/6"×7"	2'9"	M	Leopoldina Rly, Brazil	
9266	1936	RC	6V/6"×7"	2'9"	M	Leopoldina Rly, Brazil	
9267	1938	RC	6V/6"×7"	2'9"	M	FMSR	261.01
9268	1938	RC	6V/6"×7"	2'9"	M	FMSR	261.02
9269	1938	RC	6V/6"×7"	2'9"	M	FMSR	261.03
9284	1937	L	2V/6¾"×9"	2'6"	Std	London Brick Co., Calvert	1
9294	1936	L	2V/6¾"×9"	2'6"	Std	Leys Malleadle Castings Co., Derby	3
9295	1938	RC	6V/6"×7"	2'9"	M	FMSR	261.04
9296	1938	RC	6V/6"×7"	2'9"	M	FMSR	261.05
9297	1938	RC	6V/6"×7"	2'9"	M	FMSR	261.06
9299	1936	L	4H/11"×12"	2'9"	M	Egyptian S. Rlys (c)	276
9300	1936	L	4H/11"×12"	2'9"	M	Egyptian S. Rlys (c)	277
9301	1936	L	4H/11"×12"	2'9"	M	Egyptian S. Rlys (c)	278
9302	1936	L	4H/11"×12"	2'9"	M	Egyptian S. Rlys (c)	279
9304	1937	L	2V/6¾"×9"	1'8"	2'0"	Hendy Merthyr Coll. Co., Clydach	

VERTICAL BOILER LOCOMOTIVES

Works No.	Built	Type	Cyls	D.W.	Gauge	Customer	No./Name/Notes
9321	1937	L	2V/6¾"×9"	1'8"	2'0"	London Brick Co., Arlesley	3
9322	1937	L	2V/6¾"×9"	1'8"	2'0"	London Brick Co., Arlesley	2
9334	1937	RC	6V/6"×7"	2'6"	3'6"	Tanganyika Rlys 150 hp	

The missing works numbers in the foregoing series were mainly road vehicles, but commencing with 9363 the series is continuous except for the following:
9402–9501 were steam road lorries for Argentina
9502 was a steam dump truck for Penderyn Quarries, Aberdare
9503–9510 were blank.

Works No.	Built	Type	Cyls	D.W.	Gauge	Customer	No./Name/Notes
9363	1945	L	2V/6¾"×9"	2'6"	Std	BTH Rugby 150 hp	
9364	1945	L	2V/6¾"×9"	2'6"	Std	Cammell Laird, Birkenhead	4
9365	1945	L	2V/6¾"×9"	2'6"	Std	Wm. Cory & Sons, Erith	(Belvedere)
9366	1945	L	2V/6¾"×9"	2'6"	Std	Tottenham & District Gas Co.	11 P
9367	1946	L	2V/6¾"×9"	1'8"	Std	Brit. Rein. Concrete Eng., Ltd, Stafford	BRC
9368	1946	L	2V/6¾"×9"	2'6"	2'0"	Bonyo Sabank Sisal Estate, Kenya	80 hp
9369	1946	L	2V/6¾"×9"	2'6"	Std	R.O.F. Hooton, Wirral	
9370	1947	L	2V/6¾"×9"	2'6"	Std	Sheffield Corp Electricity Works	1 100 hp
9371	1947	L	2V/6¾"×9"	2'6"	Std	Sheffield Corp Electricity Works	2 100 hp
9372	1947	L	2V/6¾"×9"	1'8"	2'0"	Electrical Engineer Jodphur, India	80 hp
9373	1947	L/BE	2V/6¾"×9"	2'6"	Std	Cafferata & Co., Hawton	6 ST. MONANS
9374	1947	L/BE	2V/6¾"×9"	2'6"	Std	Roads Reconstruction Co., Frome 100 hp	784/1 P
9375	1947	L/BE	2V/6¾"×9"	2'6"	Std	Altrincham Gas Co.	
9376	1947	L	2V/6¾"×9"	2'6"	Std	Ind Coope & Allsopp, Burton	7
9377	1947	L	2V/6¾"×9"	2'6"	Std	Bolton Corp. Gas Works	GRADWELL 100 hp
9378	1947	L	2V/6¾"×9"	2'6"	Std	Peter Spence & Sons, Farnworth	HOWARD SPENCE 2
9379	1947	L	2V/6¾"×9"	2'6"	Std	Mansfield Standard Sand Co.	"
9380	1947	L	2V/6¾"×9"	2'6"	Std	D. Adamson & Co., Dukinfield	"
9381	1947	L	2V/6¾"×9"	2'6"	Std	McKechnie Bros, Widnes	LITTLE ENOCH
9382	1948	L	2V/6¾"×9"	2'6"	Std	Gypsum Mines Ltd, Mountfield	ENTERPRISE "
9383	1948	L	2V/6¾"×9"	2'6"	Std	McKechnie Bros, Widnes	"
9384	1948	L	2V/6¾"×9"	2'6"	Std	Ind Coope & Allsopp, Burton	ENDURANCE
9385	1948	L	2V/6¾"×9"	1'8"	2'0"	Hong Kong	8 P
9386	1948	L	2V/6¾"×9"	2'6"	Std	Roads Reconstruction Co., Frome	789/2
9387	1948	L	2V/6¾"×9"	2'6"	Std	Roads Reconstruction Co., Frome	794/3
9388	1948	L	2V/6¾"×9"	2'6"	Std	Eccles Slag Co., Appleby	
9389	1948	L	4V/6¾"×9"	2'6"	3'6"	Griffin Eng Co., S. Africa	Twin 0-4-4-0T

SENTINEL WAGGON WORKS LTD

Works No.	Built	Type	Cyls	D.W.	Gauge	Customer	No./Name/Notes
9390	1948	L	2V/6¾"×9"	2'6"	Std	Liverpool Corp. Trading Estate, Kirkby	CITY OF LIVERPOOL 100 hp
9391	1949	L/BE	2V/6¾"×9"	2'6"	Std	Road Reconstruction Co., Frome	1262 "
9392	1949	L/BE	2V/6¾"×9"	2'6"	Std	Midland Iron Co., Rotherham	"
9393	1950	L/BE	2V/6¾"×9"	2'6"	Std	Edgar Allen & Co., Tinsley	"
9394	1950	L/BE	2V/6¾"×9"	2'6"	Std	N.C.B. Monk Bretton Colly.	SENTINEL NO.3
9395	1950	L/BE	2V/6¾"×9"	2'6"	Std	N.C.B. Manton Main Colly.	MANTON NO.2
9396	1950	L/BE	2V/6¾"×9"	2'6"	Std	Leys Malleable Castings Co., Derby	4
9397	1950	L/BE	2V/6¾"×9"	2'6"	Std	N.C.B. Kirkby Colly.	BONNIE DUNDEE "
9398	1950	L/BE	2V/6¾"×9"	2'6"	Std	Vobster Quarries, Somerset	752 SENTINEL
9399	1950	L/BE	2V/6¾"×9"	2'6"	Std	N.C.B. Wingfield Manor Colly.	BALMORAL CASTLE "
9400	1950	L/BE	2V/6¾"×9"	2'6"	Std	N.C.B. Barnsley Main Colly.	SENTINEL NO.1
9401	1950	L/BE	2V/6¾"×9"	2'6"	Std	N.C.B. Wharncliffe Colly.	(SENTINEL NO.2) 2
9511	1951	RC	6V/6"×7"	2'9"	Std	Egyptian S.R.	Art. Railcars 335 hp
9512	1951	RC	6V/6"×7"	2'9"	Std	Egyptian S.R.	Art. Railcars 335 hp
9513	1951	RC	6V/6"×7"	2'9"	Std	Egyptian S.R.	Art. Railcars 335 hp
9514	1951	RC	6V/6"×7"	2'9"	Std	Egyptian S.R.	Art. Railcars 335 hp
9515	1951	RC	6V/6"×7"	2'9"	Std	Egyptian S.R.	Art. Railcars 335 hp
9516	1951	RC	6V/6"×7"	2'9"	Std	Egyptian S.R.	Art. Railcars 335 hp
9517	1951	RC	6V/6"×7"	2'9"	Std	Egyptian S.R.	Art. Railcars 335 hp
9518	1951	RC	6V/6"×7"	2'9"	Std	Egyptian S.R.	Art. Railcars 335 hp
9519	1951	RC	6V/6"×7"	2'9"	Std	Egyptian S.R.	Art. Railcars 335 hp
9520	1951	RC	6V/6"×7"	2'9"	Std	Egyptian S.R.	Art. Railcars 335 hp
9521	1950	L	2V/6¾"×9"	1'8"	2'6"	Madras Irrigation Project, India	
9522	1950	L	2V/6¾"×9"	1'8"	2'6"	Madras Irrigation Project, India	
9523	1951	L	2V/6¾"×9"	1'8"	2'6"	Madras Irrigation Project, India	
9524	1951	L	2V/6¾"×9"	1'8"	2'6"	SDA Power Station, United Provinces	
9525	1951	L	2V/6¾"×9"	1'8"	2'6"	SDA Power Station, United Provinces	
9526	1951	L	2V/6¾"×9"	2'6"	Std	N.C.B. Dinnington Main Colly.	DINNINGTON NO.3 100 hp
9527	1951	L	2V/6¾"×9"	2'6"	Std	EMGB, Northampton	PLANTAGENET "
9528	1952	L	2V/6¾"×9"	2'6"	Std	NCB Shawcross Colly.	1952 "
9529	1952	L	2V/6¾"×9"	2'6"	Std	N.W.G.B. Warrington	L.G. No.4
9530	1952	L	2V/6¾"×9"	2'6"	Std	N.C.B. New Hucknall Coll.	STIRLING CASTLE
9531	1952	L	2V/6¾"×9"	2'6"	Std	N.C.B. Newstead Coll.	GLAMIS CASTLE
9532	1952	L	2V/6¾"×9"	2'6"	Std	N.C.B. Newstead Coll.	WINDSOR CASTLE
9533	1952	L	2V/6¾"×9"	2'6"	Std	E.E.C. Rugby	PEEPING TOM II

Works No.	Built	Type	Cyls	D.W.	Gauge	Customer	No./Name/Notes
9534	1952	L	2V/6¾"×9"	2'6"	Std	N.C.B. Holditch Coll.	(preserved)
9535	1952	L	2V/6¾"×9"	2'6"	Std	N.C.B. Silverdale Coll.	853 TIMOTHY
9536	1952	L	2V/6¾"×9"	2'6"	Std	Chesterfield Tube Co. Ltd	854 SUSAN P
9537	1952	L	2V/6¾"×9"	2'6"	Std	Chesterfield Tube Co.	L.31
9538	1952	L	2V/6¾"×9"	2'6"	Std	*To Barrow Hematite Steel Co. Ltd	24
9539	1952	L	2V/7"×9"	2'6"	Std	Parkgate I.&S.Co., Rotherham	25
9540	1952	L	2V/7"×9"	2'6"	Std	Parkgate I.&S.Co., Rotherham	LION
9541	1952	L	2V/6¾"×9"	2'6"	Std	N.C.B. Garw Coll.	VANGUARD
9542	1952	L	2V/6¾"×9"	2'6"	Std	N.C.B. Garw Coll.	No.1
9543	1952	L	2V/6¾"×9"	2'6"	Std	N.C.B. Donisthorpe Coll.	No.2
9544	1952	L	2V/6¾"×9"	2'6"	Std	N.C.B. Ellistown Coll.	
9545	1952	L	2V/6¾"×9"	2'6"	Std	B.E.A. Skelton Grange, Yorks	No.26
9546	1952	L	2V/7"×9"	2'6"	Std	Parkgate I.&S. Co., Rotherham	SENTINEL 1
9547	1952	L	2V/6¾"×9"	2'6"	Std	Tunnel Portland Cement Co., Pitstone	MANTON No.2
9548	1952	L	2V/6¾"×9"	2'6"	Std	N.C.B. Manton Main Coll.	No.10
9549	1952	L	2V/6¾"×9"	2'6"	Std	N.C.B. Denby Hall Coll.	100
9550	1952	L	2V/7"×9"	2'6"	Std	R.T.B. Ltd, Ebbw Vale	
9551	1952	L	2V/6¾"×9"	2'6"	Std	B.E.A. Skelton Grange, Yorks.	50
9552	1953	L	2V/6¾"×9"	2'6"	Std	N.C.B. Manvers Main Coll.	
9553	1953	RC	6/6"×7"	2'6"	3'6"	Nigerian Rlys	
9554	1953	RC	6/6"×7"	2'6"	3'6"	Nigerian Rlys	
9555	1953	L	2V/6¾"×9"	2'6"	Std	N.C.B. Wingfield Manor Coll.	BARROWGILL CASTLE
9556	1953	L	2V/6¾"×9"	2'6"	Std	Craven Bros. Ltd, Reddish	No.9 CRAVEN
9557	1953	L	2V/6¾"×9"	2'6"	Std	N.C.B. Wentworth Coll.	SENTINEL No.4
9558	1953	L	2V/6¾"×9"	2'6"	Std	*To Armstrong Whitworth, Gateshead	A.W. No.1
9559	1953	L	2V/6¾"×9"	2'6"	Std	Rugby Portland Cement Co., Stanbridgeford	No.1
9560	1953	L	2V/7"×9"	2'6"	Std	Scottish Gas, Falkirk	
9561	1953	L	2V/6¾"×9"	2'6"	Std	R.B. Tennent, Whifflet, Coatbridge	JOHN
9562	1954	L	2V/6¾"×9"	2'6"	Std	Tyne-Tees Shipping Co., Stockton	No.4
9563	5/1954	L	2V/6¾"×9"	2'6"	Std	Short Bros, Pallion	
9564	1954	L	2V/6¾"×9"	2'6"	Std	Rugby Portland Cement Co., Stanbridgeford	No.2
9565	1954	L	2V/6¾"×9"	2'6"	Std	C.E.A. Willington, Burton	
9566	1954	L	2V/6¾"×9"	2'6"	Std	Gjers Mills, Middlesbrough	1 AYRESOME
9567	1955	L	2V/6¾"×9"	2'6"	Std	N.C.B. Nailstone Coll.	No.3
9568	1954	L	2V/7"×9"	2'6"	Std	R.T.B. Ebbw Vale	101
9569	1954	L	2V/6¾"×9"	2'6"	Std	N.C.B. Cynheidre Coll.	
9570	1954	L	2V/6¾"×9"	2'6"	Std	N.C.B. Barrow Barnsley Coll.	SENTINEL No.5

Works No.	Built	Type	Cyls	D.W.	Gauge	Customer	No./Name/Notes
9571	1954	L	2V/6¾"×9"	2'6"	Std	N.C.B. Great Mountain Coll.	CARADOC
9572	1954	L	2V/6¾"×9"	2'6"	Std	N.C.B. Cross Hands Coll.	
9573	1954	L	2V/7"×9"	2'6"	Std	R.T.B. Ebbw Vale	102
9574	1954	L	2V/7"×9"	2'6"	Std	R.T.B. Ebbw Vale	103
9575	1954	L	2V/7"×9"	3'2"	Std	★To N.W.G.B. Bradford Rd, Manchester	
9576	1954	L	2V/6¾"×9"	3'2"	Std	N.C.B. Babbington Coll.	5
9577	1955	L	2V/6¾"×9"	3'2"	Std	I.C.I. (Metals) Dowlais	
9578	1955	L	2V/6¾"×9"	3'2"	Std	N.C.B. Bestwood Coll.	4
9579	1955	L	2V/6¾"×9"	3'2"	Std	N.C.B. Langwith Coll.	SENTINEL No.1
9580	1955	L	2V/6¾"×9"	3'2"	Std	N.C.B. Holmewood Coll.	SENTINEL No.2
9581	1955	L	2V/6¾"×9"	3'2"	Std	N.C.B. Derwenthaugh Coll.	89
9582	1955	L	2V/6¾"×9"	3'2"	Std	Barrow Hematite Steel Co.	L.30
9583	1955	L	2V/6¾"×9"	3'2"	Std	N.C.B. Derwenthaugh Coll.	87
9584	1955	L	2V/6¾"×9"	3'2"	Std	N.C.B. Derwenthaugh Coll.	88
9585	1955	L	2V/6¾"×9"	3'2"	Std	Millom & Askham Iron Co.	4
9586	1955	L	2V/6¾"×9"	3'2"	Std	Millom & Askham Iron Co.	5
9587	1956	0–6–0T			Std	Dorman Long, South Bank Middlesbrough	S.1/1
9588	1956	0–6–0T			Std	Dorman Long, South Bank Middlesbrough	S.2/2
9589	1956	0–6–0T			Std	Dorman Long, South Bank Middlesbrough	S.3/3
9590	1956	0–6–0T			Std	Dorman Long, South Bank Middlesbrough	S.4/4
9591	1956	0–6–0T			Std	Dorman Long, South Bank Middlesbrough	S.5/5
9592	1956	0–6–0T			Std	Dorman Long, South Bank Middlesbrough	S.6/6
9593	1954	L		2'6"	Std	Shipbreaking Industries Ltd, Faslane	(1)
9594	1955	L		2'6"	Std	Gjers Mills & Co. Ltd, Middlesbrough	2 AYRESOME
9595	1955	L		2'6"	Std	C.E.G.B. Stella N. Station	24
9596	1955	L		2'6"	Std	Courtaulds Ltd, Flint	
9697	1955	L		2'6"	Std	C.E.G.B. Stella N. Station	25
9698	1955	L		2'6"	Std	Gjers Mills & Co. Ltd, Middlesbrough	3 AYRESOME
9699	1956	L		3'2"	Std	Courtaulds Ltd, Grimsby	WILLIAM
9600	1955	L		3'2"	Std	Gjers Mills & Co. Ltd, Middlesbrough	
9601	1956	0–6–0TG		3'2"	Std	Dorman Long, South Bank Middlesbrough	7
9602	1956	0–6–0TG		3'2"	Std	Dorman Long, South Bank Middlesbrough	8
9603	1956	0–6–0TG		3'2"	Std	Dorman Long, South Bank Middlesbrough	9 0–6–6–0T
9604	1956	0–6–0TG		3'2"	Std	G.K.N. East Moors	
9605	1956	0–6–0TG		3'2"	Std	G.K.N. East Moors	
9606	1956	0–6–0TG		3'2"	Std	G.K.N. East Moors	
9607	1956	L				Barrow Hematite Steel Co.	L.33
9608	1956	L				Barrow Hematite Steel Co.	L.32

Works No.	Built	Type	Cyls	D.W.	Gauge	Customer	No./Name/Notes
9609	1956	L				Millom Hematite Ore & Iron Co.	6
9610	1956	L				Millom Hematite Ore & Iron Co.	7
9611	1956	L				Settle Limes Ltd, Horton-in-Ribblesdale	
9612	1957	L				Pilkington Bros, St. Helens	SENTINEL No.1
9613		6W.L				Gjers Mills & Co. Ltd, Middlesbrough	5 AYRESOME
9615	7/1956	L				Oxfordshire Ironstone Co.	PHYLLIS
9616	1957	L				N.C.B. Barrow Coll.	SENTINEL No.6
9617	1956	L			Std	W.M.G.B. Nechells, Birmingham	10
9618	1/1957	L			Std	Seaham Harbour Dock Co.	TEMPEST
9619	1957	L			Std	Dorman Long, Lackenby	VANE
9620	1957	L			Std	Colvilles Ltd, Clydebridge	2/19
9621	1957	L			Std	Colvilles Ltd, Clydebridge	2/20 P
9622	1958	L			Std	National Smelting Co., Swansea Vale	SWANSEA VALE No.1
9623							
9624	blank						
9625							
9626							
9627	1957	L			Std	Whitehead I.&S. Co., Newport Mon.	
9628	1957	L			Std	R.B. Tennent, Whifflet, Coatbridge	ROBIN
9629	1957	L			Std	Tees-side Bridge & Eng. Wks, Cargo Fleet	TEES-SIDE No.5
9630	1957	L			Std	J. Brown & Co. Ltd, Clyde Bank	No.5
9631	2/1958	L			Std	R.B. Tennent, Whifflet, Coatbridge	THE DOCTOR
9632	1957	L			Std	W.M.G.B. Walsall	P
9633	1957	L/ 0-6-0TG			Std	Dorman Long, South Bank By-Products Wks	
9634							
9635							
9636							
9637							
9638							
9639	blank						
9640							
9641							
9642							
9643							
9644							
9645							

Works No.	Built	Type	Cyls	D.W.	Gauge	Customer	No./Name/Notes
9646	⎫						
9647	⎬ blank						
9648	⎪						
9649	⎭						
9650	1957		0-6-0F			Dorman Long, Lackenby	
9651	1957		0-6-0F			Dorman Long, Sth Bank By-Products Wks	
9652	1957		0-6-0F			Dorman Long, Sth Bank By-Products Wks	
9653	1957		0-6-0F			Dorman Long, Sth Bank By-Products Wks	

FOOTNOTES

*4W-4WTG articulated

(a) Special type. Standard vert. engine mounted on a gearbox driving direct on to the axle.
(b) Articulated.
(c) Engine units only. Built into 2-2-2-2 tender locos by N.B. Loco. Co. 24413-6/38.

†Demonstration loco.

VERTICAL BOILER LOCOMOTIVES

CONVERSIONS

Works No.	Date	From Type	From Make	From Wks No.	To	Gauge	Customer	No./Name
5666	1924	0-4-0ST	MW	1091/88	0-4-0TG	Std	T.E. Gray, Isebrook	
5667(a)	2/1924	0-6-0ST	MW	848/82	0-6-0TG	Std	London Brick Co., Arlesey	SENTINEL
5679(b)	1924	0-4-0ST	RP	13111/88	0-4-0TG	Std	Tottenham & District Gas Co.	No.6
5988	1925	0-4-0ST	LE	230/97	0-4-0TG	Std	Sir Hedworth Williamson's Limeworks Ltd	PHYLLIS
6005	1925	0-4-0ST	HC	527/99	0-4-0TG	Std	Thomas Butlin & Co. Ltd, Irthlingboro	HUGH
6006	1925	0-4-0ST	?	?	0-4-0TG	Std	Ravenhead Brick & Tile Upholland	UPHO
6144		0-4-0ST		?	0-4-0TG	Std	Castner Kellner Alkali Co.	
6154	1926	0-4-0ST	D	2051/84	0-4-0TG	Std	Weardale Steel, Iron & Coke Co.	2
6155	1925	0-4-0ST	MW		0-4-0TG	Std	Coalbrookdale Co. Ltd	
6183		0-4-0ST	HC	406/	0-4-0TG	Std	Stanton Ironworks Co.	HOLWELL No.4
6218	5/1925	0-4-0ST	HC	683/03	0-4-0TG		Sir Hedworth Williamson's Lime Works Ltd	CHARLES HEDWORTH
6219	1927	0-4-0P	MW	1954/18	0-4-0TG	Std	Road Reconstruction Ltd, Vobster Quarry	
6220	1929	0-4-0ST	BAG	1344/91	0-4-0TG	3'9½"	B.P.C.M. Johnson's Branch, Greenhithe	CEMENT
6309			?	?	0-4-0TG	3'0"	Powell Tillery Steam Coal Co. Ltd	
6310	1926	0-4-0ST	AB	282/86	0-4-0TG	Std	Ford Paper Mills, Sunderland	
6661	1926	0-4-0ST	BE	317/09	0-4-0TG	Std	Glascote Coll. Co. Ltd	
6662	1926/7	0-4-0ST	YE	628/02	0-4-0TG	Std	Frodingham Iron & Steel Co. Ltd	
6807	1928	0-4-0ST	MW	1472/00	0-4-0TG	Std	J.S. Peters, Merstham	
6828	1928	0-6-0ST	RS	1648/65	0-6-0TG	Std	Clay Cross Co.	GERVASE
6951	1927	0-4-0ST	N	1562/70	0-4-0TG	Std	Beckton Gas, Light & Coke Co.	3
7973	1929	Steam lorry		(Leyland)	0-4-2TG	Std	Derbyshire Wagon Co.	2
8749	1932	"			0-4-0TG	3'0"	Cafferata & Co. Ltd	
9169	1935		S	6776/	4wVBTG	Std	Taylor Bros (Sandiacre) Ltd	

(a) Reb. by Blackwells, Northampton
(b) Reb. at Tottenham by Church & Sons, Stamford Hill

ALEXANDER SHANKS AND SON LTD
DENS IRON WORKS
ARBROATH

Established in 1840, the range of products manufactured in the Dens Iron Works was very wide indeed; from five catalogues in the writer's possession, dated 1904, 1906, 1919, 1920, and 1938, it is observed that this firm was advertising horizontal steam engines, high-speed vertical engines, triple-expansion engines, steam and hand cranes (including gantry cranes), the traditional agricultural portable engine, marine engines and Scotch boilers and ships' ash hoists; while in later years diesel engines and lawn mowers formed a major part of their output. In a catalogue issued in the 1870s Shanks and Son offered to supply four- and six-coupled saddle tank locomotives suitable for contractors' use, and eleven such locomotives have been traced, all built between 1872 and 1877.

In addition to building the normal type of locomotive as mentioned above, the firm also introduced between 1870 and 1880 a series of vertical boiler locomotives, and these are illustrated by *Fig. 31* which is from a woodcut in an early catalogue. These locomotives had cross tubes in the boiler, and were geared 3 to 1, being made in several sizes suitable for gauges of 2 ft 11 in. upwards; no other dimensions are known, but the details of the design are clearly shown in the illustration. One of these locomotives worked at the Carmyllie Quarry, near Arbroath, about the period 1910–1920.

Alexander Shanks and Son Ltd went out of business in 1968, and the premises were taken over by Giddings and Lewis-Fraser Ltd, the records of the old firm being handed over to The Signal Tower Museum, Ladyloan, Arbroath.

SILLEY, COX AND COMPANY, LTD
FALMOUTH

Established in 1868 as Cox, Farley and Co., this firm has been engaged in marine engineering and ship repairing since that date. In 1918 the Falmouth Docks and Engineering Co. required a further locomotive, and this was built by Cox from Sara and Burgess drawings, the latter firm having gone out of business by this time. The locomotive is illustrated here by *Plate 58*.

W. SISSON AND CO. LTD
SISSON ROAD
GLOUCESTER

The Cardiff Railway was essentially a dock undertaking, but about 3¼ miles from the docks on the main line of the Rhymney Railway a branch was constructed by the Cardiff Railway in 1909 to join the Taff Vale Railway near Treforest. For some reason, however, the junction at Treforest was taken out*, and it was not until 1911 that the line was opened for public traffic as far as

---

*Interested readers should see *The Cardiff Railway* by E.R. Mountford (Oakwood Press) for the reason.

ALEXANDER SHANKS & SON, DENS IRON WORKS, ARBROATH.

IMPROVED GEARED LOCOMOTIVE.

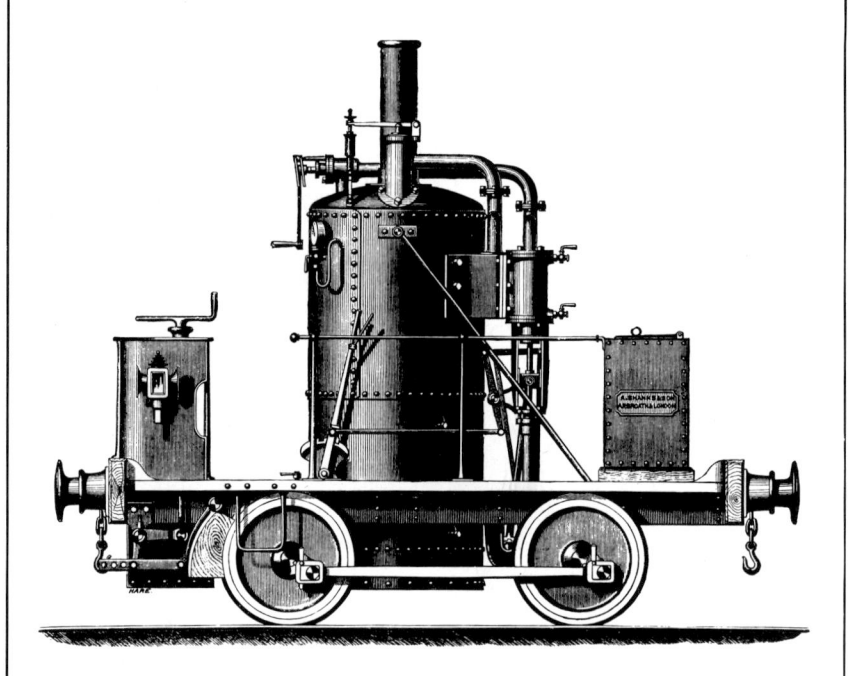

LOCOMOTIVES, with vertical boilers, having cross tubes, and geared in the proportion of say 3 to 1, are frequently used by contractors, and for light work where an inexpensive engine is desired. ALEXANDER SHANKS & SON have made these engines of the form here shown, of various sizes, and for railway gauges, of 2 feet 11 inches and upwards. It is not expected that this class of engine will be so economical in working as the ordinary Tank Locomotive. In districts, however, where fuel is cheap, and where the work required is not heavy, the engine will be found to answer very well. Enquiries for this class of engine should be accompanied with a full description of the work they are intended to perform.

LONDON OFFICE, 27 LEADENHALL STREET, E.C.

Fig. 31 A. Shanks & Son Ltd geared locomotive c. 1870–1880.   *Signal Tower Museum*

Plate 58 Silley, Cox & Co's geared locomotive built 1918 for Falmouth Docks (similar to the Sara & Burgess design. *The Executors of the late G. Alliez*

Rhydyfelin Halt, and the short length thence to Treforest Junction was never used. Steam railmotors were introduced for working the passenger service from the Rhymney Railway station at Cardiff to Rhydyfelin Halt, and two were supplied to the Cardiff Railway for this purpose by the Gloucester Railway Carriage and Wagon Company Ltd.

These railmotors carried sixteen first class and forty-eight third class passengers, and were delivered in February, 1911. The distance between bogie centres was 46 ft; the length over the bodywork was 65 ft and the length over the buffers 68 ft 11¼ in. The power-bogies, *Plate 59*, came from the works of W. Sisson and Co. Ltd, the well-known marine engine builders of Gloucester; three units were supplied, Works Nos. 971–73, one of which was kept as a spare. These had four-coupled wheels of 4 ft diameter on a wheelbase of 8 ft, and cylinders 12 in. in diameter with a stroke of 16 in. The boilers, of the vertical multi-tubular type, were constructed to Sisson's order by Abbott and Co. Ltd of Newark-on-Trent, and had an outside diameter of 4 ft 6 in. at the foundation ring, tapered slightly for 6 ft upwards. The upper portion was enlarged to 6 ft diameter; the firebox and tubes were of copper. The total height of these boilers was 9 ft 6 in., and the

Plate 59 Power bogie built in 1911 by W. Sisson & Co. for a Cardiff Railway railmotor.
W. Sisson & Co.

total heating surface amounted to 660 sq.ft, with a grate area of 11.5 sq.ft. The steam pressure was 160 lb. psi.

In service these railmotors normally worked in conjunction with a trailer coach, but after only three years they proved to be inadequate for the traffic, and were replaced about 1914.

JOHN SLEE AND COMPANY
EARLESTOWN ENGINEERING WORKS
WARRINGTON

John Slee & Co. was a firm of General Engineers and John Slee was also a Director of the Plynlimon & Hafan Tramway. Although no locomotive had been built by this firm, in May 1897, a locomotive of very unorthodox design was delivered at the Llanvihangel station of the Cambrian Railways for use on the new Plynlimon and Hafan Tramway. This was a 2ft 3in. gauge line, 7 miles 26 chains in length, serving Graywacke Stone Quarries on the western slopes of the Plynlimon range. The locomotive was named VICTORIA (see *Plate 60*) had a four-cylinder engine, a vertical boiler, and was carried on four coupled wheels, the whole being enclosed in an attractive all-over cab.

At one time there was some uncertainty as to the layout of the four cylinders, one theory being that two cylinders drove each axle, but this would have filled the rear of the cab and left little room for the driver and fireman. An examination of the original large photograph reveals that one vertical cylinder was arranged on each side driving on to the leading crankpin with connecting rods having marine-type big ends, whilst the coupling rods had bushed ends. The other two

Plate 60   *Victoria* built in 1897 by John Slee & Co. for the Plynlimon & Hafan Tramway.
National Library of Wales

cylinders were mounted inside the frames at an angle of approx. 20 degrees to the vertical, forwards, driving on to cranks on the same axle.

Although having the same general appearance of either a Cochran or a Sharp-Palmer boiler, the one installed in this locomotive must have been very different internally, the fire-door being on the opposite side to the chimney, while the flat plate at the top, secured by only 18 widely spaced studs and nuts, would appear to have been part of the boiler cladding. What looks like a central flue was probably a safety-valve casing.

The general dimensions, which cannot be guaranteed as accurate, were as follows:

Wheelbase	6 ft
Overall length	12 ft 6 in.
Diameter of Wheels	1 ft 6 in.

Apparently the locomotive was short of steam even when two of the cylinders were isolated, even then, it put up a very poor performance and a more orthodox type was purchased.

Reference

M.J. Messenger

T. SMITH & SONS (RODLEY) LTD
RODLEY
NR. LEEDS

Established in the 1860s by Thomas Smith who took his sons into partnership in 1902, the main business was the manufacture of steam cranes. Mention is made in J.S. Brownlie's book *Railway Steam Cranes* of a locomotive crane supplied to South America, but no further information is available.

SOUTH EASTERN RAILWAY COMPANY
ASHFORD WORKS

The Ashford Locomotive Works of the South Eastern Railway was opened in 1847, and during that year a certain amount of repair work was undertaken there, but in 1848 construction began on the first locomotive actually completed in the new Works. This was a locomotive remarkable for the unusual design of vertical boiler and for its small overall dimensions, and was intended for the use of the Directors and Chief Engineer on their periodical tours of inspection. The locomotive is illustrated by *Fig. 32* but few dimensions are known. It possessed outside cylinders 5¾ in. in diameter with a stroke of 9 in., uncoupled wheels of 3 ft 6 in. diameter, and the boiler had a diameter of 2 ft 6 in. The water tank capacity was 130 gallons and the driver stood in a recess immediately over the axle of the carrying wheels. The construction of this locomotive had been started in the old workshops at Bricklayer's Arms and after transfer to Ashford it remained a stock job until its completion in 1850.

Fig. 32 First locomotive built for the SER at Ashford Works in 1850.

    The locomotive was frequently used in the London area during the 1858–9 period and is reported to have been capable of a fair turn of speed, which may account for it being known to the staff as the "Flying Dutchman", and its active life lasted until 1866 having spent its time from 1853 on the Reading branch for permanent way service. It was put into store until 1877 when it was converted into a stationary engine and sent to Redhill. It was sold for scrap in 1888.
    Its SER number was 126. Although completed at Ashford it seems that the majority of the building work must have been carried out at the Bricklayers Arms Works as D.L. Bradley in his book *Locomotives of the S.E.R.* (RCTS 1963) states that the cost at this Works was £438 10*s*. 8*d*. and to finish it off, Ashford spent £25. According to the *Ashford Works Centenary* booklet its design is attributed to a Marine Engineer of the name of Fernihough.

ROBERT STEPHENSON AND COMPANY
FORTH STREET WORKS
NEWCASTLE-UPON-TYNE

The Works, the first Locomotive Manufacturer's in the world, established in 1823 by George Stephenson who had already built some locomotives at various collieries. Most of the responsibility for managing the Works fell on the shoulders of his son, Robert, his father being engaged away from home on railway construction and other projects.

A locomotive called the TWIN SISTERS was the first six wheeled engine supplied by Robert Stephenson & Co., at a cost of £500 to the Liverpool and Manchester Railway Company. It had two vertical boilers placed one behind the other, and cylinders at the rear inclined downwards with the connecting rod driving on to crankpins on the leading wheels, all six wheels being coupled by side rods. According to a letter written by Robert Stephenson at Liverpool to Michael Longridge on 1st December, 1828, the boilers were made at Laird's Boiler Works in Liverpool and shipped to Carlisle for transportation to Stephenson's Works at Newcastle. These boilers were intended to burn coke.

The completed locomotive was despatched on 2nd July, 1829, the Works No. being 13. The *Manchester Guardian* of 25th July refers to it in these words:

> This engine, which is one constructed by Mr Stephenson, the Engineer of the Railway, arrived about the time we mentioned and has since been regularly at work. We have had several opportunities of seeing it and consider it decidedly the best locomotive engine we have ever seen. It has two cylinders, each 9 in. in diameter, with a stroke of 2 ft and works at a pressure of 50 lb. on the square inch. We have more than once seen it driving before it twelve wagons, each weighing a ton, and each carrying 4 tons of clay, and when propelling this weight, amounting altogether to 54 tons, it travelled with great ease at the rate of 6 or 7 miles an hour.

This locomotive was used during the construction of the Railway and afterwards for ballasting purposes. The only known illustration of this locomotive is an

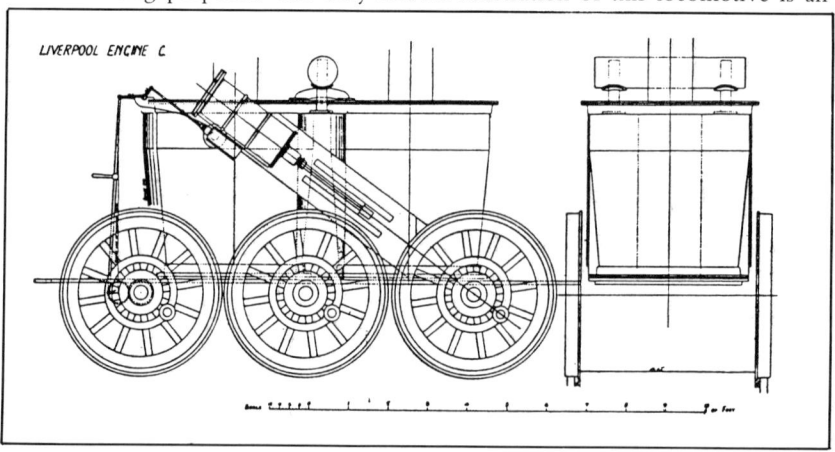

Fig. 33 R. Stephenson & Co's *Twin Sisters* built 1829 for the Liverpool & Manchester Railway.

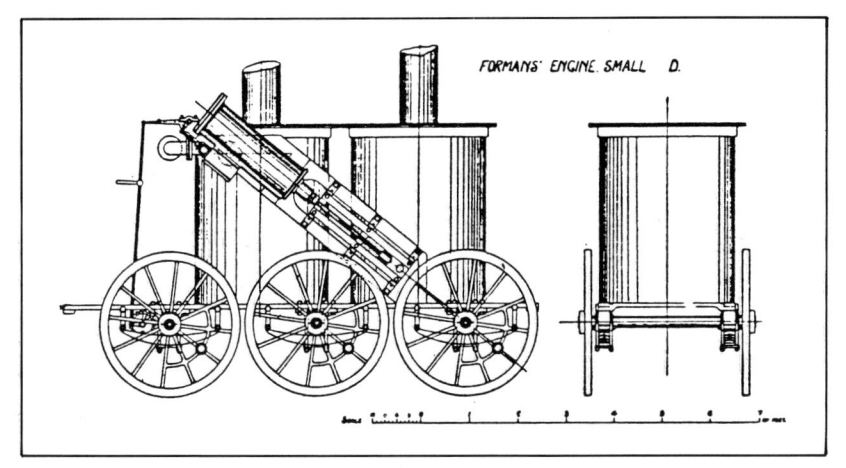

Fig. 34 Twin boiler locomotive built by R. Stephenson & Co. in 1829 for Penydarren ironworks.

incomplete original drawing (*Fig. 33*) and no contemporary technical description is known.

A second, but smaller, locomotive of this type was designed for William Forman, of the Penydarren Ironworks and intended for a 3 ft gauge tramroad. The original drawing is reproduced here in *Fig. 34* but it is doubtful whether this locomotive was completed in its original form as another drawing dated July 1828 shows an alternative suggestion for a single horizontal cylindrical boiler, while other drawings still preserved show further proposals for altering this locomotive to a wider gauge of 4 ft 6 in. This locomotive, which carried Works No. 16 and cost £375, was delivered on 18th July, 1829.

Two crane locomotives were supplied to The Consett Iron Co. The first a 0–4–0VBCT (Works No. 2853/1897), the second a 2–4–0VBCT (Works No. 2854/1898). They carried Consett numbers E. No.8 and E. No.9 respectively.

In 1902 a new Factory was completed at Darlington to cope with large orders received. In 1937 R. Stephenson & Co. Ltd, purchased the locomotive department of R. & W. Hawthorn Leslie & Co. Ltd, the firm becoming R. Stephenson & Hawthorns Ltd. In 1962 it became part of English Electric Co. Ltd at Darlington, the Forth Street Works having closed in 1960.

STOTHERT & PITT LTD
BATH

Founded in 1779 by George Stothert as an ironmongery business, an iron foundry was also set up in 1815. A Robert Pitt started as an apprentice in the foundry in the 1830s and subsequently he became a partner. After the firm became Stothert & Pitt, they moved to the Lower Bristol Road site, manufactur-

Fig. 35 Stothert & Pitt Ltd's special 15 ton locomotive steam crane built 1891 and supplied to Bolckow Vaughan & Co.

ing cranes, tanks, pumps, turntables and a variety of railway material.

Many cranes were despatched to the South Wales area including special ingot handling locomotive cranes in the 1880s, and to the Cleveland area by 1891. Their outside cylinders were situated between the uncoupled wheels and drove one axle. The crane was operated by a separate pair of cylinders and a vertical boiler supplied the steam to all cylinders. 15 ton cranes of this type were supplied to the Landore Siemens Steel Co. in 1891 and others went to the N.E. coast area (see *Fig. 35*), but it is not known how many were built.

Reference

The Evolution of a Family Firm: Stothert & Pitt of Bath by H. Torrans

T.M. TENNANT AND COMPANY
BOWERSHALL IRON AND ENGINE WORKS
LEITH, NEAR EDINBURGH

Between the early 1850s and 1863 this firm had three addresses recorded in the Edinburgh directories, and were listed first as machine makers, then engineers, and finally when established at the fourth address in 1866, as manufacturers of rolling stock and railway plant.

Messrs Tennant and Co. built a number of vertical boiler contractors locomotives, but the only reference to this company as builders of such machines known to the writer is in *The Locomotive* for May, 1927, and no details have been discovered since that date. This firm was well known as the builder of the Thompson three-wheeled road steamers, and as these engines were built between the years 1867 and about 1873 it is probable that any locomotives built would be contemporary in date.

The road steamers were fitted with patent vertical "pot" boilers, the fireboxes of which had a large copper sphere suspended from the crown. At a later date this design of boiler was discarded for one of the "Field" tube type. Whether either of these two kinds of boiler were used on the contractors' locomotives is not known. A sectional drawing of a "pot" boiler will be found on page 191 of *Steam Locomotion on Common Roads* by W. Fletcher, 1890. The business of T.M. Tennant and Co. was wound up in the early months of 1878.

WILLIAM WILKINSON & CO. LTD
HOLMHOUSE FOUNDRY
WIGAN

In 1881, William Wilkinson, of the Holmhouse Foundry, Wigan, patented a somewhat remarkable locomotive designed for tramway operation and with two main objects in view – first, to get rid of the exhaust steam without the expense of a condenser and, secondly, to make every part of the machine easily accessible.

These locomotives, the first of which was built in the year of the Patent, had vertical boilers with "Field" tubes, and of 3 ft 6 in. diameter, and made in several sizes from 5 ft 1 in. to 7 ft high. The boilers had a cast iron superheating vessel fixed in the firebox, and the exhaust steam first passed into two receivers, one on each side of the boiler, and then passed into the superheater in the firebox before escaping up the chimney. This method of getting rid of the steam nuisance in the public streets was not very successful, and so in 1886 Wilkinson patented a roof condenser as an accessory.

The engine was of the vertical launch type, made in various sizes with cylinders variously 6 in. in diameter by 7 in. stroke, 6¾ in. diameter by 10 in. stroke, 7¼ in. diameter by 11 in. stroke and 7½ in. diameter by 12 in. stroke. The drive was by means of a pinion on the crankshaft engaging with a spur wheel on one axle, the two axles being coupled by rods. The gear ratio was either 2 or 2½ to 1. Wheelbases varied from 5 ft 6 in. to 5 ft 8 in., and weights from 5¾ to 9 tons; overall measurements were, 11 ft to 12 ft long, 5 ft 6 in. to 6 ft 8 in. wide, and about 9 ft high.

These locomotives created a very favourable impression among tramway engineers, and Messrs Wilkinson supplied 63 of them; of these 59 have been accounted for as follows:

Date	Tramway	No.	Gauge
1881–86	Wigan and District Tramways Co. Ltd	Twelve	3 ft 6 in.
1882–83	Huddersfield Corporation Tramways	Six	4 ft 7¾ in.
1882	Nottingham and District Tramways Co. Ltd	One	4 ft 8½ in.
1883	Birmingham and Aston Tramways Co. Ltd	Two	3 ft 6 in.
1883	Dublin Southern District Tramways Co.	Two	5 ft 3 in.
1883	Manchester, Bury, Rochdale & Oldham Steam Tramways Co.	Nine	4 ft 8½ in.
1883	" "	Eight	3 ft 6 in.
1885	" "	Two	3 ft 6 in.
1886	" "	Two	3 ft 6 in.
1883	South Staffordshire Tramways	Seven	3 ft 6 in.
1883	Giants Causeway, Portrush and Bush Valley	Two	3 ft
1896	Giants Causeway, Portrush and Bush Valley	Two	3 ft
1884	Brighton District Tramways Co.	Two	3 ft 6 in.
1884	Plymouth, Devonport & District Tramways Co.	Two	3 ft 6 in.

It should be noted that the Manchester, Bury, Rochdale and Oldham Tramways Co. Ltd operated 30 miles, 22 chains of tramway, of which about 9½ miles was of 4 ft 8½ in. gauge, and the remainder of 3 ft 6 in. gauge.

The demand for these locomotives outstripped the capacity of the patentee's workshops, which were never very large, and indeed, the boilers of some of the locomotives built there were supplied by Hough and Sons, Newtown Boiler Works, Wigan, so accordingly licences were granted to Thomas Green and Sons, Leeds; Black, Hawthorn and Company, Gateshead; and to Beyer, Peacock and Co. Ltd, Manchester, and the Wilkinson type locomotives built by these firms are dealt with under these headings.

The design however, failed to compete successfully with the Kitson tram locomotive, and after some 206 had been built their manufacture ceased in 1886, except for the two built in 1896 for the Giants Causeway, Portrush and Bush Valley Tramway Co. (*Plate 61*).

When working on routes with steeply graded sections, the steam tram locomotive was often at a serious disadvantage in wet weather with greasy rails, for in the early days there were no statutory stopping places, and if any wayfarer signalled the demand to stop the signal had to be obeyed even if on a steep incline. On attempting to restart the locomotive would, in all probability, skid and race its wheels, only to be held up at once by the automatic brake which acted above a certain speed. This would perhaps happen several times before the locomotive got going again. The Wilkinson locomotives, being geared, were generally good starters, and their designer was probably the first to attempt to work steep gradients of 1 in 11½, 1 in 12, and 1 in 13 by steam power, but with a view of obtaining a more even torque and improving the hill-climbing powers, Wilkinson designed and built the unusual locomotive shown in *Fig. 36*.

In this locomotive the two-cylinder vertical engine was placed at the rear of the frame and the drive to the rear axle was by a worm, this worm being of Siemens

WILLIAM WILKINSON & CO. LTD 163

Plate 61 W. Wilkinson & Co. Ltd: *Dunluce Castle* built 1896 for the Giant's Causeway, Portrush & Bush Valley Railway & Tramway. *L. & G.R.P. David & Charles*

Fig. 36 Experimental tram engine built c.1884 for Street Tramways by W. Wilkinson & Co. Ltd. *Institution of Civil Engineers*

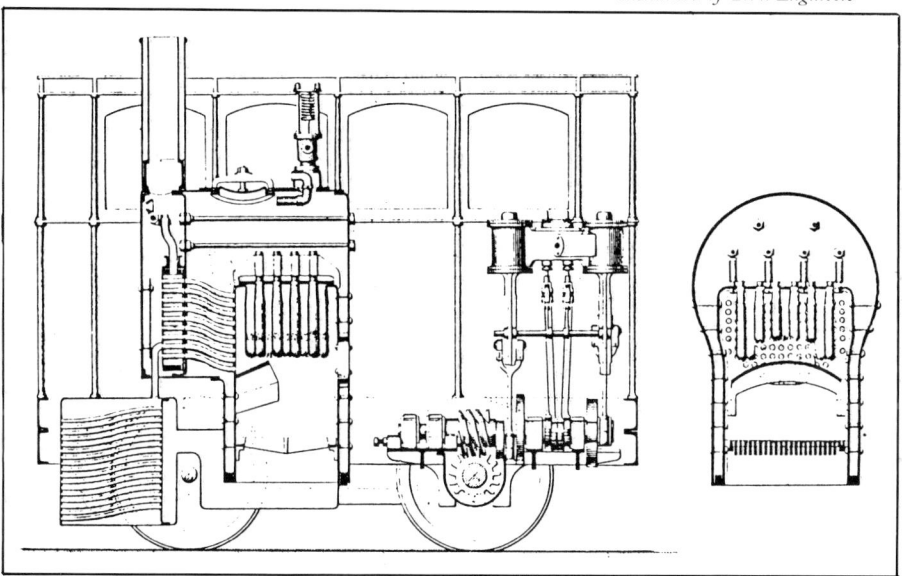

steel. The worm wheel ran in an oil bath, there being special thrust bearings provided for the crankshaft to absorb the heavy end thrust caused by starting and on the over-run with steam shut off. The gear ratio was 7½ to 1. It was predicted by contemporary engineers that the use of a worm drive would cause the wheels to lock when the throttle was closed, but Wilkinson reported that in practice the locomotive coasted quite freely. The complete engine could be removed for overhaul in two hours by releasing six bolts. The axles were coupled by rods and at 8 mph the piston speed was 436 feet per minute, while a speed of 16 mph could be attained.

The second unusual feature in the design was the boiler, which was a combination of the horizontal and vertical element, with the vertical predominating; its construction will be clearly understood from the drawing. The height from foundation ring to top was 6 ft 2 in.; distance from front tube plate to back plate, inside, 3 ft 5 in.; diameter of horizontal portion, inside, 3 ft 9 in.; length of horizontal tubes, 12 in., with reverse curve to allow for expansion and contraction. The inside firebox was 2 ft 1 in. long by 2 ft 7 in. wide at bottom and 2 ft 9½ in. at top, by 3 ft high, and had a series of "Field" tubes suspended from the crown. The working pressure was 50 lb. psi, and the boiler had an evaporative efficiency of 9.7 lb. of water per 1 lb. of coke, with feed water at 62 degrees Fahrenheit.

Other dimensions were: coupled wheels, 3 ft 2 in.; wheelbase, 6 ft; overall length, 12 ft 8 in.; overall height to top of chimney, 10 ft 9 in. All the above dimensions, except the tubes and wheels, should be regarded as approximate only, having been scaled from the original drawings on a scale of $3/8$ in. to 1 ft.

The air-cooled condenser, placed low down at the front, had tubes with between 200 and 300 sq.ft of cooling area, and the air for combustion passed through these tubes on its way to the closed ashpan. It will be noticed that these condenser tubes, like those in the horizontal part of the boiler, had a reverse curve to allow for expansion and contraction. All steam not condensed passed into a superheater in the smokebox, the superheater tubes being exactly coincident with the boiler tubes. Under certain conditions of working, it was found that there was such an amount of expansion that the condenser condensed the greater portion of the steam and little was left to provide a sufficient draught for the fire. To counteract this the locomotive was fitted with a variable blast pipe so that the nozzle could be restricted, when necessary, to maintain the blast.

The date of this unusual locomotive is not known with any certainty, but it had been built and run on trials before 1885.

DE WINTON & CO.
UNION WORKS
THE SLATE QUAY
CAERNARVON

The date of founding of this engineering business is uncertain, but the Directory of Liverpool and Environs for January 1844 lists five iron and brass foundries in Caernarvon one of which was that of Owen Thomas at the Slate Quay. Thomas was joined about 1861 by Jeffreys Parry de Winton who had been an apprentice at Messrs Fawcett Preston & Co. of York Street, Liverpool, and was

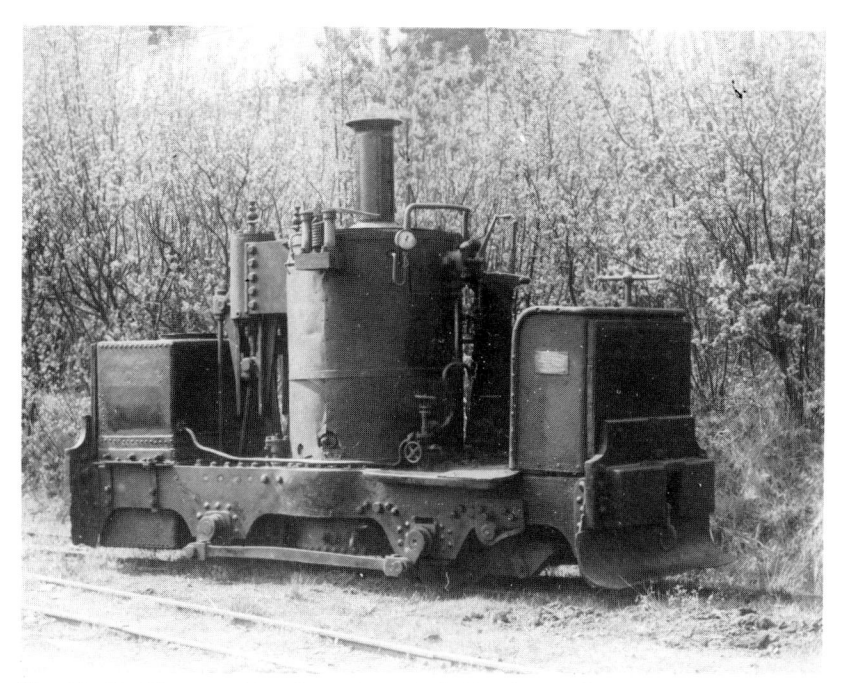

Plate 62 De Winton & Co.: *George Henry* built 1877 for Penrhyn Quarries, Bethesda.
D. Stoyel

an accomplished engineer. The firm then became well-known as builders of marine engines, horizontal and vertical stationary engines, boilers of both Scottish and Lancashire types, cooling tanks, air compressors, stone crushing machines, gold mining machinery and locomotives.

The writer's interest in the products of de Winton and Co. dates back to 1925, but a chance meeting with the chief draughtsman of the Penmaenmawr and Welsh Granite Co. in August 1945 lead to an extensive correspondence with the managers and engineers of all the quarry companies working at that time, together with a number of retired employees. From this, much original information was obtained regarding the vertical boiler locomotives built at the Union Works. Although primarily intended for the narrow gauge lines in the local slate and granite quarries of Caernarvonshire and Merioneth, these small locomotives were afterwards supplied for use further afield, and for gauges up to 4ft 8½in.

Exactly how many were built is not known, perhaps about 60, but two-cylinder and 2 single-cylinder examples have been traced, all built between c.1869 and 1897, although in a number of cases no details are available other than the fact that a quarry did at one time own such a locomotive.

Of the single-cylinder design little is known beyond the fact that they had direct drive and double-flanged wheels, and being very small could be used close up to the working face of the quarries for supplying steam to rock drills. Two were owned by the Lower Glyn-Rhonwy Slate Quarries at Llanberis.

What may be called the "standard" 1 ft 11½ in. gauge locomotive of the two-cylinder type (*Plate 62*), had solid plate frames outside the disc wheels, and being without springs the bearings were fixed directly to these frames, being literally simple plummer blocks. An interesting detail here is that an inspection of all the available photographs will reveal that hardly two frames were exactly alike and the spacing and arrangement of the rivets varied greatly.

At the front was the small water tank, at the other end the coal bunker, with the boiler mounted very low in the centre between the axles. The fire was fed through a trapdoor in the footplate and the coal slid down a chute on to the grate. These boilers were 2 ft 7½ in. in diameter and 4 ft 10½ in. high, made of Low Moor iron and fitted with seventy-six tubes of 1½ in. diameter; the grate area was 34 sq.ft. The Ramsbottom safety valve, fitted on a bracket on the left-hand side, was normally set to blow-off at 120 lb. psi. The valve gear was originally Joy's, but later Stephenson's gear was adopted in conjunction with a special form of slide valve designed by Charles Cousins, chief draughtsman during the 1880s; the reversing quadrant was on the right-hand side of the footplate. Other dimensions were: wheels 1 ft 8 in. diameter; wheelbase – this varied from 4 ft to 4 ft 4 in.; length over frames 8 ft 6 in.; overall width 3 ft 6 in. and the height to the top of the chimney was 6 ft 9 in.

On most locomotives the chimney was in the top centre of the boiler above the smoke-box, but as condensed steam and rainwater was found to run down the short chimney and cause the top-tube plate to corrode the design was altered in

Plate 63   De Winton & Co.: *Victoria* built 1897 for Pen-yr-Orsedd Quarry, Nantlle.
F. Jones

Plate 64 De Winton & Co.: *Arthur* built 1895 for Pen-yr-Orsedd Quarry, Nantlle.
Real Photographs Co.

the later examples to provide for a smokebox placed staggered fashion in advance of the boiler top. The two vertical cylinders were fixed to the boiler front by two steel plates, one on either side of, and partially embracing, the boiler. The drive was direct on to the front axle without gearing, the connecting-rod big-ends being of the marine type.

The VICTORIA, built in 1897, differed in being fitted with a free-standing launch type engine and this can be seen in *Plate 63*, which also shows the offset type of smokebox. It is thought that this was the last de Winton locomotive to be built.

A drastic variation from the standard design was made in the case of the ARTHUR, built for the Pen-yr-Orsedd Quarries, Nantlle, in 1890 and illustrated here in *Plate 64*. In this design the water tank was placed close to the boiler, and the free-standing engine at the front end of the frame with the drive from the crankshaft to the front axle by outside cranks and coupling rods. Whether this particular locomotive was the only one produced to this pattern is not known.

The 3 ft gauge series seen in *Plate 65*, were slightly larger and had inside frames. The dimensions were: boiler 2 ft 10 in. in diameter and 5 ft 3½ in. high, grate 2 ft 1¼ in. diameter; working pressure 120 lb. psi; wheels 1 ft 8 in. in diameter; wheelbase 4 ft 5 in.; length over frames 11 ft 7 in. and overall width 4 ft 3 in. The price of one of these locomotives in 1894 was £430.

On locomotives for both the 1 ft 11½ in. and 3 ft gauges, the frames were sometimes formed with an outward bulge to accommodate the boiler. The original cylinder dimensions of all these locomotives are doubtful as most of

Plate 65 De Winton & Co.: *Watkin* built 1893 for 3 ft gauge quarry lines of Darbishires Ltd, Penmaenmawr. *Author*

them were re-bored at least once, but the most recent measurements available show that cylinders of 6¼ in. bore by 10 in. stroke, and 6¼ in. bore by 12 in. stroke were to be found on the 1 ft 11½ in. gauge. The dimensions on the 3 ft gauge locomotives were 5¾ in. bore by 10 in. stroke, and 6¾ in. bore by 12 in. stroke. The crankshafts were made in one forging complete with the four eccentrics and the turner responsible for finishing them prided himself on being able to centre and turn one complete in only 11 days.

Weights are likewise uncertain, as some locomotives had, in later years, thick slabs of steel plate laid flat on the top of the frames on either side of the boiler to increase the adhesion. Two of the Penmaenmawr locomotives that were so treated weighed 5 tons 15 cwt., but otherwise the average weight on both the narrow gauge appears to have been 4½ tons empty and 5 tons in working order.

The only example of a reputed standard gauge de Winton locomotive known to the writer is illustrated in *The Locomotive* for 1905, page 138, but here the "S" shaped wheel spokes and the conical smokebox do not seem to be de Winton features. It is of interest to record that although the last de Winton locomotive was built in 1897 (Works No. 201), the firm quoted for the supply and delivery of one to the phosphate company operating on Christmas Island about 1900. The Union Works closed down in 1902.

The details of all the vertical boiler locomotives that have been traced are tabulated below, but it should be remembered that some locomotives are known to have been transferred between quarries, as for example the Cilgwyn Quarry locomotive GERTRUDE of 1877 was sold to the Gloddfa Glai Quarry in 1898, while the two at Pen-y-Bryn Quarry passed to the Pen-yr-Orsedd Quarries. The Gorseddau Junction and Portmadoc Railway locomotive was sold about 1894 to the Borth Stone Company, while the locomotive at the Swanscombe cement works was bought second-hand in 1890.

Probably most of those locomotives that survived into recent times had been re-boilered, and three examples at Penmaenmawr are known: the PENMAEN (1927), LLANFAIR (1933) and WATKIN (1928), the boilers being supplied by Lumbys of Halifax: these were identical to the original boilers, except for the number of tubes. The Pen-yr-Orsedd locomotive CHALONER received a new boiler in 1927.

Fortunately at least seven de Winton locomotives have been preserved: the PENMAEN is in the care of Kingston Minerals Ltd. at Penmaenmawr; the WATKIN is at Llanwryst (J.O. Williams); the GEORGE HENRY is in Towyn Narrow Gauge Museum. Both LLANFAIR and KATHLEEN are at The Narrow Gauge Railway Centre of North Wales, Blaenau Ffestiniog and PENDYFFRYN is at Brecon Mountain Railway.

In Bedfordshire, the CHALONER works passenger trains, during week-ends in summer, on the Leighton Buzzard Narrow Gauge Railway.

DE WINTON VERTICAL BOILER LOCOMOTIVES

Date	Name	Owner	Cyls	DW	Gauge	Withdrawn
1876	FLORINDER	Alexandra Quarry, Rhosgatfan			1ft 11½in.	
1877	EFA	Alexandra Quarry, Rhosgatfan			1ft 11½in.	
1881	REVOLUTION	John Bazley, White & Bros, Swanscombe	6"×10"	1'7"	3ft 5½in.	1924
1878	PENMAEN	Brundrit & Co., Penmaenmawr	5¾"×10"	1'8"	3 ft	1943
1893	PUFFIN	Brundrit & Co., Penmaenmawr	5¾"×10"	1'8"	3 ft	1934
1895	LLANFAIR	Brundrit & Co., Penmaenmawr	6¾"×11½"	1'8"	3 ft	1942
		Braich Slate Quarry			1ft 11½in.	
1876	LIZZIE	Cilgwyn Slate Quarry, Carmel			1ft 11½in.	1900
1877	GERTRUDE	Cilgwyn Slate Quarry, Carmel			1ft 11½in.	
1880	MADGE.	Cilgwyn Slate Quarry, Carmel			1ft 11½in.	1902
1874		Croesor Granite Co.				
1880	MOELEILIA	Caedmadoc Slate Quarry				
1876	TOMMY	Clay Cross Co., Crich	8"×		3ft 3in.	
1891	LILIAN	Darbishires Ltd, Penmaenmawr	5¾"×10"	1'8"	3 ft	1933
1892	LOUISA	Darbishires Ltd, Penmaenmawr	5¾"×10"	1'8"	3 ft	1936
1892	ADA	Darbishires Ltd, Penmaenmawr			3 ft	1931
1893	WATKIN	Darbishires Ltd, Penmaenmawr	6¾"×11½"	1'8"	3 ft	1944
1894	HAROLD	Darbishires Ltd, Penmaenmawr			3 ft	1938
	WELLINGTON	Dinorwic Slate Quarry Co. Ltd			1ft 10¾in.	
c.1869		Dorothea Slate Co., Talysarn			1ft 11½in.	
c.1870		Dorothea Slate Co., Talysarn			1ft 11½in.	
1874	GLYN	Dorothea Slate Co., Talysarn			1ft 11½in.	
	PADARN	Lower Glyn-Rhonwy Slate Co., Llanberis			1ft 11½in.	
		Lower Glyn-Rhonwy Slate Co., Llanberis			1ft 11½in.	
c.1895	EMILY	Llanberis Slate Co.			1ft 11½in.	
1896	CAERNARVON CASTLE	Llanberis Slate Co.			1ft 11½in.	
	FREDA	Greaves Llechwedd Slate Quarry, Blaenau Festiniog			1ft 11½in.	
		Greaves Llechwedd Slate Quarry, Blaenau Festiniog				
1875		Gorseddau Junction & Portmadoc Rly			1ft 11½in.	
1875	MARY OAKELEY	Oakeley Slate Quarries, Blaenau Festiniog			1ft 11½in.	1911
c.1876	ALICE	Penrhyn Quarries, Bethesda			1ft 11½in.	1904
1876	GEORGINA	Penrhyn Quarries, Bethesda			1ft 11½in.	1911
1876	INA	Penrhyn Quarries, Bethesda			1ft 11½in.	
1876	LORD PENRHYN	Penrhyn Quarries, Bethesda			1ft 11½in.	1909

Date	Name	Owner	Cyls	DW	Gauge	Withdrawn
1876	LADY PENRHYN	Penrhyn Quarries, Bethesda	6¼"×10"	1'8"	1ft 11½in.	1911
1876	KATHLEEN	Penrhyn Quarries, Bethesda	6¼"×10"	1'8"	1ft 11½in.	1939
1877	GEORGE HENRY	Penrhyn Quarries, Bethesda	6¼"×10"	1'8"	1ft 11½in.	
1877	INVERLOCHY	Pen-yr-Orsedd Quarries, Nantlle	6"×10"	1'8"	1ft 11½in.	1937
1880	GLYNLLIFON	Pen-yr-Orsedd Quarries, Nantlle			1ft 11½in.	1933
1893	GELLI	Pen-yr-Orsedd Quarries, Nantlle			1ft 11½in.	1945
1894	PENDYFFRYN	Pen-yr-Orsedd Quarries, Nantlle			1ft 11½in.	
1895	ARTHUR	Pen-yr-Orsedd Quarries, Nantlle	7"×12"	1'8"	1ft 11½in.	
1897	VICTORIA	Pen-yr-Orsedd Quarries, Nantlle			1ft 11½in.	
	BALADEULYN	Pen-yr-Orsedd Quarries, Nantlle			1ft 11½in.	
	STARSTONE	Pen-yr-Orsedd Quarries, Nantlle			1ft 11½in.	
1875	RHYMNEY	Pen-y-Bryn Slate Quarry		1'10"	1ft 11½in.	
1877	CHALONER	Pen-y-Bryn Slate Quarry	6"×12"	1'8"	1ft 11½in.	
		Talysarn Slate Co. Ltd			1ft 11½in.	
c.1878	VRON	Vron Slate Quarry			1ft 11½in.	
1875		Welsh Granite Co.			1ft 11½in.	
1870		Glendwr Slate Mills, Brynewyn			1ft 11½in.	
1876	ADDA	Alexandra Slate Co., Rhosgatfan			1ft 11½in.	
1876	EVA	Alexandra Slate Co., Rhosgatfan			1ft 11½in.	
1879	MURIEL	Glanrafon Slate Co.			1ft 11½in.	
	CATHERINE	Premier Glyn-Rhonwy Slate Co. (Glyn Ganol, Llanberis)			1ft 11½in.	
	FANNY	Rhos Slate Co., Capel Curig			1ft 11in.	
1896?		Park Croesor Slate Quarry			1ft 11½in.	
		Park Croesor Slate Quarry			1ft 11½in.	

A possible addition to the above list is a 2ft 6in. gauge locomotive advertised for sale in January 1878 on behalf of The Diamond Rock Boring Co. Ltd. This followed completion of their contract on the Llynvi & Ogmore Railway probably in connection with the Cymmer Tunnel work. It is unclear whether this locomotive was coupled to a drilling rig or used to convey spoil. (Ref: *The Industrial Locomotive*, Vol.3, No.34, p.202; No.35, pp.232–4 and Vol.4, No.43, pp.155–7). The vertical cylinders were quoted as 6" diameter by 12" stroke.

THE YORKSHIRE ENGINE COMPANY LTD
MEADOW HALL WORKS
SHEFFIELD

The Yorkshire Engine Co. was established in 1865 and the first locomotive was completed in 1866, but between that date and 1956 only about 800 were built, for the firm also had a lucrative trade in large colliery winding engines and in the supply of iron and steel forgings together with a large number of replacement boilers. It is known that the firm built two vertical boiler locomotives, but the details that have survived in the archives of the makers are meagre in the extreme, and apart from six photographs and brief notes in the Progressive No. Book and Drawing Office Order Book, most of the information on these locomotives has been gleaned from other sources. These locomotives differed considerably in design and each one may be considered as experimental.

A tramway locomotive, to be built under the Patent of Mr Loftus Perkins, was ordered on 9th October, 1873, in the name of T. Vancamp, and this was delivered early in 1874 to the Belgian Street Tramway Company, Brussels. For details of its construction we are indebted to a contemporary engineer, the late D.K. Clark, who recorded this locomotive in his *Tramways: Their Construction and Working*. The vertical boiler and vertical engine were placed side by side and along each side of the frames was an air-cooled condenser, consisting of a series of ½ in. copper tubes set vertically: into them the exhaust steam was discharged. The two condensers together presented between 700 and 800 sq.ft of cooling surface to the action of the atmospheric air. The upper ends of the tubes were closed, except for a small opening, left for the escape of possible vapour.

The boiler was constructed on Loftus Perkin's patented water-tube system, consisting of bent wrought-iron tubes 2¾ in. in diameter inside, and ⅜ in. thick, and proved to a pressure of 2500 lb. psi. The engine worked at the high pressure of 500 lb. psi with compound cylinders, one single-acting of 2 in. diameter and the other one double-acting of 4⅜ in. diameter, with a gear ratio between the crankshaft and intermediate shaft of 3 to 1. From this intermediate shaft the drive to the wheels was by coupling rods. The wheels were 2 ft in diameter, while the total weight in working order was only 4 tons.

Fortunately it has been possible to illustrate this locomotive by the two photographs reproduced here as *Plates 66 and 67*, which clearly show the principal constructional details. The guard-rails round the sides and at the ends seem to indicate that this locomotive was not enclosed in the usual all-over cab. After trials in Belgium, this locomotive was returned to England and was in store at the Meadow Hall Works in 1883.

We now have to consider a second and little-known tram locomotive, and Mr Ockendon, when chief draughtsman at the Meadow Hall Works, informed the writer that no documentary evidence existed relating to this locomotive, other than that it is referred to in the Drawing Office Order Book as No. 3300, dated March, 1878, and was for "1 Tramway Engine to drawings and Manager's instructions". In the Progressive No. Book it is No. 358 of 1878. The locomotive was tested on 29th October, 1878 and handed over to the Sheffield Corporation when it ran trials on the Newhall Road to Staneforth Road section of the

Plate 66 Yorkshire Engine Co's Loftus Perkins high pressure locomotive built 1874 for Belgian Street Railway Co. Brussels. *Sheffield Public Libraries*

Sheffield Tramways (*Plate 68*). This locomotive had cylinders of 7 in. diameter by 12 in. stroke, and a weight of 4 tons 15 cwt., increased in working order to 6 tons. It appears to have been returned to the makers, as it was reported to be in store at the Meadow Hall Works until 1883, when it underwent trials in Huddersfield.

The later history of this locomotive has been fully chronicled by D.L. Smith in his articles in *The Locomotive* during 1943 and 1946 and from these we learn that in 1883 it was acquired by the Wigtownshire Railway, then transferred to the Girvan & Portpatrick Junction Railway in 1886, but did little work there, and after being out of use for nine years was finally put to stationary work at the George Hotel, Stranraer.

Rolls Royce took over the firm in 1965 and work was transferred to their Sentinel Works at Shrewsbury.

Plate 67 Another view of the same locomotive. *Sheffield Public Libraries*

Plate 68 Locomotive built 1878 for experimental work on the Sheffield Tramways.
Yorkshire Engine Co.

Miscellanea

Firms not included in this book that have been credited with having built locomotives with vertical boilers are:

Appleby Brothers, Southwark
Brown and May, North Wiltshire Foundry, Devizes
Ellis H. & J., Salford (probably boiler only)
Gorton and Company, (boiler makers)
Lochgelly Iron and Coal Co. Ltd. Fife. (See I.R.S. Handbook N *Industrial Locomotives of Scotland*, p.57)
Riley Brothers, Middlesbrough

but the evidence for this is inconclusive.

The two machines built by Arthur Cudworth, St Mark's Engineering Works, Wrexham, about the year 1900, and supplied to W.B. Davis and Sons (Wagon) Limited, of Langwith Junction for working on double-flanged wheels and permanently coupled to traversers, cannot really be classed as locomotives.

Mention must be made of an advertisement by C.D. Phillips of the Emlyn Engineering Works, Newport, that appeared in Machinery Register for December 1895–May 1896. "22240. Coffee Pot locomotive, 3 ft gauge, 12 ft from rails to top of chimney. Made by a Canterbury firm. £75." During the period 1878 to 1895 there were eight engineering firms listed in Canterbury Directories, but the maker of the above locomotive has not been identified. However, in view of the definite knowledge that the Thanington Engineering Works, Wincheap Street, Canterbury, built a vertical boiler steam roller, one is inclined to consider this firm as the most likely builder of the advertised locomotive.

Another possible builder of a vertical boiler locomotive is Davey Paxman. A photograph reproduced as *Plate 69* at Brownlee & Co., Havelock, New Zealand is reputed to be a Davey Paxman locomotive for the 4 ft gauge imported in 1869 and set aside in 1886.

Plate 69 Davey Paxman 4 ft gauge locomotive imported into New Zealand in 1869 photographed at Brownlee & Co. Havelock c.1875. *P.A. Mahoney Collection*

Index

Articulated vehicles 46, 93, 124, 138, 145, 149
——, double 135
——, Gresley 120

Baguley-Clarkson design 10
Baguley-Devlin 11
Bogie
  Fox's pressed steel 106
  power 46, 86, 93
  power Baguley-Devlin 11, 13
Boiler types and makers
  Abbot & Co. (Newark) Ltd 120
  Bengal 121
  Broadbent 91
  Clarkson 10, 81
  Cochran 17, 52, 156
  Field 96, 98, 100, 161, 164
  Fletcher's patent 59
  Hanging tubes 36, 42
  Hartley & Sugden 56
  Lancashire 164
  Launch 161
  Lumby 169
  Merryweather 56, 100
  Perkins 70, 172
  Perkins, Loftus 83
  Pot 161
  Scottish 165
  Shand Mason 97
  Sharp & Palmer 156
  Spencer Hopwood 12
  Square multi-tubular 21
  Thimble tube-Clarkson 10
  Woolnough 120

Collieries
  Babbington 147
  Baglan Hall 38
  Bagworth 56
  Barnsley Main 145
  Barrow Main 148
  Barrow Barnsley 146
  Bestwood 147
  Candie 42
  Chell 74
  Cross Hands 147
  Cynheidre 146
  Denby Hall 146
  Derwenthaugh 147
  Dinnington Main 145
  Donisthorpe 146

Easthouses 119
Ellistown 146
Garforth 133
Garw 146
Glamorgan Coal Co. 39
Glascote 150
Glyn Neath 39
Great Mountain 147
Hartshay 33
Hendy Merthyr 143
Holditch 146
Holmewood 147
Kirkby 145
Langwith 147
Manton Main 145, 146
Manvers Main 146
Monk Bretton 145
Nailstone 146
New Gorsllan 132
New Haden 74
New Hucknall 145
Newstead 145
Peasley Cross 38
Pelaw Main 132
Penallt 39
Pilsley 46, 139
Sanquhar & Kirkconnel 96
Silverdale 146
Shawcross 145
Wentworth 146,
Wharncliffe 145
Wigglesworth 127
Wingfield Manor 145, 146
Compound 112, 118, 172
——, triple expansion 68
——, vee type 10
——, Willans 21
Contractors
  Balfour Beatty & Co. Ltd 83, 128, 132
  Budd & Holt 32
  Carlye 42
  Carmichael, A.H. 128
  Cochrane & Sons 15
  Ireland & Co. 38
  Jackson, E.J. 42
  Jackson, John 42
  Offer, Stephen 74
  Parry & Co. 77
  Proudfoot, David 42
  Scott 42
  Smith & Knight 38

Walker, T.W. & J. 107, 109
Wrigg, Henry 37
Crane locomotive 26, 51, 96, 139, 159

Demonstration loco 142, 143, 149

Engine
  double 120, 124
  launch 167
  single 120
  Stanley 110
  Super Sentinel 120
  uniflow 6
Engine names
  ADA 170
  ADDA 171
  ALEXANDER 137
  ALICE 129, 170
  ANN 133
  ARTHUR 167
  A.W. No.1 146
  1 AYRESOME 146
  2 AYRESOME 147
  3 AYRESOME 147
  5 AYRESOME 148
  BALADEULYN 171
  BALMORAL CASTLE 145
  BANG UP 46, 48
  BANKS OF DON 140
  BARBY 131
  BARROWGILL CASTLE 146
  (BELVEDERE) 144
  BIDDY 131
  BILLY 118
  BLACKBIRD 117
  BOB 38
  BONNIE DUNDEE 145
  B.R.C. 144
  BRILLIANT 129
  BRITANNIA 137
  BRITANNIE 128
  BRITISH QUEEN 137
  BRITTANY 132
  BRONLLWYD 77
  BRUNO 39
  CAERNARVON CASTLE 170
  CARADOC 147
  CARBARCENO 25
  CATHERINE FANNY 171
  CELERITY 137
  CEMENT 150

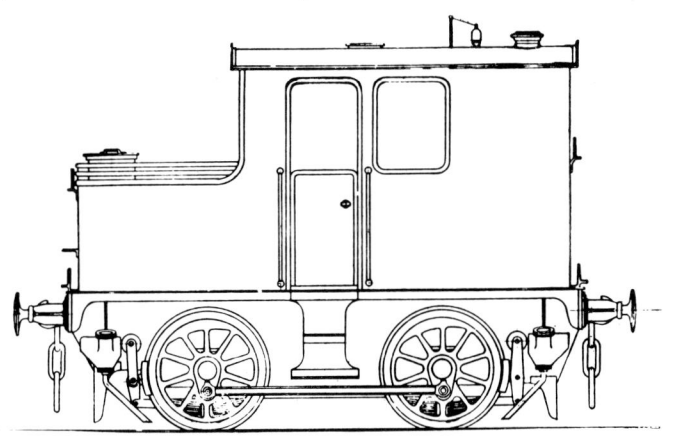

Clayton Type A locomotive, *see page 45.*

CITY OF LIVERPOOL 145
CHALONER 169, 171
CHARLES HEDWORTH 150
CHARLTON 142
CHEVY CHASE 46
CLEVELAND 135
CLYDESDALE 135
COETMOR 77
COMET 46
COMMERCE 135
CONDÉ 25
CORNWALLIS 138
COURIER 135
No.9 CRAVEN 146
CRITERION 138
DARTON 140
DEFIANCE 138
DILIGENCE 138
DINNINGTON No.3 145
EAGLE 135
EBOR 133
ECLIPSE 133
EDITH 39
EFA 170
ELGIN 103
EMERALD 138
EMILY 170
ENDURANCE 144
ENTERPRISE 144
EPPLETON 75
EVA 171
EXPEDITION 135
EXPRESS 1
FAIRFIELD 2
FAIR MAID 135
FELSPAR 9
FLORINDER 170
FLOWER OF YARROW 135
FREDA 170
GELLI 171
GEORGE HENRY 169, 171
GEORGINA 170
GERTRUDE 170
GERVASE 150
GLAMIS CASTLE 145
GLYN 170
GLYNLLIFON 171
GRADWELL 144
GREENWICH 136
HARK FORWARD 135
HAROLD 170
HASSALL 131
HENDON 132
HERO 133
HIGH FLYER 133
HIGHLAND CHIEFTAIN 135
HOLWELL No.4 150
HOPE 135
HOWARD SPENCE 144
HUGH 150
INA 170
INDEPENDENT 138
INDUSTRY 138
INTEGRITY 133
INVERLOCHY 171
IVANHOE 15
JOAN 132
JOHN 146
JOYCE 132
JUMBO 129
KATHLEEN 169, 171

LADY PENRHYN 171
LA MOYE 127
LANGHAR 137
LA PLATA 93
LAZARUS 9
L.G.4 145
LIBERTY 133
LILIAN 128, 170
LION 146
LITTLE ENOCH 144
LIZZIE 170
LLANFAIR 170
LORD PENRHYN 170
LOSSIEMOUTH 103
LOUISA 170
LYONS 75
MABEL 40
MADGE 170
NANTON No.2 145, 146
MARY 112
MARY OAKELEY 57, 170
MAUREEN 131
MAY ENGESTRÖM 136
MOELEILIA 170
MOLLY 132
MONA 77
MURIEL 171
NEPTUNE 133
NETTLE 134
NEW FLY 137
NORFOLK 138
NORMANDIE 127
NORTH BRITON 138
NORTH STAR 133
NOVELTY 28
NUTTY 136
OLD BLUE 138
OLD JOHN BULL 138
OTTO 39
PADARN 170
PARAGUAY 93
PAT 62
PEARL 137
PEEPING TOM II 145
PENDYFFRYN 171
PENMAEN 170
PERSEVERANCE 31, 133
PHENOMENA 138
PHOENIX 133
PHYLLIS 148, 150
PILOT 46
PLANTAGENET 145
PORTELET 126
PRINCE REGENT 137
PROTECTOR 137
PUFFIN 170
QUEEN ADELAIDE 28
QUEEN OF BEAUTY 140
QUICKSILVER 138
RAILWAY 46
RAJAWAU 141
RAPID 46
RECOVERY 138
RED ROVER 133
REDSTONE 52
RETALIATOR 138
REVOLUTION 170
RHYMNEY 171
RISING SUN 137
RIVAL 137
ROBIN 148

ROB ROY 133
ROCKINGHAM 133
RODNEY 133
ROYAL CHARLOTTE 137
ROYAL EAGLE 135
ROYAL FORRESTER 137
ROYAL SAILOR 46
RUBY 135
SAFAGA 142
SENTINEL 132, 145, 150
SENTINEL No.1 145, 146, 147, 148
(SENTINEL No.2) 145, 147
SETNINEL No.3 145
SENTINEL No.4 146
SENTINEL No.5 146
SENTINEL No.6 148
SIFTA 60
STARSTONE 171
STEAM TRAM 56
STIRLING CASTLE 145
ST MONANS 144
SWANSEA VALE No.1 148
SWIFT 137
SURPRISE 137
SUSAN 146
TALLY HO 133
TEAZLE 133
TEES-SIDE No.5 148
TELEGRAPH 137
TEMPEST 148
THE DOCTOR 148
THE DON 15
THE PIONEER 119
TIMES 137
TIMOTHY 146
TINY 116
(TOBY) 129
TOMMY 170
TORBAY 118
TRAFALGAR 133
TRANSIT 46
TRAVELLER 135
TRUE BLUE 133
TRUE BRITON 133
TWEEDSIDE 135
TWIN SISTERS 158
UMPIRE 135
UNION 46, 113
UPHO 150
URUGUAY 93
VALIANT 129
VANE 148
VANGUARD 146
VICTORIA 155, 167, 171
VRON 171
WASDALE 119
WATERLOO 135
WATER WITCH 133
WATKIN 170
WELLINGTON 46, 170
WHEELOCK 134
WILMENSEN 25
WILLIAM 147
WILLIAM IV 28
WINDSOR CASTLE 145
WONDER 46
WOODPECKER 135
WOOLWICH 132
YORKSHIRE HUSSAR 133

INDEX

Firms and customers
Abbot & Co. (Newark) Ltd 64, 120, 153
A.B. Sawmills 42
Adams & Benson 136
Adamson Alliance Co. Ltd 115
Adamson D. & Co. 144
Adamson J. & Co. Ltd 114
Aitken & Morcom 127
Allan T. & Sons 40
Alley & McLellan 119
Alpha Cement Ltd 9
Anglo Newfoundland Dev. Co. 129
APCM Dunstable 127
Appleby Bros 176
Armstrong Whitworth 146
Arnold H. & Sons 9
Arrol, Sir William & Co. Ltd 43
Atkinson Vehicles Ltd 6
Atkinson-Walker Wagons Ltd 81
Avonside Engine Works 55
Bairds & Dalmellington Ltd 96
Barclay, Andrew Sons & Co. Ltd 106
Barnsley Corp. Scout Dyke Reservoir 132
Barrow Haematite Steel Co. Ltd 57, 146, 147
B.E.A. Skelton Grange 146
Bedworth Coal & Iron Co. 40
Belfast Harbour Comm. 40, 41
Berry Hill & Stapleford Sand Co. 132
Beyer Peacock & Co. Ltd 67, 162
Bird, Wm. & Co. 37, 38
Black Hawthorn & Co. 51, 67, 162
Blackwells 83, 150
Blaenavon Co. Ltd 42
Blaxter Quarries Ltd 9
Board of Public Works, Dublin 41
Bolckow Vaughan & Co. 160
Bonyo Sabank Sisal Estate 144
Borth Stone Co. 169
Bosanquet Curtis & Co. 42
B.P.C.M. Greenhithe 150
Bradley & Turton Ltd 28
Brand, Charles & Son 43
B.R.C. Engineering Ltd 144
Bridgewater Trustees 40
Briggs, Richard & Son 39, 41, 42
British Tar Products Co. Ltd 133
Brodie, Michael & Co. 41
Brotherhood 37
Brown & May 176
Brown, James & Co. Ltd 41
Brown, J.B. & Co. 37
Brown, John & Co. Ltd 106, 148
Brownlee & Co. 170
Brundit & Co. 77, 170
Brunner Mond 131, 134
Brush Electrical Engg. Co. Ltd 57, 93
Bryant & May 3
B.T.H. Rugby 144
Budd & Holt 32
Buddon Jennings & Co. 39
Burnley, W. & F. & Co. 40
Burstall & Hill 31
Butler, John & Co. 32
Butler, Samuel & Co. 13, 32
Butlin, Thomas & Co. Ltd 150
Butterley Co. 39

Cafferata & Co. 140, 144, 150
Cammell Laird & Co., Birkenhead 128, 129, 134
Cammell Laird & Co., Nottingham 119
Castle Dyke Iron Co. 42
Castner Kellner Alkali Co. 150
C.E.A. Willington 146
C.E.G.B. Stella North 147
Chaplin A. & Co. 27, 30, 33, 49, 51
Chapman & Furneaux 23, 26
Chatwood Safe Co. 139
Chesterfield Tube Co. 146
Christchurch Meat Co. 42
Church & Sons 150
City of London Contract Corp. 24
Clarke Chapman Crane & Bridge Div. 43
Clarkson Steam Motor Ltd 10, 81
Clay Cross Co. 128, 150, 170
Clayton & Shuttleworth 44
Clayton Forge 44, 46
Clayton Wagons Ltd 11, 44, 47
Clyde Crane & Booth 43
Coalbrookdale Co. 128, 150
Cochran & Co. 16
Cochrane & Co. 38
Cochrane Grove & Co. 49
Cochrane's Ltd 49
Cochrane's (Middlesbrough) Foundry Ltd 49
Coghill, J. & Co. 38
Cohen, Geo. 600 Group 32
Cohen, Geo. Sons & Co. Ltd 44
Colonial Co. Ltd 39, 40
Colvilles Ltd 148
Compagnie Miniere Belge Antwerp 40
Connor & Alley 42
Consett Iron Co. 23, 26, 43, 51, 96, 159
Cory Wm. & Sons 132, 136, 142, 144
Coulthard, Ralph & Co. 23
Courtaulds Ltd 147
Cox & Co., Nairobi 139
Craven Bros. Ltd 146
Cudworth, A. 176
Cumberland Iron Mining & Smelting Co. 57
Darbishires Ltd 77, 168
Davey Paxman 176
Davis W.B. & Sons (Wagons) Ltd 176
Davy & Co. 38
Davy H. & Donath R. 39, 40
Davy, Humphrey 39
Derbyshire Wagon Co. 150
De Winton 52, 57, 77
Diamond Rock Boring Co. 171
Dick, W.B. & Co. 24
Dinas & Co., Wolsingham Park 40
Dorking Greystone Lime Co. 74
Dorman Long
——, Lackenby 148, 149
——, Middlesbrough 132, 147
——, South Bank 147–149
Dowlais Iron Co. 23, 26
Downing of Barnsley 45
Donya Sabouk Sugar Estates, Kenya 133

Duckering R. Ltd 47
Dunlop Rubber Co. Ltd 131
Earle G. & T. Ltd 45, 131
Easton Gibb & Co. 42
Eccles Slag 144
Edgar Allen Engg Ltd 119, 145
Edwards Bros. 36, 38
Edwards, J.C. Ltd 127
E.E.C. Rugby 145, 159
Egyptian Phosphate Co. 142
Elder A.L. & Co. 41
Electrical Engineer Jodphur 144
Ellis, H. & J. 176
Equator Sawmills 132
Evans, William & Co. 131
Fairlie Engine & Steam Carriage Co. 55
Falmouth Docks Engg. Co. 117, 151
Fawcett Preston & Co. 164
Field & Mackay Clee Hill 128
Ford Paper Mills 150
Forrest & Barr 38
Fraserburgh Harbour Comm. 40
Frodingham Iron & Streel Co. Ltd 150
Fry, J.S. & Sons Ltd 136
Gartverrie Fireclay Co. 42
Gjers Mills 74, 146–8
G.K.N. East Moors 147
Glaisdale Iron Works 39
Glamorgan Coal Co. Ltd 39
Glendwr Slate Mills 171
Gloucester Railway Carriage & Wagon Co. 64, 153
Goode, Sir John 40
Gorton & Co. 176
Gossage, Wm. & Sons 136, 139
Granger, J. & W. 42
Gray & Buchanan 16
Gray, T.E. 150
Green, E., Nottingham 56
Green, Thomas & Sons 67, 162
Greenlaw Mindin Co. 131
Griffin Engg. Co. 144
Gypsum Mines Ltd 144
Haigh & Sons 158
Hanna, Donald & Wilson 42
Hanomag 74, 139
Hartley, Arnoux & Fanning 82
Hawthorn Leslie & Co. Ltd 23 159
Hay & Chopping 107
Hayes & Co. (Stockport) Ltd 131, 132
Head Ashley & Co. 70
Heenan & Froude 136
Hendon Paper Co. 132
Hellibors A. & J., Kronsas 41
Hogg Curtis Campbell & Co. 41, 42
Hough & Sons 162
Huon Timber Co. 107
Hudson R. & Sons Ltd 84, 135
Hunslet Engine Co. 88
Hunslet Group 18
Hurst Nelson & Co. 83
Hutchinson & Ritson 3
I.C.I. (Metals), Dowlais 147
Ind Coope & Allsop 144
Indian Stores Dept 130, 134
Isham Ironstone 83

VERTICAL BOILER LOCOMOTIVES

Ivybridge China Clay Co. 6, 9
James & Shakespear, London 41
Jennings & Co. 39
Johore Steam Saw Mills 39
Kelhead Lime Co. 33
Kettering Coal & Iron Co. Ltd 124
Keyworth J. & H. & Co. 38
Kilsyth Coal Co. 42
Kingowira Sisal Estate 127
Kingston Minerals Ltd 169
Kitson & Co. 21, 94, 162
La Guaiya Corp. 143
Laird's Boiler Works 158
Landore Siemens Steel Co. 160
Landré & Glinderman 38
Law & Blount 38
Leatham Flour Mills, York 9
Lee Wm. Son & Co. 41
Lellan S. & W. 38
Leys Malleable Castings Ltd 127, 143, 145
Liebig's Extract of Meat Co. 38
Linthorpe-Dinsdale Smelting Co. 49
Liverpool Corp. Trading Estate 145
Llwydarth Tinplate Co. 42
Lochgelly Iron & Coal Co. Ltd 176
Loftus Iron Co. 49
Logan, John & Co. 42
London Brick Co.
——, Arlesley 143, 144, 150
——, Calvert 133, 136, 143
——, Fletton 131
——, Stewartby 130, 136, 143
Londonderry Estates Co. 74
Losh Wilson & Bell 39
Lowca Engineering Co. 57
Low Temperature Carbonisation Co. 140
Macclesfield Corp. Trentabank Reservoir 131, 132
Malcolm A. & Co. 40
Manning Wardle 83
Mansfield Standard Sand Co. 144
Marston Valley Brick Co. 143
McDonald A. & K. 38
McKechnie Bros. 144
McKendrick Ball & Co. 37, 41
McKinnel, James A.B. 33
McMillan Estates 139
Meeson & Co. 37
Merryweather & Sons 98
Midland Iron Co. 145
Millom & Askham Iron Co. 147
Millom Hematite Ore & Iron Co. 148
Millward & Co. 57
Minerals Concentration Co. Ltd 139
Mobbs, Henry Northampton 42
Mountsorrel Granite Co. 42
Murrietta & Co. 93
National Coal Board 145–147
National Smelting Co. 148
Newbie Brickworks Annan 15
New Lowca Engg. Co. Ltd 57
Nicholls Matthews & Co. 40
Northampton Sewage Works 55
Northumberland Whinstone Co. 127, 130
Oldbury Carriage & Wagon Works 96

Oswald & Co. 42
Outram, Benjamin & Co. 33
Oxford & Shipton Cement Ltd 9
Oxfordshire Ironstone Co. 148
Oxted Greystone Lime Co. 131
Palmer Mann & Co. 60
Parkgate Iron & Steel Co. 146
Pathankoj Bajri Stone Supply Co. 126
Penmaenmawr & Welsh Granite Co. 77, 170
Penydarren Ironworks 159
Perran Foundry 117
Perry J. & Co. 39
Peters J.S., Merstham 150
Phillips C.D. 176
Pickering, R. & T. 106, 110
Piel & Walney Gravel Co. 14
Pilkington Bros 148
Port of Par Ltd 118
Powell Tillery Steam Coal Co. Ltd 150
Poznan City Council 132
Ransome Sims & Head 112
Ransome Sims & Jefferies 112
Ravenhead Brick & Tile Upholland 150
Reader of Nottingham 56
Redfern, Alexander & Co. 39
Riley Bros 176
Roads Reconstruction Co., Frome 144, 145, 150
Robertson & Henderson 54
Robinson & Majoribanks 39
Rochdale Corp. Waterworks 40, 129, 131
R.O.F. Hooton 144
Rolls Royce 174
Rosehaugh Co. 127
Rothwell & Co. 113
R.T.B. Ebbw Vale 146, 147
Rugby Portland Cement 146
Russell, John & Co. 134
Ruston & Hornsby 56
Sara & Burgess 151
Sara & Co. 116
Saunders Roe Ltd 88
Scandia 85
Seaham Harbour Dock Co. 74, 148
Seend Iron Works 40
Sentinel Waggon Works 83, 110
Settle Limes Ltd 147
Shap Granite Co. 9, 119
Sharpe, R. & Sons 38
Sharp Stewart & Co. Ltd 55
Sheffield Corp. Electricity Works 144
Sheffield Corp. Longsett Reservoir 15
Shipbreaking Industries Ltd, Faslane 147
Short Bros, Pallion 146
Singapore Municipal Council 6, 9
Smith-Clayton Forge Ltd 44, 46
Smith Fleming & Co. 38
Smith, Thomas Stamping Works 44
Soc. Anonyme des Acieries de Longwy 41
Sommerville W. & Son Ltd 41
Spence, Peter & Sons 144
Spence & Buddon 38

Springs Mines Ltd, Transvaal 130, 135
Standard Bank, Nairobi 136
Stanton Iron Works 107, 150
Starbuck Carriage & Wagon Co., Birmingham 97
Staveley Coal & Iron Co. 106, 139
Steetley Lime Co. 136
Stephenson, Robert & Hawthorns Ltd 88, 159
Stevenson Iron & Coal Ltd 42
Stewart & Co. 37
Stromnas Bruks 136
Swanscombe Cement Works 169
Swanston & Co. 41
Tata Steel Works 143
Taylor Bros. (Sandiacre) Ltd 150
Tees-side Bridge & Engg Cargo Fleet 148
Tennent R.B., Whifflet 146, 148
Thanington Engg Works 176
Thomas, Richard Clydach 126
Thompson & Co. 33
Thorpe, Titus & Ainsworth 81
Tintern Abbey Tinplate Co. Ltd 42
Tredegar Iron Co. 57
Treffrey Estates 129
Tulk & Ley 57
Tunnel Portland Cement Co. 146
Tyne-Tees Shipping Co. 146
Union Cold Storage 134
Vickers Armstrong Ltd 5
Vulcan Foundry 55
Walker Bros (Wigan) Ltd 6, 9, 119
Wallace J. & Co. 42
Walleroo & Moonta Mining 85
Walleroo Copper Co. 41
Watt, James & Co. 38
W.D. Tidworth 132
Weardale Coal & Iron Co. Ltd 74
Weardale Steel Iron & Coke Co. 150
Wellman Cranes Ltd 43
Whitehead Iron & Steel Co. 148
Wilkinson Wigan 21, 23
Wilson Geo. & Co. 39
Williams S. & Son 127
Williamson, Sir John Hedworth Limeworks 150
Wimshurst & Co. 38, 39, 42
Wimshurst Hollick & Co. 39–41
Woodside Brickworks (Croydon) Ltd 130
Yeoman, Joseph 42
York & Co. 37, 38
York W. & T. 38
Yorkshire Amalgamated Products 132, 139
Yorkshire Engine Co. 55, 68

Gas Works
Adelaide 130
Altrincham 144
Beckton 150
Bolton 144
Bradford Road, Manchester 147
Cambridge 139
Croydon 132
Edinburgh 41
Falkirk 146
Kensal Green 127, 142
Motherwell & Wishaw 135

INDEX

181

Nechells 148
Northampton 41, 145
North Thames 128
Ryde 28
Tottenham 9, 139, 143, 144, 150
Walsall 148
Warrington 145
Grantham car 54, 96

Inspection cars 78, 100, 112, 121, 135
Inspection loco 78, 80, 101, 111, 121, 135

Persons
Aldes, Os 40
Armstrong, William George 5
Ball, Henry 37
Barclay, Andrew 16
Bennett, A.R. 2
Bentley, J. 15
Beresford, F. 33
Beyer, C.F. 19
Bostock, J.H. 40
Bourne, J.F. 37
Bradley, D.L. 157
Bradley, F. 27
Braithwaite, J. 28
Brooks, Edward 15
Brownlie, John S. 114, 155
Burgess, John 117
Campbell, R. 39
Casperton, H.W. 39
Cegielski, Mr. 11
Chaplin, A. 116
Churchward, G.J. 64
Clark, D.K. 70, 92, 97, 172
Clark, R.H. 88
Clarkson, Thomas 10
Clayton, Nathaniel 44
Clifford, Charles 106
Coey, R. 62
Cousins, Charles 166
Cowans, John 51
Deeley, R.M. 102
Dendy Marshall, C.F. 30, 31
Devlin, S.R. 11
Devu, Pierre 38
De Winton, J.P. 164
Dickinson, R.E. 54
Doble, A. 121
Dollfus, C. 31
Donkin, Armourer 5
Drummond, Dugald 89
Eastwood, Edward 106, 109
Ericsson, John 28
Fairlie, Robert 55
Ferguson, W. 28
Fernihough, Mr 157
Fletcher, Henry A. 59
Fletcher, W. 161
Foden, Edwin 59
Forman, William 158
Fowler, John 85
Fraser, J.S. 55
Gabrielli, A. 42
Glaenzeret, Perrand 127
Grantham, John 97
Gregory, Wm. 39
Griffen, Mr 126
Harding, G.P. 97
Harley, W.A. 41

Harrison, E. 88
Henderson, Mr 54
Heslop, Thomas 57
Hick, Benjamin 113
Hills, A.J. 52
Hinder, S. 32
Holt, D.G. 38
Holt, W.L. 25
Hood, A. 39
Howie, W. 38
Hughes, H. 57
Hughes, Owen 77
Hunter, C.W. 15
Jacks (Dealer) Karachi 137
Jamieson (Lord Provost) 54
Jessop, W. 33
Kennedy, W. 15
Kensington, J. 25
Lee, C.E. 77
Lee, Mr 66
Longridge, Michael 158
Lund, C. 25
Markham, C.P. 106
Martin, J. 38
McKendrick, J. 37
Mitchell, James 103
Mountford, Eric 151
Murray, D. 38
Neilson, Walter 103
Ockenden, Mr 172
Oliver, John 106
Oliver, J.G. 132
Oliver, William 106
Outram, B. 33
Patterson, H.C. 16
Paxman, J. 16
Peacock, R. 19
Pearce Higgins, S.H. 96
Perkin, Loftus 68, 83, 172
Perrett, Edward 91
Perrott, E.W. 40
Pickersgill, Mr 16
Pitt, A. Robert 159
Redstone, Mr 52
Riddle, J.H. 15
Robertson, Mr 54
Robinson, J.G. 61
Rogers, J. Kennedy 41
Rowan, W.R. 85
Rushton, T.L. 75
Russell, G. 116
Samuel, James 1, 108
Sara, E.B. 117
Sara, Nicholas 117
Scott, Mr 42
Sheldon, Edward 51
Shuttleworth, Joseph 44
Simon, H. 39
Simpson, David 119
Sissons, W. 153
Smith, A.W. 133
Smith, D.L. 173
Smith, T. 156
Stead, W. 57
Stephenson, George 75, 158
Stephenson, Robert 158
Stevens, H.F. 110
Stevenson, G.E. 39
Stothert, G. 159
Thomas, Owen 164
Torrans, H. 160

Van Bruam 40, 42
Vancamp, T. 172
Vaughan, T. 38
Walker, John S. 119
Wallis-Taylor Mr 88
West, T. 114
Wilkinson, William 66, 161
Willans, Kyrle 21, 83
Willans, Peter W. 83
William, J.O. 169
Wilson, H. 25
Winby, F.C. 25
Wood, N. 32
Woods, E. 40, 97
Wright, J. 33

Quarries
Alexandra Slate 170, 171
Bazley White, John & Bros 170
Braich Slate 170
Blaxter, Elsdon 9
Brundit & Co. 170
Caedmadoc Slate 170
Caernarvon Granite 57
Carmyllie 151
Ceiriog Granite 132
Cilgwyn 170
Clay Cross Co., Crich 170
Cliffe Hill Granite 131
Croesor Granite 170
Darbishires Ltd 170
Dinmor 139
Dinorwic Slate 170
Dorothea Slate 170
Gatelawbridge 33
Glanrafon Slate 171
Gloddfa Glai 169
Glyn Ganol Llanberis 171
Graiglwyd 77
Graywracke 155
Greaves Llechwedd Slate 170
Grin 128
Hessle 45
Hilts 33
Little Orme 77, 128
Llanberis Slate 52, 170
Lord Penrhyn's Slate 77
Lower Glyn-Rhonwy 170
Mendip Mountain 127
Oakeley Slate 57, 170
Park Croesor Slate 171
Penmaen Mawr 77, 165
Penrhyn 77, 170, 171
Pen-y-Bryn 171
Pen-yr-Orsedd 166, 167, 171
Raynes & Co. 132
Rhos Slate 171
Talysarn Slate 171
Trevor 52
Vobster 145, 150
Vron Slate 171
Welsh Granite 77, 171

Railbus 120, 142
Railcars & railmotors 1, 9, 16, 17, 46, 55, 60–62, 64, 82, 85, 89, 93, 102, 103, 110, 119, 120, 126–129, 131–146, 153

Railways
Ahmadpur-Katwa Lt 139, 141

VERTICAL BOILER LOCOMOTIVES

Argentine N.E. 128, 137
Australian Commonwealth 126
Axholme Joint 140
Bahia & San Francisco 38
Bankura-Damodar 139, 141
Baroda State 127
Barry 103, 106
Barsi Lt 128, 129, 136, 139
Belgian National 142
Belgian State 139, 140
Bengal Nagpur 127, 128
Bhavnagar State 130
Bolton & Leigh 113
Bombay, Baroda & Central India 136
Brecon Mountain 52, 169
Bristol & Exeter 2
British North Borneo Co. 129
Buenos Ayres Midland 141
Buenos Ayres Pacific 81, 100, 129
Buenos Ayres Western 132
Cadeby Lt 56
Cambrian 155
Cardiff 151, 153
Central Argentine 127
Central of Peru 137
Ceylon 127, 129, 131, 132, 134, 135
Cheshire Lines Comm. 137
Chilean Transandine 100
Chimboti, Peru 129
Chusan 137
Clogher Valley 6, 9, 81
Colombian National 120, 142
Cork & Bandon 3
County Donegal Jt Comm. 81
Czechoslovakian 127
Danish State 39
Der Spoorweg Maatschappij 141
Derwent Valley Lt 127
Eastern Bengal 130
Eastern Counties 1, 29, 103
Eastern of France 143
East Indian 5, 133
Egyptian Delta Lt 9, 126, 128, 129, 130, 134
Egyptian Govt. 47
Egyptian State 142, 143, 145
Entre Rios 127, 133, 137
Federated Malay States 137, 141, 143
Ferrocarril de la Provincia de Buenos Ayres 93
Gavle Dala 126
Girvan & Portpatrick Jt 174
Gold Coast 132, 136, 139
Gorseddau Jt & Portmadoc 170
Great Central 44
Great Eastern 87
Great Indian Peninsula 131
Great Northern 32
Great Northern of Ireland 93, 106
Great North of Scotland 16
Great Southern of Ireland 47, 131, 132
Great Western 32, 42, 82, 117, 129
Gribscov 85
Harnosand 127
Helsingor, Denmark 126
Iraq 129, 136
Isle of Wight 27
Jaywick Lt 110

Jersey 127
Jersey Eastern 128, 132
Jersey Railways & Tramways Ltd 119
Jodhpur State 136
Kalighat-Falta 139, 141
Kent & East Sussex 110
Leighton Buzzard Lt 169
Leopoldina 121, 134, 143
Liverpool & Manchester 29, 30, 158
Llynvi & Ogmore 171
London & North Eastern 46, 119, 120, 125, 127–30, 132–5, 137–143
London & North Western 27
Londonderry & Enniskillen 3
London Midland & Scottish 119, 131, 135–142
——, NCC 127
London & South Western 89
Malmesbury 32
Midland 18, 106
Monmouthshire 27
Montrose & Bervie 38
Morayshire 103
Newfoundland 127, 134
New Zealand Govt. 126
Nigerian 136, 139, 146
Nitrate 127
Nizam's Govt. 131
Nor Oeste Peru 128, 136
Northern of France 142
North West of India 128, 132, 141
Nyasaland 142
Orki Div. India 126
Oudh & Rohilkund 78
Pachitea 128
Palestine 133, 135
Paraguay Central 142
Paris Orleans 126
Penrhyn 77
Peruvian Central 142
Polish State 136
Pontiloff 85
Portsdown & Horndean Lt 89
Rhymney 151, 153
Rother Valley 110
Roumanian State 141, 142
Salvador 129
Sao Paulo 141, 142
Shackerstone 56
Shanghai Nanking 136, 137
Somerset & Dorset Jt 136
South African 126
South Devon–Sutton Harbour 116
South Eastern 157
Southern–Dyke Branch 120, 142
St. Helens & Runcorn Gap 29
Sudan Govt. 128
Taff Vale 151
Tanganyika, 136, 139, 140, 144
Tasmanian Govt. 141–143
Trinidad 141
Vale of Glamorgan 103
Victoria Govt. 83, 85
West Australian Govt. 139
Wigtownshire 174
Worcester & Hereford 42
Zaffra Huelva 136

Tramcars 54, 88, 91, 97, 119, 161, 172

Tramways
Alford & Sutton 22, 24
Belgian Street Tramway 172
Birmingham & Aston 162
Bradford 66
Bradford & Shelf 66
Brighton District 162
Burnley & District 91, 117
Carthagena-Herrerias 139
Copenhagen 85
Coventry & District 21, 66
Dublin & Lucan 91
Dublin Southern District 162
Dundee & District 54
Edinburgh Corp. 54
Gateshead & District 24, 25
Giants Causeway Portrush & Bush Valley 162
Glenelg & South Coast 85
Greenock & Gourock 54
Huddersfield Corp. 25, 162, 173
Kerang & Koendrook 136
Leeds 66, 70
Leith 54
London 97
Manchester, Bury, Rochdale & Oldham 20, 21, 24, 66, 162
Minas Huelle–Santander 25
New South Wales 85
North Shields & Tynemouth 24, 66
North Staffordshire 21, 25
Nottingham & District 91, 162
Partick & Whiteinch 54
Pernambuco 93
Plymouth, Devonport & District 162
Plynlimon & Hafan 155
Portsmouth Corp. 88
Ryde Pier Co. 28
Sheffield Corp. 172
Southern of Paris 97
South Staffordshire 21, 66, 162
Stirling 54
Stirling & Bridge of Allen 54
Sydney N.S.W. 21
Tynemouth 25
Vale of Clyde 54
Wantage 97
Wigan & District 162
Wisbech & Upwell 125, 139

Valve gear
Joy's 166
Link Motion 18, 100, 110
Modified Dodds Wedge Motion 12, 45
Stationary Link 2
Stephenson Link 13, 166
Walschaert's 61, 64, 83, 89, 93, 106

Wilkinson's patent 20